# 5 STEPS TO A 5

# AP Environmental Science

# 5 STEPS TO A 5™

# AP Environmental Science

Courtney Mayer, MEd

McGraw Hill

ISBN        978-1-266-70866-4
MHID        1-266-70866-9

The series editor was Grace Freedson, and the project editor was Del Franz.

Series design by Jane Tenenbaum.

# CONTENTS

**STEP 5**

**Build Your Test-Taking Confidence**

# PREFACE

Welcome to the *5 Steps to a 5 AP Environmental Science* (APES) review book! This book contains the information you need to be successful on the APES exam. I have written this book so that it is completely aligned to the most recent College Board curriculum framework. All the practice questions in the chapters, on the diagnostic exam, and on the two practice exams are written as closely to how they will be tested on the actual exam as possible.

Keep in mind that the test will be difficult, but with hard work and a plan in place, you will have a very good chance at earning college credit. This book will take you step-by-step through each topic and each type of question. There are different strategies on how you should approach your studying depending on when you start studying and how much time you have to devote to your studies spelled out in Chapter 2. Pick the strategy that works best for you and stick with it!

This book has all the major concepts, clear and easy-to-understand examples, and test questions that are written with the skills outlined by the College Board. There are other books out there with similar information about AP Environmental Science, but this one truly aligns to exactly the information you will be tested on. I have written the chapters to be conversational, which is exactly how I teach my students in class. After 15 years of teaching this course to thousands of students, I have learned the best ways to remember the concepts and have had feedback from my students on ways that help them. All of this is incorporated into the book. I have also pointed out throughout the chapters the way the information will be tested. For example, if a particular concept will be tested with your reading a short text, I tell you that; if it is tested using a graph or data table, I point that out as well. The fewer surprises you encounter when you sit down to take the test, the more successful you will be.

Make sure to not only take the two practice exams after you have reviewed all the concepts, but read the explanations, even on the questions you got right, to make sure you truly understand the concepts and why the answer was correct. The multiple-choice section constitutes 60 percent of your score and the free-response section 40 percent. Make sure you pay special attention to the types of free-response questions you will be given. Do not blow this part off, as it counts for almost half of the test. Read the details of how the free-response questions will be scored carefully and make sure to go into detail as you answer. Remember, the reader/grader can't call you and ask you questions about your answer. Practice this now, with this book and its examples, so you will do well on this part of the exam.

Let's get started. First, take the diagnostic exam and go through each answer and explanation. See which chapters and topics you need to work on most and where you just need to review. There are some topics that you will know better than others, and using the diagnostic exam with the "Analyzing Your Performance on the Diagnostic Exam" page, you can prioritize the chapters you have the most difficulty with. You might also want to form a study group with others from your class since studying with others helps many students. Good luck on the exam and happy studying!

# ACKNOWLEDGMENTS

I would like to thank those who made this book possible: my husband, David, and my children, Caitlin, Colin, and my daughter-in-law Rachel, all of whom allowed me to spend countless hours over the holidays working on it. I would also like to thank my parents, Dr. Michael Masser and Carolyn Elkins, for always supporting me. Thank you, Grace Freedson and Grace Freedson's Publishing Network, for offering so many writing opportunities over the years, including this book, and for always trusting me in my writing abilities. Thank you to my amazing science editor and friend, Elisa McCracken, for painstakingly going through every chapter and every question to make sure it was aligned to the new curriculum from the College Board and to my editor, Del Franz, for making all the changes that needed to be made to make this book a success. I would also like to thank Kristin Shapiro and Matt Wells for helping me with updating the FRQs on the full-length exams so that they are aligned. Their suggestions helped immensely!

# ABOUT THE AUTHOR

Courtney Mayer taught science courses for 23 years, including AP Environmental Science for 15 years at Churchill High School in San Antonio, Texas, and currently at UT High School in Austin, Texas. She is a College Board consultant for AP Environmental Science in the southwestern region. She has presented all over the United States and in China. Courtney is also a College Board consultant for Analytical Reading and Writing Strategies in Science, Designing Investigations and Experiments, Analyzing and Interpreting Quantitative Data, AP Course Skills and Practices, and is on the writing committee for the Pre-AP Biology Curriculum and a consultant for the College Board's National Faculty and Cross-Curricular Instruction. Courtney is a reader and table leader at the AP Environmental Science reading where she scores free-response questions for thousands of students. She was honored in 2011 with the College Board's AP Award for helping promote and continue the mission set by the College Board.

Courtney has published 11 books, all around science topics, particularly AP Environmental Science. Courtney graduated with a degree in Wildlife and Fishery Science from Texas A&M University in 1992, and she received her Master of Education in Administration from Lamar University.

# INTRODUCTION: THE FIVE-STEP PROGRAM

## The Basics

At this point, you are either in an AP Environmental Science class, planning on taking one, or already schooled in many biological and ecological sciences and believe you may be able to get AP college credit with extra focus on the environmental sciences. All are good reasons to take the AP Environmental Science Exam! Solid effort and review of the material and questions offered in the *5 Steps to a 5: AP Environmental Science* study guide will give you a leg up and help ensure your score is the best it can be with the time you have to study.

## Organization of the Book

This book takes you on a journey of the five steps needed to get ready for the AP exam in environmental science. Each step will provide skills and approaches helpful in achieving a perfect 5.

First, you will be introduced to the five-step plan described in the book. Chapter 1 gives some background on the AP Environmental Science exam. Chapter 2 lays out three study plans based on the amount of time you have before the test. Chapter 3 has a diagnostic exam to give you an idea of how much you know already. In Chapter 4, various tips and different types of AP exam questions are presented.

Chapters 5 to 13 offer a broad overview of the information important in an AP Environmental Science course. Although this is meant as review, some information may be new to you depending on your previous classes, teachers' particular focus, and how up-to-date you are on global environmental concerns. A summary, key ideas, and keywords are presented at the beginning of each chapter. A rapid review, along with multiple-choice and free-response questions and answers, are also included.

Following the informational chapters, two practice exams are provided with both question types (i.e., multiple choice and free response) found on the AP Environmental Science exam. After going through the study guide, you will be able to test your knowledge level on questions similar to those asked on past AP Environmental Science exams. Should you find areas where your memory or understanding fog, check your answers with the explanations and note where you need to refresh. Go back to the subject chapters and review the information.

## The Five-Step Program

### Step 1: Set Up Your Study Program

The first step contains an overview of the AP Environmental Science exam and an outline of associated topics. It also offers a timeline to help with your exam review planning.

- **The School-Year Timeline:** An entire school year: September to May
- **The One-Semester Timeline:** One semester: January to May
- **The Six-Week Timeline:** Six weeks: Quick exam brushup

### Step 2: Determine Your Test Readiness

This step offers a diagnostic exam for a "sneak peek" at your test readiness. Take your time with the questions and do your best. Remember, the diagnostic exam is intended to help you see how much you already know and how much preparation you need before you take the real exam.

### Step 3: Develop Strategies for Success

Here the different question types are described with strategies for doing your best on the multiple-choice and free-response questions. You'll learn how to read and analyze the questions and whether or not to guess. How to organize your responses on the free-response questions is also presented.

### Step 4: Review the Knowledge You Need to Score High

This step presents the bulk of the environmental science information you'll need to know to score well on the revised AP Environmental Science exam. Since teachers and classes in different geographical areas may focus on one topic more heavily than another, this material helps fill in your knowledge gaps. The topics covered in Chapters 5 to 13 parallel those presented in a year long AP class.

### Step 5: Build Your Test-Taking Confidence

The final step in AP Environmental Science preparation gives you a chance to take a practice exam with advice on how to avoid common mistakes. Practice exam questions are not from actual AP Environmental Science exams but mirror test material and question format.

## Introduction to the Graphics Used in This Book

To emphasize particular strategies, we use several icons throughout this book. An icon in the margin will alert you that you should pay particular attention to the accompanying text. We use these three icons:

This icon points out a very important concept or fact that you should not pass over.

This icon calls your attention to a strategy that you may want to try.

This icon indicates a tip that you might find useful.

STEP 1

# Set Up Your Study Plan

CHAPTER 1

# What You Need to Know About the AP Environmental Science Exam

**IN THIS CHAPTER**

**Summary:** Learn what's on the AP Environmental Science exam, how it is scored, and basic test-taking information.

**Key Ideas**

✪ Before taking the AP Environmental Science course, you should have at least one year of a life science (for example, biology) and one year of a physical science (for example, chemistry).

✪ Eighty multiple-choice questions account for 60 percent of your score on the AP Environmental Science exam; three free-response (essay) questions account for the remaining 40 percent.

✪ You will receive a score of 1 to 5 on the AP exam. Most colleges will award credit for a score of 3, 4, or 5.

✪ There is no guessing penalty; if you don't know an answer to a multiple-choice question, you should try to eliminate incorrect answer choices and then guess.

# The Advanced Placement (AP) Exams

The Advanced Placement Program (AP) is designed to allow high school students to earn credit for college-level courses by showing they have mastered the subject matter through their performance on an AP exam. Started in 1955, the program now encompasses dozens of AP exams across a range of disciplines. A complete list of the 38 AP courses offered and exams given is available at AP Central on the College Board website (https://apcentral .collegeboard.org/courses).

## Who Creates the AP Environmental Science Course and Exam?

The College Board (www.collegeboard.com) is responsible for creating and administering the AP exams. For the AP Environmental Science course and exam, it is guided by members of the AP Environmental Science Development Committee, which is composed of leading educators in environmental science at both the high school and college levels. AP environmental science teachers around the country follow a basic course curriculum that covers everything that will be on the AP exam. The AP course is designed to be the equivalent of a one-semester introductory environmental science college course. It includes biology, geology, chemistry, Earth science, and geography and fulfills a laboratory science requirement.

All questions developed for the exam go through a rigorous review process to ensure that they are accurate, fair, and valid. As part of this process, the questions are tested on actual students. In fact, some of the questions you will encounter are actually questions that are being tested for use on a future AP exam and do not count on your test score. But since there is no way of knowing which questions these are, you should do your best on all questions.

## Why Take the AP Environmental Science Exam?

The most obvious reason to take an AP exam is that you can earn college credit while you are still in high school, but there are other reasons as well. By taking an introductory college course in high school, you satisfy a prerequisite for many more advanced courses. This means you can jump right into more advanced courses in your field of study in college. Furthermore, since you are taking a college-level course in high school for free, you save a bundle of money over what it would cost to take the course in college. If you are taking several AP courses, you may even be able to finish college early. But even if you don't do well enough on the AP exam to earn college credit, you will still impress college admission officials. Your college application will show you have experienced a college-level course, are serious about school, and are not afraid of hard work.

Since you have bought this book, you are probably already enrolled in the AP Environmental Science course at your school. It is not a requirement that everyone enrolled in the course take the AP Environmental Science exam, but you should. Of course, doing well on the test is the only way to get college credit. Even if you think you will not do well enough to pass the test, have confidence in yourself; you may do better than you expect. And if you don't get a good score, you don't have to report it to the colleges to which you plan to apply.

Most students taking the AP Environmental Science exam are also taking biology, geology, chemistry, or other related science classes. An interesting thing about environmental science is that many subjects merge when studying the environment. Nature contains many interconnected components and concepts. In fact, most environmental jobs in the real world call for a general knowledge of all these areas when a job application is being considered.

# Frequently Asked Questions About the AP Environmental Science Exam

### Are There Any Prerequisites for the AP Environmental Science Course?

Students who take AP Environmental Science should have already completed one year of life science and one year of physical science (for example, one year of biology and one year of chemistry). Students should also have at least a year of algebra because of the quantitative analysis that is required in the course.

### Is There a Lab Requirement?

Yes. It is required that the students spend at least 25 percent of instructional time engaged in laboratory inquiry or fieldwork investigations.

### What Is the AP Classroom?

The AP Classroom is the name given to the online platform designed to the used by teachers and students during the AP course. It includes an online library of real AP exam questions from previous tests. Questions for every unit provide feedback, allowing you to check on your progress. The sign-up process includes entering a code provided by your teacher that is unique to your class so your teacher can monitor your progress, give you online assignments, and create unit tests. To start the sign-up process, go to www.collegeboard.com/apstudents.

### What Type of Questions Are on the AP Environmental Science Exam and How Long Is It?

The exam actually consists of two separate tests: Section 1 and Section II. The first section of the exam includes 80 multiple-choice questions and accounts for 60 percent of your total score. You have 90 minutes to complete this section of the test. Part II of the exam consists of three free-response questions and accounts for 40 percent of your final score. You have 70 minutes for this section. In total, the exam is 2 hours and 40 minutes.

### What Can I Expect Regarding the Multiple-Choice Questions?

The chart below shows what is on the test and the amount of your total score each part comprises.

| Unit 1: | The Living World: Ecosystems | 6–8% |
|---------|------------------------------|------|
| Unit 2: | The Living World: Biodiversity | 6–8% |
| Unit 3: | Populations | 10–15% |
| Unit 4: | Earth Systems and Resources | 10–15% |
| Unit 5: | Land and Water Use | 10–15% |
| Unit 6: | Energy Resources and Consumption | 10–15% |
| Unit 7: | Atmospheric Pollution | 7–10% |
| Unit 8: | Aquatic and Terrestrial Pollution | 7–10% |
| Unit 9: | Global Change | 15–20% |

Source: The College Board

The multiple-choice section includes both individual and set-based questions. The set-based questions will have two or three multiple-choice questions relating to a chart, graph, map, etc., that you are given. This visual representation of data is called a "stimulus" by the test creators. There will be three to four question sets based on quantitative data (tables, charts, graphs) and three to four question sets based on qualitative information (models, representations, maps). You can also expect two sets of questions that will include text-based sources.

### What Can I Expect Regarding the Free-Response Questions?

There are three free-response or essay questions and each of them is worth 10 points. In the first essay question you will be asked to design an investigation. In the second question, you will be asked to analyze an environmental problem and propose a solution. For the third, you will have to use calculations to propose a specific solution to an environmental problem.

Each free-response question typically has multiple parts. Be sure to answer all parts of each question and label your answer to each part. If you are asked to "propose two realistic solutions to reduce greenhouse gas emissions," you should be sure to give exactly two realistic solutions. Giving only one solution, no matter how comprehensive, will not earn you full credit. And, more important, giving three solutions, when only asked to give two, will not earn you any extra credit. Stick to exactly what you are asked to do.

### How Is the Exam Graded?

The multiple-choice questions are graded by a computer, but the essay questions are graded by humans. At the AP Reading in June, the free-response questions are read by environmental science college faculty and expert AP teachers at the high school level. A group of readers are assigned to each question; the three essay questions you write will be evaluated by three teams of teachers. Readers are carefully trained in their question and their work is monitored throughout the reading for fairness and consistency. Scores on the free-response questions are weighted and combined with the results of the multiple-choice section of the exam that was scored by computer. The raw score is converted into a score of 1–5; this is your final score on the AP Environmental Science exam. In July, you will receive your AP score for the exam you took in May.

### What Does the Score Mean?

Your AP score can be interpreted as follows:

| AP SCORE | RECOMMENDATIONS | COLLEGE GRADE EQUIVALENT |
|:---:|:---|:---:|
| 5 | Extremely well qualified | A |
| 4 | Well qualified | A–, B+, B |
| 3 | Qualified | B–, C+, C |
| 2 | Possibly qualified | n/a |
| 1 | No recommendation | n/a |

Source: The College Board

Colleges and universities are responsible for setting their own policy of what score you will need on the AP exam to receive credit. Most colleges and universities will award credit for a score of 3 or higher; however, elite colleges often require a score of 4 or better. Check the AP credit policy of each college or university to which you are applying. A search engine to do this is available at the College Board website: go to apstudent.org/creditpolicies.

## How Do I Sign Up for the Exam?

The deadline for registration for the exam is in October or November. Signing up is easy; your name and personal data is taken from the information you input when you registered for the AP Classroom. Schools receive personalized registration labels for each student taking the exam; you will no longer need to bubble in your personal information. The cost to students to take the exam in 2020 was $94. Students who sign up late pay an additional $40. If you cancel your registration to take the exam, that will also cost $40.

## Is There a Guessing Penalty on the Exam?

No. In times past there was a guessing penalty; a fraction of a point was subtracted for each incorrect answer but not for an unanswered question. But this is no longer the case. Points are given for each correct answer and no points are subtracted for a wrong answer. For that reason, if you don't know an answer, you should try to eliminate as many answer choices as possible and then guess. If you are running out of time, you should randomly guess the answers. You have a 25 percent chance of getting an answer correct simply by guessing. Never leave an answer blank.

## Is a Calculator Allowed?

A four-function, scientific, or graphing calculator is allowed on both sections of the exam. But only certain types and brands of calculators are allowed. Check the College Board website for a list of approved calculators at https://apstudents.collegeboard.org/exam-policies-guidelines/calculator-policies. Alternatively, just search for "approved calculators" on the website.

No calculator will be allowed that has the option to communicate with the world outside the exam room. Therefore, the calculator on your cell phone will not be allowed. You must have your own calculator; you will not be allowed to share calculators with a friend. Be sure your calculator is fully charged before the test.

A calculator will be a big help on questions that ask for a specific answer and on the third free-response question where you will have to use calculations to propose a solution to an environmental problem. But just because you *can* use a calculator, doesn't mean you *should*. You won't find it helpful on most of the questions on the exam—only when a specific calculation is asked for.

## What Should I Bring to the Test?

1. Two sharpened No. 2 pencils with erasers for all your responses on your multiple-choice answer sheet. Be sure the eraser will erase pencil marks completely without smudging.
2. Two pens with black or dark blue ink for writing your essays in the exam booklet.
3. A watch will allow you to pace yourself by keeping track of the time in case the exam room does not have a clock or the exam room's clock is not correct. Make sure your watch does not have Internet access, does not have an alarm, and does not beep.
4. An approved calculator. (You can actually bring two of these. If yours suddenly quits working for some reason, you'll have a backup.)
5. If you don't attend the school where you're taking the exam, you must bring a current government-issued or school-issued photo ID.

## What Should I Not Bring to the Exam Room?

1. Most types of electronic equipment (phones, smartwatches, laptops, cameras, recording devices, etc.) are prohibited. Approved calculators are the only exception.
2. Scratch paper; instead, you can write on blank areas of the exam booklet. Do *not* write anything on the exam answer sheet except to bubble in the answers.
3. Food or drink.

# CHAPTER 2

# How to Plan Your Time

IN THIS CHAPTER

**Summary:** The right preparation plan for you depends on your study habits, your own strengths and weaknesses, and the amount of time you have to prepare for the test. Take the diagnostic test in the next chapter to assess your strengths and weaknesses and get started.

**Key Ideas**

✪ Create a study plan that best suits your needs. It should take into account your strengths and weaknesses, your study habits, and the amount of time you have to prepare for the AP Environmental Science exam.

✪ The first step in creating your study plan is to take the diagnostic test in the next chapter; it will help identify where you need to prioritize your review.

✪ Your study plan will depend on when you start your test preparation. You can choose a full school year, a one-semester, or a six-week timeline for your plan.

# Your Personalized Study Plan for the AP Environmental Science Exam

Your study plan will be unique to your needs—your strengths and weaknesses and the amount of time you have to review. It's up to you to decide how you want to use this book to study for the AP Environmental Science exam. This book is designed for flexibility; you can work through it in order or skip around however you want. In fact, no two students who purchase this book will probably use it in exactly the same way.

The first step in developing your plan is to take the diagnostic test in the next chapter. This practice exam closely mirrors the multiple-choice section of the actual exam. The diagnostic test lets you experience what the multiple-choice section is like and also tells you what you are reasonably good at and what things you need to practice. Identify your weakness and focus on these first.

Also helpful in identifying strengths and weaknesses are the chapter summary and the key terms and ideas that begin each content review chapter. Use these to test yourself to determine if you need to carefully review the chapter or if your knowledge will allow you to skip it and move on to chapters that you need to study more completely.

# Three Timelines for Preparing for the AP Environmental Science Exam

Besides your strengths and weaknesses, another factor to consider is the amount of time you have to prepare for the test. This includes not only how long you have before the exam, but also the amount of time you have to devote to the review effort. For example, for students who are taking more than one AP course and have to divide their study time among many demands, it is especially important to prioritize the areas they need to review.

Below are three timelines for study plans based on how long you have before the test. Decide on a timeline for your study plan and get started.

## The School-Year Timeline

Choose this timeline if you like taking your time going through the material. Following this plan will allow you to practice your skills and develop your confidence gradually. You should go through the chapters in the book as you go through the units of your course. Take the diagnostic exam during winter break, the first practice exam during spring break, and the final practice exam a week before the actual exam. You will be able to see your progress!

This book is filled with explanatory material and practice exercises. Beginning to work through the chapters at the beginning of the school year will allow you to get to all the material in the book and maximize your preparation for the exam.

## The One-Semester Timeline

Starting in the middle of the school year should give you ample time to review and prepare for the exam. Begin by taking the diagnostic test in the next chapter; this will give you an idea of what the test is like. You'll get a sense of how hard the test will be for you, how much time you need to devote to practice, and which type of questions or tasks you most need to review. Then skip around in this book, prioritizing the chapters that you most need to review or that you find most difficult. Take the first practice exam during spring break and the final practice exam a week or a few days before you take the actual test.

## The Six-Week Timeline

OK, maybe you procrastinated a bit too long. But this might not be a problem if you are doing well in your AP Environmental Science class. In fact, preparation for the exam is included in most AP classes, so you may be better prepared for the exam than you realize.

Start by taking the diagnostic test in the next chapter to find out what the actual test will be like and to identify the chapters you most need to review. With limited time, it is especially important to prioritize wisely the areas you need to review. If you found the practice test difficult, try to devote as much time as possible to reviewing the chapters you found most difficult, paying special attention to the practice problems in these chapters. Save time to take the practice exams at the back of this book; take the final one a few days before you take the actual test. Even if you did well on the diagnostic test, you should take both practice exams; taking them will give you experience in pacing yourself within the time limits of the exam.

### When to Take the Practice Exams

Most students should take the diagnostic test in Chapter 3 when they begin test preparation. Taking the test will show you what the actual exam will be like and, based on your performance, you can identify your strong points as well as the weaknesses on which you'll need to focus. Take the first practice exam at the end of this book during spring break or midway through your test preparation to measure your progress and see if your priorities should change. Take the final practice exam a week, or perhaps only a few days, before the actual test.

The practice tests are perhaps the most important part of this book. Taking them will accomplish all of the following:

- Give you practice with all the different types of questions you'll encounter on the AP Environmental Science exam.
- Allow you to measure your progress and identify areas you need to focus on in your test preparation.
- Allow you to practice pacing yourself with the time limits imposed on the test.

Below are some things to remember as you plan your test-prep effort, regardless of when you start and how long you plan to practice:

- Establish a specific calendar of review so you stay on schedule and check off tasks as you complete them.
- Use your mobile phone to time yourself every time you take a timed test.
- Take advantage of the practice tests in this book. They are your friends.
- Don't stay up the night before the test trying to do some last-minute cramming; this may be counterproductive.

Good luck!

STEP **2**

# Determine Your Test Readiness

CHAPTER **3**  Take a Diagnostic Exam

# CHAPTER 3

# Take a Diagnostic Exam

**IN THIS CHAPTER**

**Summary:** In the following pages you will find a diagnostic exam that is modeled after the multiple-choice section of the actual AP exam. Take it as you begin your review for the AP Environmental Science Test. Use it to prioritize which chapters you will need to review for the actual exam.

**Key Idea**

✪ Practice the kind of multiple-choice questions you will be asked on the real exam.
✪ Check your work against the answers and explanations provided.
✪ Determine your areas of strength and weakness.
✪ Earmark the concepts to which you must give special attention.

## How to Take the Exam

When you take the diagnostic exam, try to reproduce the actual testing environment as closely as possible. Find a quiet place where you will not be interrupted. Do not listen to music or watch a movie while taking the exam! Set the timer on your cell phone for 90 minutes. If you didn't finish, note how far you have gotten so you can learn to pace yourself, but then take the extra time to complete all the questions so you can find your areas of weakness. One more thing: tear out the answer sheet provided and fill in the correct ovals with a No. 2 pencil. The AP Environmental Science Exam is a paper-and-pencil test.

## After Taking the Diagnostic Exam

Following the exam, you'll find not only the answers to the test questions, but also explanations for each answer. Don't just read the explanations for the questions you missed; you also need to understand the explanations for the questions you got right but weren't sure of. In fact, it's a good idea to read through the explanations for all the questions. Finally, complete the chapter-by-chapter analysis of your test results by filling in the boxes for the questions you missed. Then you have it—the chapters you most need to review.

# AP Environmental Science Diagnostic Exam

## ANSWER SHEET

| | | |
|---|---|---|
| 1 Ⓐ Ⓑ Ⓒ Ⓓ | 31 Ⓐ Ⓑ Ⓒ Ⓓ | 61 Ⓐ Ⓑ Ⓒ Ⓓ |
| 2 Ⓐ Ⓑ Ⓒ Ⓓ | 32 Ⓐ Ⓑ Ⓒ Ⓓ | 62 Ⓐ Ⓑ Ⓒ Ⓓ |
| 3 Ⓐ Ⓑ Ⓒ Ⓓ | 33 Ⓐ Ⓑ Ⓒ Ⓓ | 63 Ⓐ Ⓑ Ⓒ Ⓓ |
| 4 Ⓐ Ⓑ Ⓒ Ⓓ | 34 Ⓐ Ⓑ Ⓒ Ⓓ | 64 Ⓐ Ⓑ Ⓒ Ⓓ |
| 5 Ⓐ Ⓑ Ⓒ Ⓓ | 35 Ⓐ Ⓑ Ⓒ Ⓓ | 65 Ⓐ Ⓑ Ⓒ Ⓓ |
| 6 Ⓐ Ⓑ Ⓒ Ⓓ | 36 Ⓐ Ⓑ Ⓒ Ⓓ | 66 Ⓐ Ⓑ Ⓒ Ⓓ |
| 7 Ⓐ Ⓑ Ⓒ Ⓓ | 37 Ⓐ Ⓑ Ⓒ Ⓓ | 67 Ⓐ Ⓑ Ⓒ Ⓓ |
| 8 Ⓐ Ⓑ Ⓒ Ⓓ | 38 Ⓐ Ⓑ Ⓒ Ⓓ | 68 Ⓐ Ⓑ Ⓒ Ⓓ |
| 9 Ⓐ Ⓑ Ⓒ Ⓓ | 39 Ⓐ Ⓑ Ⓒ Ⓓ | 69 Ⓐ Ⓑ Ⓒ Ⓓ |
| 10 Ⓐ Ⓑ Ⓒ Ⓓ | 40 Ⓐ Ⓑ Ⓒ Ⓓ | 70 Ⓐ Ⓑ Ⓒ Ⓓ |
| 11 Ⓐ Ⓑ Ⓒ Ⓓ | 41 Ⓐ Ⓑ Ⓒ Ⓓ | 71 Ⓐ Ⓑ Ⓒ Ⓓ |
| 12 Ⓐ Ⓑ Ⓒ Ⓓ | 42 Ⓐ Ⓑ Ⓒ Ⓓ | 72 Ⓐ Ⓑ Ⓒ Ⓓ |
| 13 Ⓐ Ⓑ Ⓒ Ⓓ | 43 Ⓐ Ⓑ Ⓒ Ⓓ | 73 Ⓐ Ⓑ Ⓒ Ⓓ |
| 14 Ⓐ Ⓑ Ⓒ Ⓓ | 44 Ⓐ Ⓑ Ⓒ Ⓓ | 74 Ⓐ Ⓑ Ⓒ Ⓓ |
| 15 Ⓐ Ⓑ Ⓒ Ⓓ | 45 Ⓐ Ⓑ Ⓒ Ⓓ | 75 Ⓐ Ⓑ Ⓒ Ⓓ |
| 16 Ⓐ Ⓑ Ⓒ Ⓓ | 46 Ⓐ Ⓑ Ⓒ Ⓓ | 76 Ⓐ Ⓑ Ⓒ Ⓓ |
| 17 Ⓐ Ⓑ Ⓒ Ⓓ | 47 Ⓐ Ⓑ Ⓒ Ⓓ | 77 Ⓐ Ⓑ Ⓒ Ⓓ |
| 18 Ⓐ Ⓑ Ⓒ Ⓓ | 48 Ⓐ Ⓑ Ⓒ Ⓓ | 78 Ⓐ Ⓑ Ⓒ Ⓓ |
| 19 Ⓐ Ⓑ Ⓒ Ⓓ | 49 Ⓐ Ⓑ Ⓒ Ⓓ | 79 Ⓐ Ⓑ Ⓒ Ⓓ |
| 20 Ⓐ Ⓑ Ⓒ Ⓓ | 50 Ⓐ Ⓑ Ⓒ Ⓓ | 80 Ⓐ Ⓑ Ⓒ Ⓓ |
| 21 Ⓐ Ⓑ Ⓒ Ⓓ | 51 Ⓐ Ⓑ Ⓒ Ⓓ | |
| 22 Ⓐ Ⓑ Ⓒ Ⓓ | 52 Ⓐ Ⓑ Ⓒ Ⓓ | |
| 23 Ⓐ Ⓑ Ⓒ Ⓓ | 53 Ⓐ Ⓑ Ⓒ Ⓓ | |
| 24 Ⓐ Ⓑ Ⓒ Ⓓ | 54 Ⓐ Ⓑ Ⓒ Ⓓ | |
| 25 Ⓐ Ⓑ Ⓒ Ⓓ | 55 Ⓐ Ⓑ Ⓒ Ⓓ | |
| 26 Ⓐ Ⓑ Ⓒ Ⓓ | 56 Ⓐ Ⓑ Ⓒ Ⓓ | |
| 27 Ⓐ Ⓑ Ⓒ Ⓓ | 57 Ⓐ Ⓑ Ⓒ Ⓓ | |
| 28 Ⓐ Ⓑ Ⓒ Ⓓ | 58 Ⓐ Ⓑ Ⓒ Ⓓ | |
| 29 Ⓐ Ⓑ Ⓒ Ⓓ | 59 Ⓐ Ⓑ Ⓒ Ⓓ | |
| 30 Ⓐ Ⓑ Ⓒ Ⓓ | 60 Ⓐ Ⓑ Ⓒ Ⓓ | |

# AP Environmental Science Diagnostic Exam

### SECTION I: Multiple-Choice Questions
### Time—90 minutes

**Directions:** For the multiple-choice questions that follow, select the best answer and fill in the appropriate letter on the answer sheet.

**1.** The graph below shows the total number of endangered species per year.

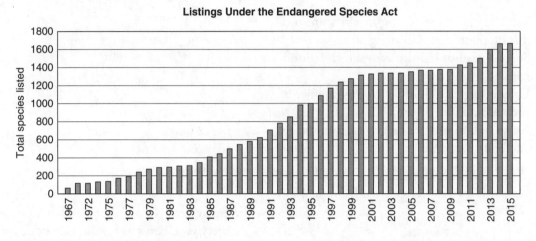

**Listings Under the Endangered Species Act**

Which of the following solutions could lead to a decrease of species on the endangered species list for future years?

(A) Introduce species to environments to compete for resources.
(B) Decriminalize poaching.
(C) Provide wildlife habitat corridors.
(D) Build roads and human habitation in wildlife areas.

**2.** The diagram below shows a convergent plate boundary.

**Convergent Plate Boundary**

What is causing the formation of the volcano near the convergent plate boundary you see in the picture above?

(A) The two continental plates are coming together and forming mountains.
(B) The ocean plate is subducting below the continental plate, melting, and rising to form a volcano.
(C) As the magma from the mantle rises, and the lithosphere is moving over a stationary hot spot, a line of volcanic islands is forming.
(D) Land is being formed at a divergent plate boundary as magma rises.

**3.** "Loud noises from cities are becoming a huge problem for animal species. The sounds of vehicles and construction are causing changes to animals' migratory routes, as well as causing problems to how they interact within their own species. This noise can have devastating effects to our biodiversity."

Which of the following statements would most likely support the author's claim?

(A) Vehicles and construction in cities are producing photochemical smog.
(B) Species need to learn to adapt to the sounds coming from cities.
(C) Urban sprawl is leading to environmental problems.
(D) Noise pollution is caused by transportation and construction.

**4.** Which of the following changes would most likely occur if the rat was removed from the food web?

**A Food Web**

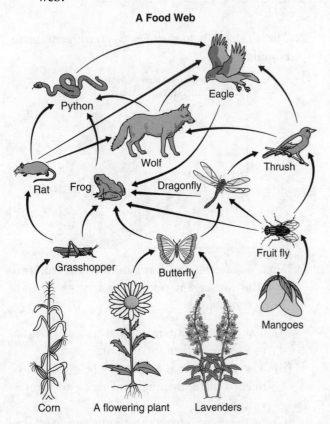

(A) Increase in grasshoppers and a decrease in pythons
(B) Decrease in frogs and a decrease in eagles
(C) Increase in eagles and an increase in thrushes
(D) Increase in lavenders and an increase in corn

**5.** If the producers in an ecosystem convert 2,000 kCal of energy stored in organic compounds, which of the following would most likely be the amount of energy available to the secondary consumers?

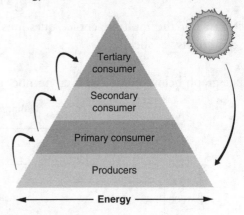

(A) 2,000
(B) 200
(C) 20
(D) 2

**6.** Soil erosion costs the world billions of dollars every year. Reasons for this economic cost include the number of pollutants washing into rivers and the loss of farmland due to erosion. A group of students decides to set up an experiment to see if they can reduce the amount of soil that is eroded after a rainfall.

Which of the following would the students discover as a benefit of reducing soil erosion?

(A) Soil filters and purifies water when protected from erosion.
(B) Soil can help reduce the effects of ozone depletion.
(C) Less soil erosion can help increase runoff and decrease infiltration.
(D) Clear-cutting can reduce the impacts of soil erosion.

**7.** People that live in the northern part of the United States can reduce their energy cost by lowering their thermostat by 2° in the winter. This reduces their energy costs by about 8 percent in many homes. If the family was paying $150 per month, how much will their bill be if they lower the thermostat by 2°?

(A) $12
(B) $187.50
(C) $37.5
(D) $138

8. Which of the following is true about persistent organic pollutants (POPs)?

(A) POPs break down easily in the environment.
(B) POPs are found naturally on Earth.
(C) POPs can travel very long distances through the food chain.
(D) POPs cause nervous system damage.

9. Which of the following is a nonpoint source pollutant that might affect the air quality of a major city?

(A) Automobile exhaust
(B) Mercury from a coal burning power plant
(C) A camper's campfire
(D) Fertilizer runoff from a CAFO

10. Which of the following best describes an environmental disadvantage of aquaculture?

(A) Aquaculture leads to overfishing.
(B) Aquaculture can generate wastewater and contaminate waterways.
(C) Aquaculture can be cost prohibitive.
(D) Aquaculture helps build resistance to disease in wild populations of fish.

11. A country has a growth rate of 3 percent. How many years will it take for the population to double?

(A) 3 years
(B) 23 years
(C) 30 years
(D) 210 years

12. A country is going through the demographic transition and has lowered its total fertility rate (TFR) from 6.0 to 3.2 in 50 years. Which of the following could have affected the decline in TFR?

(A) The government put in place strict laws on who could receive access to family planning.
(B) Women have married at younger ages.
(C) Good nutrition and medical attention are not accessible for many.
(D) Women have gained more access to education.

13. Which of the following would be the most effective solution for reducing ozone depletion?

(A) Encourage the manufacturers to utilize alternative chemicals.
(B) Utilize chlorofluorocarbons in industrial processes.
(C) Eat lower on the food chain so methane is reduced from cattle farming.
(D) Ensure landfills are capped and gases can't be released into the atmosphere.

14. The graph below would be best used to compare to which of the following environmental concerns?

**Global Average Temperature**

(A) Depletion of the stratospheric ozone levels
(B) Increase of tropospheric ozone levels
(C) Rising sea levels from melting ice sheets
(D) Decreases in insect-borne vector diseases

15. One island is 30 km away from the mainland and another is 10 km away. They are both virtually the same size. Which of the following would be correct about the number of species living on the islands?

(A) The numbers would be generally the same and would include species from the mainland.
(B) There would be fewer species on the island farther away and more species on the island closer to the mainland.
(C) There would be more species on the island farther away and fewer species on the island closer to the mainland.
(D) The numbers would be generally the same but neither island would have species from the mainland.

**16.** Based on the diagram below, which of the following best describes what happens during a thermal inversion?

(A) The air temperature is cooler near the Earth's surface than above so pollution is trapped close to Earth.
(B) Warm air rises, allowing pollution to escape to space.
(C) Warm air rises, trapping pollution close to the Earth's surface.
(D) Sinking air pressure allows pollutants to escape to space.

**17.** Coyotes eat rabbits as one of their main sources of food. Which of the following would be true of coyotes?

(A) Coyotes are herbivores.
(B) Ten percent of the energy from the rabbit will go to the coyote when it eats the rabbit.
(C) The coyote and the rabbit are in a mutualistic symbiotic relationship.
(D) If you removed the coyote from the food web, rabbits would decline in numbers.

**18.** Michelle likes to take a walk and enjoy nature. It calms her down, allows her to think about the next day, and she is able to get exercise while doing it. Which ecosystem service is Michelle benefiting most from?

(A) Provisioning
(B) Regulating
(C) Cultural
(D) Supporting

**19.** A student is on a walk and decides to test some of the soil they find. After testing the student discovers it is 10 percent sand, 60 percent silt, and 30 percent clay. Which of the following soil types would the student classify the soil as?

(A) Silty clay loam
(B) Clay loam
(C) Sandy clay loam
(D) Clay

**20.** The image below shows the different layers of the atmosphere.

What layer is where chlorofluorocarbons have destroyed ozone?

(A) Troposphere
(B) Stratosphere
(C) Mesosphere
(D) Thermosphere

**21.** The diagram below shows a typical nuclear power plant.

**Nuclear Power Plant**

Which letter corresponds to the part of the plant where steam is used to turn a turbine?

(A) A
(B) B
(C) C
(D) D

**22.** Which of the following best describes why tidal energy is a renewable energy source?

(A) There is only a certain amount of tidal energy that can't easily be captured once it is used.
(B) Tidal energy is only available in certain places on Earth; therefore, it is considered nonrenewable.
(C) Each day, as the tides go in and out, tidal energy can be captured; it doesn't run out and can be replaced.
(D) Tidal energy can damage ecosystems so it is nonrenewable.

**23.** Lake trout like cold, oxygen-rich waters due to their bodies' need for high amounts of oxygen. Which of the following would be the most damaging to lake trout?

(A) Thermal pollution from a nuclear power plant
(B) Persistent organic pollutants working their way up the food chain
(C) A thermal inversion from atmospheric pollution
(D) Acid rain decreasing the pH of the lake

**24.** Around December, fishermen off the coast of South America would discover that the normal numbers of fish they would catch would diminish every three to seven years. Which of the following is the best explanation of why this was happening?

(A) Individual sport fishing was occurring in the region.
(B) Fallout from local coal-burning power plants was generating acid rain.
(C) Warmer waters were causing the fish to move to colder waters.
(D) Large predators such as sharks were frequenting the region.

**25.** The diagram below shows how Earth is tilted on its axis.

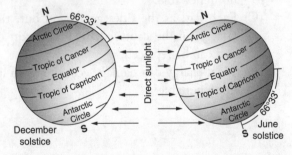

Which best explains why the Arctic Circle would have the lowest solar radiation per unit area in December?

(A) During December, the Arctic Circle receives the most direct sunlight.
(B) During December, the Arctic Circle has the longest days of the year.
(C) The Antarctic Circle is in the Southern Hemisphere so it is tilted toward the sun in December.
(D) During December, the Arctic Circle is tilted away from the sun so it receives the lowest solar radiation compared to anywhere else on Earth.

**26.** A farmer wants to discover why every year they have to put more and more pesticides on their crops to keep the pests from destroying them. Which of the following best describes the problem the farmer is trying to solve?

(A) The pests are breeding faster than ever due to climate change.
(B) The farmer has switched to a crop that the pests like more than the previous crop.
(C) The pests are becoming resistant to the pesticide through artificial selection.
(D) It is an El Niño year and the pests have moved due to increased rainfall along the coasts.

**27.** The greenhouse effect is a process that occurs when gases in Earth's atmosphere trap the sun's heat. This is important to life on Earth. Which of the following is one of the main greenhouse gases?

(A) Helium
(B) Methane
(C) Radon
(D) Lithium

**28.** The carbon cycle is shown in the diagram below.

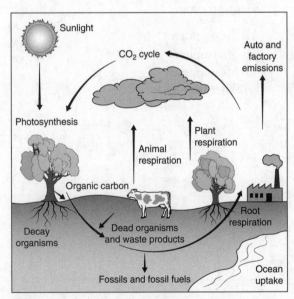

Which of the following is a place where carbon is added to the atmosphere?

(A) Photosynthesis
(B) Fossils and fossil fuels found underground
(C) Ocean uptake
(D) Animal respiration

29. A scientist is interested in seeing how high the levels of DDT are in a population of bald eagles living near a wetland. Which of the following would be a testable hypothesis the scientist could use for their investigation?

   (A) Because DDT is fat soluble, it will bioaccumulate in living organisms and will be found in the tissues of the bald eagles.
   (B) Because DDT was banned and removed from the market, it will not be found in the tissues of the bald eagles.
   (C) Because DDT is only found in primary consumers, it will not be found in the tissues of the bald eagles.
   (D) Because DDT is found in the atmosphere and soaks into the feathers as the birds fly, it will be found in the tissues of the bald eagles.

30. A gas station wants to prevent the fumes from escaping into the atmosphere as people pump gas into their vehicles. Which of the following devices would the gas station want to install?

   (A) Catalytic converter
   (B) Scrubber
   (C) Vapor recovery nozzle
   (D) Electrostatic precipitator

31. Which of the following is a benefit of using wind energy?

   (A) Steam generated from wind energy is used to turn a turbine and generate energy.
   (B) Wind turbines can be placed on land that is being used for farming or ranching to multipurpose the land.
   (C) The carbon dioxide produced from wind energy can be captured and used for carbon sequestration.
   (D) The energy created from the wind turbines can be used in hydrogen fuel cell technology.

32. In 2018/2019, Japan's greenhouse gas emissions fell to a record low. The country's greenhouse gas (GHG) emissions have declined from 1,291 $MtCO_2$ in 2017/18 to 1,244 $MtCO_2$ in 2018/19. What percent decrease has Japan seen in its GHG emissions?

   (A) 3.6%
   (B) 4,700%
   (C) 47%
   (D) 3.8%

33. The data table below shows how many animals are born every day.

| ANIMAL | HOW MANY ARE BORN EACH DAY |
|---|---|
| Humboldt penguins | 40 |
| Rabbits (UK) | 1,900,000 |
| Chickens | 62,000,000 |
| Bees (UK) | 370,000,000 |
| Nematodes | 600,000,000,000,000,000,000 |

Which of the following is most likely an animal that is an r-strategist?

   (A) Humboldt penguins
   (B) Rabbits
   (C) Chickens
   (D) Nematodes

34. Based on the data in the graph below, if a city wanted to start a recycling advertisement campaign to encourage people to recycle materials generated before they ended up in the local landfill, what would be the material the city would spend the least time convincing people to recycle?

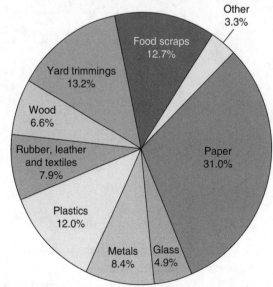

Percentage of Materials Sent to Local Landfills

   (A) Paper
   (B) Yard trimmings
   (C) Plastics
   (D) Glass

**35.** The graph below shows the number of spruce trees per hectare of land over the years of glacial retreat in Glacier Bay, Alaska.

Based on the graph, when was the total biomass of spruce trees the greatest?

(A) 20 years since glacial retreat
(B) 80 years since glacial retreat
(C) 120 years since glacial retreat
(D) 200 years since glacial retreat

**Use the graph below to answer questions 36–37.**

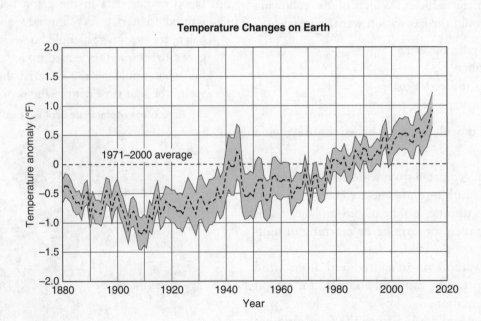

**36.** What is the trend shown in the graph?

(A) Use of chlorofluorocarbons is destroying the stratospheric ozone layer.
(B) Global temperatures have increased over the past 140 years.
(C) The negative feedback loop in the Arctic is impacting the temperatures on Earth.
(D) The circulation patterns in the Hadley cells have caused Earth's temperatures to lower over time.

**37.** Which of the following would be the best way to slow the trend that is seen in the graph?

(A) Limit the addition of greenhouse gases in the atmosphere.
(B) Discourage the use of nonrenewable energy sources.
(C) Limit the process of secondary success in land environments.
(D) Encourage people to eat higher on the food chain.

38. Stratospheric ozone depletion has led to increased UV rays reaching the Earth's surface. Which of the following would help to stop the depletion of stratospheric ozone?

(A) Limit the addition of greenhouse gases in the atmosphere.
(B) Limit the use of fossil fuels for energy production.
(C) Reduce methane gas release from landfills.
(D) Stop using chlorofluorocarbons in industry and household products.

39. A scientist is trying to determine the best way to help farmers limit the number of pests on crops while lowering the environmental effects of pesticides. The scientist sets up an experiment using predator bugs that eat the pests and then collects the following data.

| WEEK | NUMBER OF PREDATOR BUGS | NUMBER OF PEST SPECIES |
|---|---|---|
| 1 | 2,000 | 1,000 |
| 2 | 2,500 | 700 |
| 3 | 3,500 | 300 |
| 4 | 5,000 | 20 |

What method of pest management is the scientist incorporating?

(A) Using organophosphates on crops to lower pest numbers
(B) Using persistent organophosphates on crops to lower pest numbers
(C) Using integrated pest management to lower pest numbers
(D) Using terracing methods to lower pest numbers

40. Which of the following activities are humans doing that are bleaching coral reefs due to ocean acidification?

(A) Dumping untreated sewage into the open ocean
(B) Leaking oil from tanker boats
(C) Dumping plastic, forming the Pacific garbage gyre
(D) Burning fossil fuels and increasing atmospheric carbon dioxide

41. A population is growing exponentially and eventually overshoots its carrying capacity. Which of the following would be an impact of this overshoot?

(A) Starvation and disease will increase.
(B) Resources will increase to support the population.
(C) Carbon levels in the atmosphere will increase globally.
(D) Competition will decrease as the population explodes.

42. Japan's age-structure diagram is pictured below. What type of growth does the diagram demonstrate?

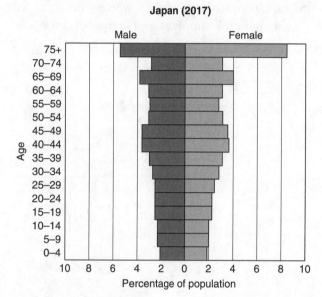

Japan (2017)

(A) Rapid growth
(B) Slow growth
(C) Stable growth
(D) Declining growth

43. Which of the following is the best example of the tragedy of the commons?

(A) Timber companies paying private tree farmers for timber.
(B) Farmers in arid climates overdrawing on water resources.
(C) Farmers negotiating usage of grazing land.
(D) Licensing sports fishermen being given regulations and limits.

**44.** Overfishing is a concern for many countries and it has lowered the biodiversity in aquatic systems. Which of the following could a country implement to solve this environmental problem?

(A) Give tax incentives to the fisherman who brings in the largest catch of the day.
(B) Extend the fishing season.
(C) Ban the use of purse seines, long-line fishing, and trawling nets that can take thousands of fish at a time.
(D) Remove all restrictions on different fishing methods.

**45.** An experiment is conducted where water is poured through a soil sample as seen in the diagram below.

Then 100 ml of water is added and after 1 hour 95 ml is found in the bottom of the jar. Which of the following is most likely the type of soil being tested?

(A) Sand
(B) Silt
(C) Loam
(D) Clay

**46.** A scientist has been asked to find out why sulfur dioxide emissions are down 73 percent from 2006 to 2015. The scientist discovers that coal-fired electricity generation is down 32 percent in that time, but this is a much larger reduction. Which of the following is most likely the device being used on power plants that are lowering the $SO_2$ emissions the greatest?

(A) Vapor recovery nozzle
(B) Catalytic converter
(C) Fluidized bed combustion and gas scrubbing
(D) Electrostatic precipitators

**47.** Use the graph below to answer the following question.

**Percentage of Population Using Solid Fuels as the Main Cooking Fuel**
The graph shows the percentage of households in each region that rely on solid fuels (wood, crop residues, dung, charcoal or coal) as the main cooking fuel. The use of solid fuels for cooking can lead to very low indoor air quality and illnesses such as pneumonia, stroke, heart disease, or lung cancer.

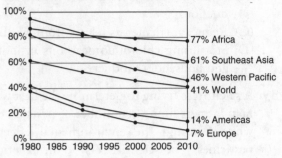

Which of the following conclusions can you draw from the graph above?

(A) People living in Africa are 77 percent more likely to suffer from diseases like pneumonia, stroke, and lung cancer than people living in high-income countries.
(B) Indoor air quality has risen in the past 30 years.
(C) Fewer people suffer from diseases like pneumonia, stroke, and lung cancer in the Americas than they do in Europe.
(D) Southeast Asia has not taken any steps in the past 30 years to lower indoor air pollution.

**48.** Nitrous oxides are considered trace gases and compose less than a tenth of 1 percent of the atmosphere. Why would scientists be concerned about the global climate impact of these trace gases?

(A) Nitrous oxides cause brain damage in children.
(B) The global warming potential (GWP) of nitrous oxide is 310, so it has a GWP of 300 times more than carbon dioxide, which has a GWP of 1.
(C) Nitrous oxides come from the production of Styrofoam and refrigerants, substances used all over Earth that lead to stratospheric ozone depletion.
(D) Nitrous oxides rise on air currents and destroy stratospheric ozone.

49. The graph below shows the energy output in kWh for a local solar energy system. Use the graph to determine which of the following statements is true.

(A) Solar energy is available all year in amounts needed to supply cities with renewable energy.
(B) The output of this energy system is the highest during the month of June.
(C) Solar energy should not be used to support local energy demands due to the low output in the winter months.
(D) This energy system can produce over 7,000 kWh per month April through August, making it a good supplement for local energy output.

50. The chart below has the ecological footprint for five different people and is measured in the number of hectares (10,000 square meters) of land required to support the activity.

| | FOOD | CARBON EMISSIONS | HOUSING | GOODS AND SERVICES | TOTAL |
|---|---|---|---|---|---|
| Person 1 | 1.8 | 2.9 | 2.4 | 1.6 | 8.7 |
| Person 2 | 3.2 | 3 | 1.6 | 1.2 | 9 |
| Person 3 | 1.4 | 2.7 | 2.2 | 2.0 | 8.3 |
| Person 4 | 2.7 | 3 | 1.5 | 2.9 | 10.1 |
| Person 5 | 2.8 | 3 | 3.4 | 1.9 | 11.1 |

If person 4 wanted to lower their ecological footprint to be more like person 1, what two activities should they change?

(A) Person 4 should increase their use of fossil fuels and food.
(B) Person 4 should decrease their housing and increase their goods and services.
(C) Person 4 should eat lower on the food chain and purchase fewer goods and services.
(D) Person 4 should increase their housing and increase their goods and services.

**Use the graph below to answer questions 51–52.**

**Global Land and Ocean Temperature Anomalies, January–December**

*Source*: National Oceanic and Atmospheric Administration

**51.** The graph above shows the trend in global temperatures from 1880 to 2010. Which of the following could be a likely consequence of the temperature changes in this graph?

(A) Sea levels will rise, flooding coastal areas.
(B) Permafrost will freeze and not allow as long a growing season.
(C) Sea ice will freeze, lowering the salt content of the surrounding oceans.
(D) Specialist species will flourish.

**52.** Which of the following most likely caused the trend you see in the data above?

(A) Increased use of fossil fuels
(B) A shift to eating lower on the food web
(C) Increased use of lead gasoline in developing countries
(D) Biomagnification up the food web of persistent organic pollutants (POPs)

**53.** The picture below shows what happens when a body of water becomes eutrophic.

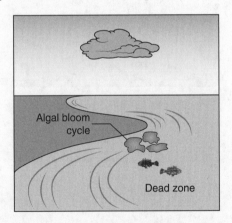

Which of the following would be the cause of what is seen in the illustration above?

(A) Increased use of fossil fuels for energy production
(B) Increased use of fertilizers from agriculture
(C) Increased thermal pollution from nuclear power plants
(D) Increased acid deposition from coal burning power plants

54. A scientist is taking water samples of a nearby lake. The scientist takes the pH of the lake water and discovers it has a pH of 6.5. Which of the following activities will the scientist most likely conclude is causing the change in lake pH?

   (A) The release of chlorofluorocarbons in the nearby town
   (B) The escape of endocrine disruptors into the lake
   (C) Limestone rock that is leaching into the lake
   (D) A high concentration of motor vehicles and coal-burning power plants in the vicinity of the lake

55. The $LD_{50}$ for table salt in humans is approximately 12,357 mg/kg. If a person weighs 200 lbs. and 1 kg = 2.2 lbs., how many grams of salt would it take to reach the $LD_{50}$ for a human?

   (A) 1,123.4 grams
   (B) 1,123,363.6 grams
   (C) 561.7 grams
   (D) 22.47 grams

56. Burning biomass would be one way to move from our dependence on fossil fuels and also decrease the waste stream. Which of the following correctly describes a concern of using biomass on a large scale?

   (A) Earthquakes can result from the heated water pumped into Earth.
   (B) Temperature inversions can result from the heat from the fires.
   (C) Deforestation and habitat destruction can result.
   (D) Helium can be released into the atmosphere.

57. The Goliath frog is the largest living frog on Earth, growing to 13 inches (33 centimeters) in length and weighing up to 7 pounds. The females lay several hundred eggs at one time with very few making it to adulthood. Adult frogs can live up to 15 years in the wild. Which of the following best characterizes this type of animal?

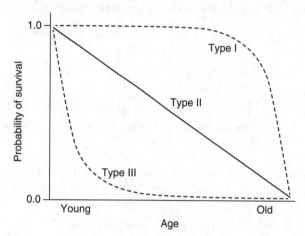

   (A) Goliath frogs are a k-selected species, displaying a Type III survivorship curve.
   (B) Goliath frogs are an r-selected species, displaying a Type I survivorship curve.
   (C) Goliath frogs are a k-selected species, displaying a Type II survivorship curve.
   (D) Goliath frogs are an r-selected species, displaying a Type III survivorship curve.

58. Which of the following would have the best success of surviving stress from environmental problems?

   (A) Populations with high genetic biodiversity
   (B) Populations with low genetic biodiversity
   (C) Populations with k-strategists
   (D) A population with low species richness

**59.** The largest watershed in the United States is the Mississippi River watershed. Pollution from farm fertilizers, soil erosion, and wastewater from sewage treatment plants are causing problems with the coastal waters at the end of this watershed. Which of the following would be an environmental concern for the estuary system at the end of the Mississippi River watershed?

(A) Increased fertilizers will bring increased fishing and tourism to the area.

(B) Low oxygen, or hypoxia, will result in the coastal waters.

(C) Runoff will lead to increased sea levels.

(D) Sewage waters will bring in estuary organisms containing disease.

**60.** A timber company is clear-cutting large acres of land to sell as lumber. Which of the following environmental consequences and economic benefits of clearcutting are correctly paired?

(A) Clear-cutting leads to soil erosion but provides the most profits.

(B) Clear-cutting leads to lower soil temperatures but provides the most profits.

(C) Clear-cutting leads to soil erosion but is costly to lumber companies.

(D) Clear-cutting leads to higher soil temperatures but is costly to lumber companies.

**61.** Surface mining removes the plants from an area leaving it vulnerable to erosion. Which of the following would be a way to remediate the loss of soil by mining?

(A) Take the slag and tailings to a certified landfill for removal.

(B) Use the overburden as agricultural filler.

(C) Reestablish the vegetation and assess and evaluate frequently.

(D) Grind up the overburden into a fine powder and spread on the area evenly.

**62.** The diagram below shows the rain shadow effect. Which of the following correctly identifies the factors behind this phenomenon?

(A) As the air mass moves to higher elevations, it expands and warms. This warm air holds more moisture so clouds form and it rains. The air mass then moves over the mountain and there is less rainfall.

(B) As the air mass moves to higher elevations, it expands and cools. This cool air doesn't hold as much moisture so clouds form and it rains. The air mass then moves over the mountain and causes catastrophic flooding concerns.

(C) As the air mass moves to lower elevations, it expands and cools. This cool air holds more moisture so clouds form and it rains. The air mass then moves over the mountain and there is more rainfall, ending droughts when they occur.

(D) As the air mass moves to higher elevations, it cools. This cool air doesn't hold as much moisture so clouds form and it rains. The air mass then moves over the mountain and there is less rainfall.

**63.** Giant pandas eat bamboo and live in a few mountain ranges in south central China in Sichuan, Shaanxi, and Gansu provinces. The koala, a marsupial, lives in eastern Australia and eats eucalyptus trees. Pigeons and doves are distributed everywhere on Earth, except for the driest areas, and eat seeds, fruits, insects, and worms. Based on the descriptions above, what can we determine about these animals?

(A) Giant pandas and koalas are specialists and pigeons and doves are also specialists.

(B) Giant pandas and koalas are generalists and pigeons and doves are specialists.

(C) Giant pandas and koalas are specialists and pigeons and doves are generalists.

(D) Giant pandas and koalas are generalists and pigeons and doves are also generalists.

**64.** If the graph below shows the numbers of lionfish found in the Western Atlantic Ocean, Caribbean Sea, and Gulf of Mexico, what could we conclude from the data?

(A) Lionfish are an invasive species that has not yet reached its carrying capacity.

(B) Lionfish are an endangered species that should be federally protected.

(C) Lionfish live in coastal regions all over the globe.

(D) Lionfish have predators that were hunted to extinction, allowing their unprecedented growth to occur.

**65.** A farmer wants to increase the number of crops they produces. To do this they use a tiller to turn over the land and prepare the ground for sowing while breaking up the soil and removing weeds. Which of the following environmental problems might the farmer encounter because of his tilling practice?

(A) Compaction of soil not allowing water to infiltrate

(B) Erosion of soil and water eutrophication

(C) Terracing leading to flooding

(D) Acid deposition from a lowered pH

**Use the graph below to answer questions 66–68.**

**Projected Total Fertility Rate by World Region**

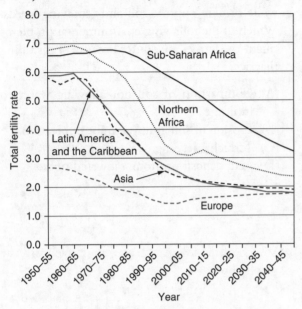

66. Which of the following can we conclude from the graph above?

   (A) Sub-Saharan Africa is at replacement level fertility in 2010.
   (B) In 1990, Northern Africa was a developed country with access for women to education and jobs.
   (C) Europe has had a low total fertility rate since 2000.
   (D) People in Latin America have more land per person than people in Europe.

67. Which of the following age-structure diagrams would most likely describe sub-Saharan Africa in 1970?

**Generalized Population Age-Structure Diagrams**

   (A) A
   (B) B
   (C) C
   (D) D

68. Which of the following environmental problems would a scientist expect to see in Northern Africa in 1960?

   (A) Habitat loss from deforestation to provide for the growing populations
   (B) Thermal pollution from nuclear power plants
   (C) Large-scale flooding from a rain shadow effect
   (D) The greenhouse effect

69. Methane is a greenhouse gas that contributes to climate change. Which of the following correctly describes methane's contribution to climate change?

   (A) Methane increases acid deposition.
   (B) Methane increases the albedo effect in polar regions.
   (C) Methane gas has the ability to trap infrared energy from the sun.
   (D) Methane gas is an endocrine disruptor in many species.

70. The graphic below shows the water (hydrologic) cycle. If we use asphalt and concrete to cover natural surfaces, which of the following would be the most likely impact on the water cycle?

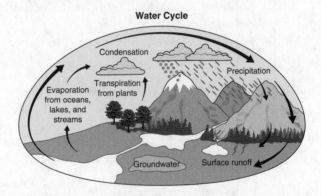

   (A) There would be less precipitation.
   (B) Evaporation would decrease.
   (C) Surface runoff would decrease.
   (D) Less water would infiltrate into the groundwater.

71. "Sea urchins belong to the phylum Echinodermata, the same group as sea stars, sand dollars, and sea cucumbers. Many saltwater aquarium enthusiasts like to introduce sea urchins into their tanks. However, adult sea urchins have a very narrow range of salt concentration. Salinity levels that are too low or too high will result in reabsorption of gametes or death."

Which of the following best identifies the author's claim?

(A) If you love salt water aquariums you should introduce sea urchins.
(B) Sea urchins have a narrow ecological tolerance for salinity.
(C) Sea urchins need warm water to survive.
(D) Sea stars, sand dollars, and sea cucumbers are fragile specialist species.

72. Many environmentalists propose removing dams from rivers because of their environmental impact. What environmental disadvantage would occur by removing dams?

(A) Air pollution could occur if we revert back to burning fossil fuels to generate energy.
(B) Sediment could build up behind where the dam used to be.
(C) Estuary systems below the dam could dry up after dam removal.
(D) The energy that had been created before the dam was removed would need to be stored for future use.

73. Use the graph below to answer the following question.

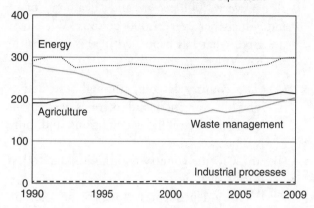

Which of the following can you derive from the graph above?

(A) The largest source of methane emissions is from industrial processes.
(B) In the past 20 years, methane emissions from energy have steadily increased.
(C) In 2009, methane emissions reached nearly 300 million metric tons carbon dioxide equivalency.
(D) Agriculture, which includes concentrated feeding operations, has increased from less than 200 million metric tons carbon dioxide equivalence to 210 million metric tons carbon dioxide equivalence.

74. Which of the following would result from the plate boundary seen below?

**Divergent Plate Boundary**

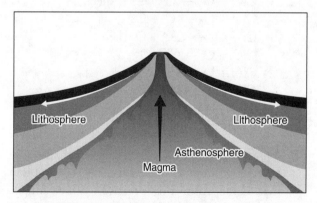

(A) Mountains would be formed.
(B) Island arcs would be formed.
(C) Sea-floor spreading would occur.
(D) Hot spots would occur.

**75.** A country had a birth rate of 20 individuals per every 1,000 persons and a death rate of 8 individuals per every 1,000 persons in 2019. In 1960 the same county had a birth rate of 40 individuals per every 1,000 persons and a death rate of 17 individuals per every 1,000 persons. What best describes what has happened in this country in the past 70 years?

(A) The country is going through the demographic transition and there is less infant mortality, better living conditions, and more women are educated.

(B) In 2019 the country is shrinking due to less births than deaths.

(C) Density-dependent factors are at work in this country.

(D) The growth rate of this country has increased.

**76.** A company produces power from coal and during the process captures the excess heat that would have been wasted. The company then uses this heat to boil water, create steam, or heat buildings. What process is the company implementing?

(A) Hydrogen fuel cell technology
(B) Passive solar generation
(C) Cogeneration
(D) Renewable energy transformation

**77.** The depletion of the stratospheric ozone layer is threatening the health of life on Earth. Which of the following chemical equations best explains the reaction that occurs in the stratosphere that breaks down ozone molecules?

(A) $ClO + O_3 \rightarrow ClO + O_3$ then
$ClO + O_2 \rightarrow Cl + O_3$
(B) $Cl + O_3 \rightarrow ClO + O_2$ then
$ClO + O \rightarrow Cl + O_2$
(C) $ClO + O \rightarrow Cl + O_2$ then
$Cl + O_3 \rightarrow ClO + O_2$
(D) $ClO_2 + O \rightarrow Cl + O_2$ then
$Cl + O_3 \rightarrow ClO_2 + O$

**78.** As we continue our reliance on fossil fuels for energy, we expand the environmental problems that come from this practice. Which of the following correctly describes an environmental problem of burning fossil fuels?

(A) Fracking is used to obtain oil and gas but leads to groundwater contamination and releases volatile organic compounds during the production process.

(B) Storage of lithium batteries used in fossil fuel production can leak and contaminate groundwater.

(C) Damming of rivers prevents migration of fish species like salmon.

(D) Storage of the radioactive waste produced from fossil fuel production can lead to radiation exposure and cancers.

**79.** "As transportation networks expand and urban areas grow, noise from sources such as vehicle engines is spreading into remote places. Human-caused noise has consequences for wildlife, entire ecosystems and people. It reduces the ability to hear natural sounds, which can mean the difference between life and death for many animals, and degrade the calming effect that we feel when we spend time in wild places."

—From "How Noise Pollution Is Wreaking Havoc on U.S. Wildlife," by Rachel Buxton in *The Nation*, July 18, 2017.

Which of the following best identifies the author's claim?

(A) Limiting energy production near wild areas will help prevent noise pollution.

(B) Noise pollution is a bigger problem in the northeastern United States than anywhere else.

(C) Animals are migrating across large areas to escape the consequences of noise pollution.

(D) Humans are causing noise pollution that is impacting animals and human relaxation.

**80.** Oceans are warming due to climate change, which is having a devastating impact on wildlife. Which of the following would be a consequence of our oceans warming?

(A) Arctic species are moving farther north.

(B) Coastal ecosystems are becoming shallower, allowing more light to penetrate farther into the waters.

(C) Aquatic animals are being impacted by noise pollution from surrounding cities.

(D) Coral bleaching is occurring, which is damaging reef systems.

**STOP. End of Part I.**

## › Answer Key and Explanations

1. **C**—Building wildlife habitat corridors can allow animals to have a place to live, find food, and migrate, which will lower the impact of human habitation.

2. **B**—As the ocean plate subducts, or is forced below the continental plate, the ocean plate melts and rises. Have you ever watched a lava lamp work? The wax (lava) is down on the bottom of the lamp where the heat source (light bulb) is found. As the heat melts the wax, the wax begins to rise up through the liquid to the top—this is like what is happening on our planet. As the ocean plate melts because of the heat in our Earth, it begins to rise, forming a volcano.

3. **D**—The author states that vehicles and construction are causing noise pollution that is harming species.

4. **A**—Rats eat grasshoppers, so removing rats would cause grasshoppers to increase. But rats are a food source for pythons, so removing the prey would decrease the predators (pythons).

5. **C**—According to the 10 percent rule, a plant (which in this case has 2,000 kCal) will be eaten by a primary consumer, giving the primary consumer 200 kCal. When a secondary consumer eats the primary consumer it only gets 10 percent of that energy, or in this case 20 kCal.

6. **A**—Soil erosion can be caused by water and wind taking soil away. It is very important to stop soil erosion if possible because of the importance of soil for plants, the ability soil has to clean and filter water, and the concern that when soil erodes it can damage the local waterways.

7. **D**—$150 × $.08 = $12 less, so $150 − 12 = $138

8. **C**—Because animals migrate long distances in the water or in wind, and because these chemicals can travel in wind and water long distances, there are POPs in almost all parts of our planet. These chemicals are passed from one species to the other in the food chain (biomagnification).

9. **A**—The car's exhaust is nonpoint source pollution. You can't point to one particular thing. You can't point with your finger to all the cars on the road. As you read the question think about it like this: is that a single thing or a bunch of things? If it is a single thing, it is most likely point; many things is most likely nonpoint.

10. **B**—The environmental problem of aquiculture is that large numbers of fish can produce huge quantities of waste (fish poop, excess fish food, etc.), which can pollute the river, lake, or ocean.

11. **B**—70/3 = 23 years

12. **D**—If girls and women have access to education, the TFR of a country will go down because women usually postpone having children until they educate themselves and possibly go into the workforce.

13. **A**—The main way we have tried to stop the problem of ozone depletion is to stop using ozone-depleting substances. The Montreal Protocol (1987) and the Vienna Convention (1985) were treaties to control the release of these substances.

14. **C**—Currently, we are in a warming trend, which has impacted the environment and human health, including rising sea levels. Rising sea levels can flood coastal communities and leave ocean organisms too deep to photosynthesize.

15. **B**—The theory states that islands closer to the mainland (where the animals/plants have moved from) and/or larger islands will have more species than islands that are farther away or smaller. The size of the island in theory matters because larger islands can support more and different species while smaller ones would be more limited.

16. **A**—A thermal inversion is a weather condition when warm, less dense air moves over dense, colder air. Because of the thermal weather condition and the dense air, pollution, particularly smog and particulates, get trapped near the ground and can't "escape" to upper atmosphere.

17. **B**—The 10 percent rule is the idea that as usable energy moves up the pyramid much of it is "lost" to the laws of thermodynamics. The first law of thermodynamics states that energy cannot be created or destroyed, but the second law states that it can be transferred or transformed. So according

to the 10 percent rule, a plant or primary producer will only transfer 10 percent of the energy to the primary consumer that eats it, let's say a rabbit. This rabbit then goes about its day hopping around, heating its body, etc., and it uses up 90 percent of the energy it received from the plant. Next, when a coyote comes around and eats the rabbit, we assume the coyote only gets about 10 percent of the energy from the rabbit because the rabbit "used up" 90 percent doing what rabbits do.

18. **C**—Cultural: These are not "things" we benefit from but rather interactions with nature, such as taking a walk or enjoying what you see or art that comes from looking at nature, etc.

19. **A**—To do this, you start with the sand and find the percentage along the bottom of the triangle, in this case 10 percent, and follow the line that goes up and to the left for sand. Then, you move to the right side of the triangle and find the line for silt, in this case 60 percent. Follow this line down and to the left until it hits the line you had drawn for sand. They should cross. Then, where they cross, if you draw a straight line to the left, where you find clay, you should be at the 30 percent line, which is your percentage of clay. Where these three lines intersected is the type of soil you have. In this case, silty clay loam.

20. **B**—The stratosphere contains the ozone that chlorofluorocarbons have destroyed as they break down ozone into $O_2$.

21. **B**—This is where steam is pumped through a pipe that is focused on the giant turbine at extremely high pressures, causing the turbine to spin. This spinning is connected to an electrical generator that generates electricity.

22. **C**—Renewable energy resources are resources that can be replaced over a relatively short time scale. These include things like solar, wind, hydroelectric, geothermal, and biomass resources. Tidal is a type of hydroelectric power source.

23. **A**—Thermal pollution is often from a nuclear power plant where large amounts of heated water are being dumped into a body of water. The heated water doesn't have to have any pollutants in it, but just being warm can cause problems. This is because warm water can't hold as much oxygen as cold water. The oxygen diffuses out of the water and into the air. If organisms, such as fish, that need dissolved oxygen in the water can't get it, they might die.

24. **C**—In the Pacific Ocean, every three to seven years on average, warmer surface waters known as the El Niño–Southern Oscillation (ENSO) occur. Upwellings from the seabed in normal years bring nutrients up to the surface for the plankton to feed on; the plankton is food for the marine life up the food chain. In an El Niño year, that upwelling does not occur so the plankton is reduced and in turn, so are the fish stocks.

25. **D**—The amount of sunlight varies seasonally. The equator gets sun year-round, but as you move up or down to the poles you get less and less direct sunlight. The Arctic Circle is near the pole and during December it is pointed away from the sun.

26. **C**—One problem with many of these pesticides is that the organism that it is designed to kill builds up resistance over time. Pesticides are designed to prevent crop damage and increase crop profits. But if pesticide resistance becomes a problem, the pesticide will no longer work (or work as well) and the farmer/homeowner will have to either apply more pesticide, use stronger doses, or switch to a new type.

27. **B**

| GAS | SOURCES | GWP | ATMOSPHERIC LIFETIME |
|---|---|---|---|
| Carbon dioxide | Decomposition, respiration, burning fossil fuels, deforestation | 1 | 50–200 years |
| Methane | Burning of fossil fuels, livestock, landfills, decomposition, burning biomass, natural wetlands | 21 | 12 years |
| Nitrous oxide | Soils, livestock manure, biomass or fossil fuel combustion, wastewater management | 310 | 120 years |
| Chlorofluorocarbons | Refrigerants, aerosols, aircraft halons, solvents | 12,000–16,000 | 20–100 years |

28. **D**—As seen in the illustration, animal respiration puts carbon into the atmosphere. The rest are all examples of removing carbon from the atmosphere.

29. **A**—DDT can bioaccumulate in the fatty tissues of animals. This is because they don't break down and "accumulate" there. In addition, because animals eat other animals, these chemicals can magnify up the food chain.

30. **C**—Vapor recovery nozzles are put on gasoline pumps to capture the fumes that are produced.

31. **B**—Wind energy is a type of power that is clean, free, and can be used in areas where the land is being used for other things, such as ranching or growing crops.

32. **A**—1,244 $MtCO_2$ − 1,291 $MtCO_2$ /1,291 $MtCO_2$ × 100% = −3.6%

33. **D**—Since the nematodes have 600,000,000,000,000,000,000 babies a day, we can assume this means they have very little parental care with so many offspring, a characteristic of an r-selected species.

34. **D**—Glass is only 4.9 percent of the material generated, the lowest of all materials. The city would want to promote materials that are of greater quantities.

35. **C**—At 120 years since glacial retreat, there were over 1,500 trees per hectare, which is the greatest biomass of spruce trees on the graph.

36. **B**—Earth has had many different changes in temperature over its history. There are times when it has been much warmer and times when it has been much colder. Currently, we are in a warming trend due to global climate change.

37. **A**—Greenhouse gases from transportation, electricity production, industry, businesses and homes, agriculture, and reduction of forested land have caused temperatures to rise causing global climate change.

38. **D**—Humans produced chemicals such as chlorofluorocarbons (CFCs). Although they are heavier than air, the air currents and mixing processes of the atmosphere have carried them into the stratosphere. These CFC molecules are hit by the sun's UV energy, which breaks up the CFCs and releases chlorine atoms. The chlorine atoms then react with the $O_3$ molecules breaking up the $O_3$ and taking one oxygen atom to form chlorine monoxide and $O_2$. This process reduces the amount of ozone found in the stratosphere.

39. **C**—IPM is killing or preventing the bugs without using as much pesticide. IPM can include biological methods like predator bugs that a farmer buys to eat the pests (biocontrol).

40. **D**—The ocean absorbs carbon dioxide from the atmosphere. The carbon dioxide reacts with the ocean water creating carbonic acid. The oceans absorb almost a quarter of global $CO_2$ emissions we create from burning fossil fuels and deforestation. As the $CO_2$ enters the ocean, it causes the ocean to become more acidic (lower pH). This acidity doesn't allow animals like clams and mussels to make protective shells, due to the loss of calcium carbonate. It can impact corals since they also make protective shells.

41. **A**—The species can continue to reproduce until it goes beyond what the area can support, then the species begins to starve, is impacted by disease, etc.

42. **D**—Declining/negative growth countries: countries like Japan, Germany, Bulgaria, and Russia are considered negative or declining growth countries because there are fewer children than middle-aged adults. In these countries, mom and dad may only be having one child, so when mom and dad die the family (and country) get smaller.

43. **B**—The tragedy of the commons is that individuals tend to overexploit shared resources until the resource becomes unavailable to all.

44. **C**—Overfishing is commercial fishing in which large quantities of fish are caught faster than the species can breed and replace itself. By banning this you would stop the loss of biodiversity.

45. **A**—Permeability is the ability of a material to allow liquid to flow through it. So sand has a high permeability, since water flows easily through it. Since 95 ml of the 100 ml went through, it is most likely sand.

46. **C**—Sulfur dioxide can be removed by gas scrubbing or by using fluidized bed combustion in coal-fired power plants.

**47. B**—Indoor air quality has risen in the past 30 years. The lines on the graph are all trending down showing that the percentage of people using solid fuel for cooking is decreasing. Since the percentage is going down, indoor air quality has gone up.

**48. B**—Nitrous oxide has a GWP 310 times that of carbon dioxide as seen in the chart below.

| GAS | SOURCES | GWP | ATMOSPHERIC LIFETIME |
|---|---|---|---|
| Carbon dioxide | Decomposition, respiration, burning fossil fuels, deforestation | 1 | 50–200 years |
| Methane | Burning of fossil fuels, livestock, landfills, decomposition, burning biomass, natural wetlands | 21 | 12 years |
| Nitrous oxide | Soils, livestock manure, biomass or fossil fuel combustion, wastewater management | 310 | 120 years |
| Chlorofluorocarbons | Refrigerants, aerosols, aircraft halons, solvents | 12,000–16,000 | 20–100 years |

**49. D**—During the months of April, May, June, July, and August, according to the graph, the solar energy system produces over 7,000 kWh, making it a good energy source to supplement local energy needs.

**50. C**—Person 4 has the highest ecological footprint when it comes to food and goods and services. Eating lower on the food chain will lower the ecological footprint as would purchasing less "stuff" since that is where person 4's ecological footprint is highest.

**51. A**—One of the consequences of increased temperatures is a rise in sea levels, which can flood coastal communities.

**52. A**—Increased levels of carbon dioxide and nitrogen oxides from burning fossil fuels is leading to increased global temperatures.

**53. B**—*Eutrophication* is the term used to describe a body of water that has an abundance of nutrients (fertilizers like nitrogen and phosphorus) that have run off from the land; these nutrients "fertilize" the algae that live in the water. This is caused by agriculture runoff, runoff from fertilizers, and wastewater runoff from CAFOs. This can cause the water to become so thick and green with algae that no light can penetrate through the water. It can also cause dead zones due to the lack of oxygen in the water.

**54. D**—Coal-burning power plants, vehicles, manufacturing, and even volcanoes release nitrogen oxides ($NO_x$) and sulfur oxides ($SO_2$) into the atmosphere. When these chemicals mix with atmospheric water (like rain, snow, fog, and hail) or dust, they can become acid rain and fall to Earth. Because this is acidic (low pH), it lowers the pH of bodies of water near where the acid rain falls.

**55. A**—$200 \text{ lb} \times \dfrac{1 \text{ kg}}{2.2 \text{ lb}} \times \dfrac{12{,}357 \text{ mg}}{1 \text{ kg}} \times \dfrac{1 \text{ g}}{1{,}000 \text{ mg}}$
$= 1{,}123.4 \text{ gram}$

**56. C**—Burning biomass is burning wood and similar products. If we did this on a large scale, we could have some concerns of deforestation and habitat destruction to obtain these large wood supplies.

**57. D**—Since very few frogs make it to adulthood, they would have a Type III survivorship curve. Think of frog eggs—most get eaten, dry out, and never hatch at all. Then, tadpoles are also a major food source for many species, so lots of young frogs are also killed. However, a few make it to old age and become adult frogs. This survivorship curve is characteristic of an r-selected species.

**58. A**—Genetic diversity refers to the diversity within a species. These genetic differences often determine if the organism can withstand different environmental pressures. Genetic diversity is important because it helps maintain the health of a population.

**59. B**—Centered at the end of the Mississippi River system, the zone is one of the largest areas of oxygen-depleted coastal waters in the world. Low oxygen, or hypoxia, can be caused by pollution from farm fertilizer, soil erosion, and discharge from sewage treatment plants.

60. **A**—Clear-cutting has many environmental consequences even though, from an economic standpoint, it is a benefit since it is cheaper than other methods. Since trees have roots that hold in the soil, when we clear cut large areas of land we expose this soil, leaving it vulnerable to erosion and/or flooding.

61. **C**—Mining removes plant life, opens the soil up to erosion and runoff, and harms habitats. By reestablishing the vegetation and assessing and evaluating the replanted area frequently, you would help to "fix" the problems that were caused from the mining.

62. **D**—In the diagram, we see the ocean on the left, which provides a lot of moisture to the area. A lot of rain falls on the windward side of the mountain because as the air mass moves to higher elevations, it expands and cools. This cool air doesn't hold as much moisture so clouds form and it rains. The air mass, which has lost most of its moisture, then moves over the mountains, where there is less rainfall.

63. **C**—Giant pandas and koalas are specialists that require particular habitats and food while pigeons and doves are generalists that can live almost anywhere and eat almost anything.

64. **A**—The graph shows that lionfish are growing exponentially, so we can assume they might be invasive and that they have not yet reached their carrying capacity. Invasive species tend to be generalists and r-selected species and they become invasive because of a lack of competition, no predators, and abundant resources.

65. **B**—Tilling the soil leaves it vulnerable to erosion and if the eroded soil has fertilizers in it, it could cause eutrophication of the body of water. In addition, the farmer may add more fertilizers to combat the loss of soil, compounding the problem.

66. **C**—The graph shows that in 2000 and the years since, Europe has had a very low total fertility rate (TFR), well below replacement level.

67. **A**—Sub-Saharan Africa had a rapid growth in 1970; the first graph typifies rapid growth countries. These are countries with a lot of infants, babies, and children who can be expected to grow up and have even more children. Some examples of countries today with an age structure like this are Kenya, Nigeria, and Saudi Arabia.

68. **A**—In 1960 in Northern Africa the TFR was near 7. With a fertility rate that high it can be expected that population growth would put demands on forests to provide fuel for cooking and human habitation. Deforestation would have been occurring, leading to habitat loss.

69. **C**—Methane is a greenhouse gas that traps heat and leads to the greenhouse effect, raising temperatures on Earth.

70. **D**—If natural land is covered with asphalt and concrete, more water would run off the land and less would infiltrate the ground to fill up aquifers.

71. **B**—All organisms have a range of conditions that they can survive in. Ecological tolerances are things like temperature, salinity, sunlight, flow rate, availability of water, etc., and can apply to species or to individuals. The author states that sea urchins have a narrow ecological tolerance for salinity.

72. **A**—The benefit of hydroelectric power is that it doesn't produce any air pollution or greenhouse gases since nothing is burned. If you took down the dam, you would need to turn to other types of energy sources. If you had to replace the power produced by the dam by burning fossil fuels, you would create air pollution and further global warming.

73. **D**—The graph shows an increase in agricultural methane release from below 200 to 210 million metric tons. Animals produce a lot of methane and carbon dioxide, two things that lead to climate change.

74. **C**—The plate boundaries are divergent when the plates move apart, resulting in seafloor spreading, rift valleys, volcanoes, and earthquakes. Along these boundaries, earthquakes are common and magma (molten rock) rises from Earth's mantle to the surface. Once this magma solidifies, the result is new oceanic crust.

75. **A**—The birth rates have dropped in half from 40/1,000 to 20/1,000 and the death rates have dropped from 17/1,000 to 8/1,000. This indicates

that the country is moving through demographic transition, lowering birth rates and death rates and lowering infant mortality. More women are becoming educated and there are generally better living conditions.

76. **C**—When an energy source is used to generate both heat and electricity, it is a combined heat and power (CHP) system or cogeneration.

77. **B**—The chemical equation, which you need to know and memorize, looks like this: $Cl + O_3 \rightarrow ClO + O_2$. Next, if the ClO molecule finds a free oxygen atom, the oxygen atom will steal the O from the ClO to become $O_2$, which releases the Cl atom back into the stratosphere to destroy more ozone. The second equation looks like this: $ClO + O \rightarrow Cl + O_2$.

78. **A**—Fracking is forcing liquid at very high pressures down into the rock to cause the oil or gas to be released. This can lead to groundwater contamination because the water that is used to release the oil or natural gas can contain contaminates that then run off into waterways. In addition, this process releases volatile organic compounds during the natural gas production process.

79. **D**—The article states that humans are causing noise pollution that is impacting animals and human relaxation. Noise pollution, the author states, reduces the ability of animals to hear natural sounds and degrades the calming effect that we feel when we spend time in wild places.

80. **D**—Our oceans are getting warmer because of climate change from greenhouse gases. Corals need zooxanthellae, an algae that lives in the tissues of the coral and captures sunlight and converts it into energy for the coral animals. When the water is warmer, the zooxanthellae come under stress and can die or leave their coral host, causing the coral to die and turn white, a process known as coral bleaching.

# Analyzing Your Performance on the Diagnostic Test

The exercise below will help you quickly and easily identify the chapters in Step 4 that you most need to review for the AP Environmental Science multiple-choice exam. Revise your study plan so that you prioritize the chapters with which you had the most difficulty.

Look at your answer sheet and mark all the questions you missed. Then shade in, highlight, or mark an X in the boxes below that correspond to the question numbers that you missed. For what concepts did you miss the most questions? This is where you want to spend the most time as you review!

### Chapter 1: The Living World: Ecosystems

| 4 | 5 | 17 | 28 | 70 |
|---|---|----|----|----|

### Chapter 2: The Living World: Biodiversity

| 15 | 18 | 35 | 58 | 71 |
|----|----|----|----|----|

### Chapter 3: Populations

| 11 | 12 | 33 | 41 | 42 | 45 | 57 |
|----|----|----|----|----|----|----|
| 63 | 66 | 67 | 75 | | | |

### Chapter 4: Earth Systems and Resources

| 2 | 6 | 19 | 20 | 24 | 25 | 59 |
|---|---|----|----|----|----|----|
| 62 | 74 | | | | | |

## Chapter 5: Land and Water Use

| 10 | 26 | 39 | 43 | 44 | 50 | 60 |
|----|----|----|----|----|----|----|
| 61 | 65 | 73 |    |    |    |    |

## Chapter 6: Energy Resources and Consumption

| 7  | 21 | 22 | 31 | 32 | 49 | 56 |
|----|----|----|----|----|----|----|
| 72 | 76 | 78 |    |    |    |    |

## Chapter 7: Atmospheric Pollution

| 3 | 16 | 30 | 46 | 47 | 54 | 79 |
|---|----|----|----|----|----|----|

## Chapter 8: Aquatic and Terrestrial Pollution

| 8 | 9 | 23 | 29 | 34 | 53 | 55 |
|---|---|----|----|----|----|----|

## Chapter 9: Global Change

| 1  | 13 | 14 | 27 | 36 | 37 | 38 |
|----|----|----|----|----|----|----|
| 40 | 48 | 51 | 52 | 64 | 68 | 69 |
| 77 | 80 |    |    |    |    |    |

# Develop Strategies
# for Success

CHAPTER **4** How to Approach Each
Question Type

# CHAPTER 4

# How to Approach Each Question Type

**IN THIS CHAPTER**

**Summary:** Become familiar with the multiple-choice and free-response questions on the exam and learn tips and strategies that will allow you to score your best. Pace yourself and know when to skip a question that you can come back to later.

### Key Ideas

✪ On multiple-choice questions, you don't lose any points for wrong answers. You should fill in an answer bubble for every question.

✪ On multiple-choice questions, don't "overthink" the test. Use common sense because that will usually get you the right answer.

✪ Free-response answers must be in essay form. Outline form is not acceptable.

✪ Free-response questions are multipart questions—be *sure* to answer each part of the question or you will not be able to get the maximum possible number of points for that question.

✪ The free-response questions are graded using a positive-scoring system, so wrong information is ignored.

# Multiple-Choice Questions

You will have 90 minutes to answer 80 multiple-choice questions, which works out to about 67 seconds per question. However, some questions will take longer than others, so make sure you are watching the time and pacing yourself. The multiple-choice section accounts for 60 percent of your final AP score.

Here are some helpful tips and strategies:

- ***Don't leave questions blank***. The AP Environmental Science exam used to take off a fraction of a point for each wrong answer. This is no longer the case. You should answer each multiple-choice question. If you don't know the answer, try to eliminate options that you know aren't correct and then make your best guess. If there are only seconds left and you're not done, you should just take random guesses. There is a 25 percent chance you'll get the right answer.

- ***All questions are weighted equally***. It doesn't matter which questions you get correct, just that you get enough questions right. So, don't spend too much time on one question. If a question is taking a long time, make your best guess and move on. Mark the question in your test booklet and go back to it later if you have time.

- ***There is no logic to the order of questions***. The test doesn't start out with the easy ones and go on to the hard ones. You may get the hardest question first. That's why it's important not to waste time on any one question. Again, if a question is taking a long time, make your best guess and move on.

- ***Don't overthink the test***. If you encounter a question that you immediately know the answer to, don't ponder it, just fill in the bubble on the answer sheet and move on. Just because the question seems easy doesn't mean it is a trick question. Some of the test questions will be easy ones.

- ***Be careful about changing answers***. If you answered a question already and come back to it later on, resist the urge to change it. Make sure that you have a real reason to change it. Oftentimes you are overthinking the question and your first answer is correct. Only change your answer if you can justify your reasons for making the switch.

- ***Check your calculations***. The math on the AP Environmental Science exam isn't intended to be all that difficult and you are allowed a simple calculator. That said, it would be unfortunate to lose points because of a silly calculation error. Make sure to work carefully and check your math. Remember, the test writers know all the possible answers you could get using the numbers given, so memorize those formulas so you get the correct solution!

- ***Make sure there are no stray marks on your answer sheet***. When you erase, make sure the wrong answer is completely erased. It may seem clear which answer you intended to mark to anyone reading it, but remember that your answer sheet is not read by humans. When more than one answer to a question is perceived, the answer is counted incorrect, no matter how much darker one of the answer bubbles is.

## › Free-Response Questions

You will be given 70 minutes to write your answers to three broad questions on the free-response section of the exam. That works out to about 23 minutes per question. It is important that your answers to these questions display solid reasoning and analytical skills. Expect to have to use data or information from your laboratory experiences as you answer some of these questions. The free-response section of the test accounts for 40 percent of your final AP score.

Answers for the free-response questions must be in essay form. Outline form is not acceptable. Be sure you answer all parts of a question and label your answer as to what part it is. If the question asks for a calculation, you *must* show your work.

It is important that you read each question completely before you begin to write so you are sure what you are being asked to do. Take a moment to plan your answer, and then write all your answers on the pages following the questions in the booklet.

Question 1 will require you to design an investigation and will be worth 10 points. Question 2 will require you to analyze an environmental problem and propose a solution. It is also worth 10 points. For Question 3, you'll have to analyze an environmental problem and propose a solution, as in Question 2, but you'll be required to do calculations. It's also worth 10 points.

Some important strategies and tips to keep in mind as you write your essays:

- It is very important that you read the question carefully to make sure you understand exactly what you are being asked and what you have to do in your answer.

- There are three questions in the free-response section. However, it isn't really three questions—it is more like 15 questions since each free-response question will have four, five, six, or more parts to it. For example, question 1 will be divided into parts (a), (b), (c), and so on, and each of these parts may be broken down further and labeled (i), (ii), etc. Make sure you label carefully each section you are answering. Label it exactly as it is labeled in the question. For example, label 1a, then write your answer. Then label 1b, and so on. Do not take all the parts and create one giant super essay. This could possibly make you lose points because the grader will not know which part of the question you are responding to. Instead, label and respond; then label the next section and respond again.

- Do not leave any part of a free-response question blank. If you aren't sure of the answer, skip it for now and answer the rest of the question. Sometimes this will jump-start your thinking, causing you to remember the part you didn't know. If you still don't know, then put down your best, most thoughtful guess. Wrong answers are ignored but you just might get a point or two when you didn't think you knew it. If you leave it blank, you will definitely get zero points.

- The free-response section is graded using a "positive scoring" system. You do not lose points for saying things that are incorrect. If you are asked for one cause of eutrophication and you are unsure of your answer, give your best possible guess. A good guess is better than a blank response.

- However, just as you do not *lose* credit for wrong answers, you will not *gain* credit for doing more than asked. For example, if the question asks for two results of global warming and you are sure you have good answers, you will not get extra credit if you give three. Don't waste time giving a more complete answer than what is being asked.

- Finally, you should know the verbs that the test writers will use and how you should respond to each verb:
  - **Calculate**—This means to do math and arrive at a final answer, including using algebra, substituting numbers, and making sure you correctly label your units. Also, you *must* show your work! No work means no points. Even if you can do the calculation in your head, you must show on paper how you got to the answer. The test graders can't look into your head.
  - **Describe**—Give relevant information on a particular topic.
  - **Explain**—Give the reasons for a particular environmental problem and tell how or why the problem happened, using evidence to support your claim.
  - **Identify**—Give information about a particular topic but you won't have to explain in detail.

- **Justify**—Provide evidence to support or defend a claim and give the reasons for this justification.
- **Make a claim**—Provide a reason based on evidence or knowledge.
- **Propose a solution**—Give a solution to an environmental problem using things you learned in the class.

## Science Practices

Finally, you should know that you will be assessed using seven different science practices with varying weights on each part of the exam. Use the points below from the College Board to know what you will be asked to do.

- Practice 1—Concept Explanation will be 30–38% of the multiple-choice section and 13–20% of the free-response section.
- Practice 2—Visual Representations will be 12–19% of the multiple-choice section and 6–10% of the free-response section.
- Practice 3—Text Analysis will be 6–8% of the multiple-choice section and none of the free-response section.
- Practice 4—Scientific Experiments will be 2–4% of the multiple-choice section and 10–14% of the free-response section.
- Practice 5—Data Analysis will be 12–19% of the multiple-choice section and 6–10% of the free-response section.
- Practice 6—Mathematical Routines will be 6–9% of the multiple-choice section and 20% of the free-response section.
- Practice 7—Environmental Solutions will be 17–23% of the multiple-choice section and 26–34% of the free-response section.

STEP 4

# Review the Knowledge You Need to Score High

# CHAPTER 5

# The Living World: Ecosystems

## IN THIS CHAPTER

**Summary:** This chapter sets the foundation for all future chapters by showing the relationships and interactions with the living world.

### Key Ideas

✪ Ecosystems are the result of biotic and abiotic interactions.
✪ Energy can be converted from one form to another.

---

### Key Terms

- 10 percent rule
- Biome
- Carbon cycle
- Commensalism
- Competition
- Desert
- Ecosystem
- Food chains
- Food web
- Freshwater biomes
- Gross productivity
- Hydrologic cycle
- Mutualism
- Net productivity
- Nitrogen cycle
- Parasitism
- Phosphorus cycle
- Predator-prey
- Primary productivity
- Saltwater biomes
- Savanna
- Shrubland
- Taiga
- Temperate grassland
- Temperate rainforest
- Temperate seasonal forests
- Trophic levels
- Tropical rainforests
- Tundra

This chapter will cover about 6 to 8 percent of your AP Environmental Science Exam, or about 5 to 6 questions out of the 80 multiple-choice questions. It will be mostly a review of concepts you learned in previous years of school. This includes topics like predator-prey, biomes, nutrient and water cycles, food chains/webs, and energy flow. Most of it will be a review but there will be some new concepts.

# Introduction to Ecosystems

There are many types of relationships in environmental science. **Predator-prey** relationships are when a predator, such as a lion, eats its prey, such as a gazelle. These two organisms must exist together and each organism relies on the other. For example, Figure 5.1 shows the relationship between the lynx and the hare. The lynx would not survive without its food source, the hare. However, the lynx keeps the hare numbers in check so they don't reach high numbers and begin to starve for lack of food resources for the hare. A healthy predator-prey relationship is important in the environment.

**Symbiosis** is the relationship between two species that have a close and long-term interaction with one another. There are many types of symbiosis: mutualism, commensalism, and parasitism. Let's begin with mutualism.

In **mutualism** both species benefit from the relationship. The example you are probably most familiar with is the clownfish and anemone. Thank you, Disney®, for *Finding Nemo*! In this common example, the anemone has stinging tentacles that allow it to sting and eat its prey . . . usually small fish like the clownfish. However, the clownfish has a slimy mucus that protects her from the anemone. The clownfish benefits by eating the algae and leftover fish from the anemone and the anemone benefits by getting more oxygen to its tentacles as the clownfish swims through it.

**Commensalism** is another relationship between species when one organism benefits and the other neither benefits nor is harmed. One example you might be familiar with is the remora and the shark. The remora uses the shark for both food and for transportation. It eats food that is left over from the shark and also has a sucking disk that allows it to adhere to the body of the shark and get a free ride. The shark is not helped or harmed.

**Figure 5.1 The relationship between the lynx and the hare.**

Another example is cattle egrets and cattle. Cattle egrets eat the insects that the cattle disturb as the cattle forage. The cattle are not helped or harmed but the cattle egrets benefit.

**Parasitism** is the final example of symbiosis. In this relationship, one species benefits while the other is harmed. The common examples here are fleas, mosquitoes, and tapeworms. All of these organisms feed off a host and benefit while the host is harmed, some more than others.

Another type of relationship is **competition,** when two or more species (or between members of the same species) are all competing for the same, usually limited, resource. These limited resources are often food, water, or territory. **Intraspecific competition** is competition between members of the same species and **interspecific competition** is between members of different species. Oftentimes species will learn to coexist by living in different parts of the same habitat, sharing food, or eating at different times of the day, which is known as resource partitioning.

# Terrestrial Biomes

A **biome** is the world's major communities of plants and animals and can be made up of many different ecosystems. An **ecosystem** is the living and nonliving parts of an environment and many ecosystems may make up a biome.

**Climate** is the normal conditions of temperature, humidity, atmospheric pressure, wind, rainfall, etc. that define an area for a long period of time. Biomes are defined by the type of climate that is found in the biome.

The main terrestrial (land) biomes and their characteristics are:

- **Taiga**—A coniferous forest (pine trees), with permafrost soil, usually found between the tundra and temperate forests. This is the world's largest land biome.
- **Temperate rainforest**—Found on the coast and consists of both coniferous and broad-leaf trees. This biome is characterized by a lot of rain.
- **Temperate seasonal forests**—These forests have all four seasons and are characterized by trees that are green in the spring and summer and turn bright colors of yellow, orange, and red in the fall, losing their leaves in the winter. This biome has warm, wet summers and cold winters.
- **Tropical rainforests**—These forests are found near the equator and stay warm all year long. They are characterized by extreme amounts of rainfall all year. More than half of the world's species live in this biome.
- **Shrubland**—This biome is typically found near coasts and have hot, dry summers and cool, moist winters. Shrubland consists of shrubs and short trees with grasses. Some plants are adapted to little rainfall, such as cacti.
- **Temperate grassland**—This biome has many different types of grasses and very few trees due to the low levels of rainfall. The climate varies during the seasons from very cold to very warm.
- **Savanna**—This biome is a grassland with widely scattered trees found in tropical regions usually between the desert and rainforest. Wildfires are common and there is a wet and dry season.
- **Desert**—This biome covers about 20% of the land on our planet and is characterized by less than 50 cm a year of rain. Trees are usually absent and there is little vegetation.
- **Tundra**—This is an extremely cold climate characterized by no trees, little precipitation, short growing seasons for plants and grasses, and poor nutrients.

# Aquatic Biomes

Aquatic biomes can be broken down into freshwater and marine. The types of resources found in these biomes depend on many things, including location, temperature, sunlight, and salinity.

- **Freshwater biomes**—These include streams, rivers, lakes, and ponds. These provide humans with water and food and could be considered the most important of all the biomes.
- **Marine biomes**—These include oceans, coral reefs, kelp forests, marshland (salt marshes), estuaries, mangrove forests, and tidepools. Marine biomes cover about 75% of Earth's surface and are important in climate control, providing much of the world's oxygen and also acting as a huge carbon dioxide sink.

You will need to learn about the different cycles in nature. The APES exam will focus on four cycles: the carbon, nitrogen, phosphorus, and hydrologic (water) cycles. For each of these, you will need to be able to look at the cycle in a visual representation or model and answer questions about the cycle. This means you must be familiar with the model/picture but also familiar with the details of each cycle.

# Carbon Cycle

As seen in Figure 5.2, carbon is found in the land, water, and atmosphere. A carbon sink is where carbon is stored, for example in plants, the ocean, and soil. Carbon sources include

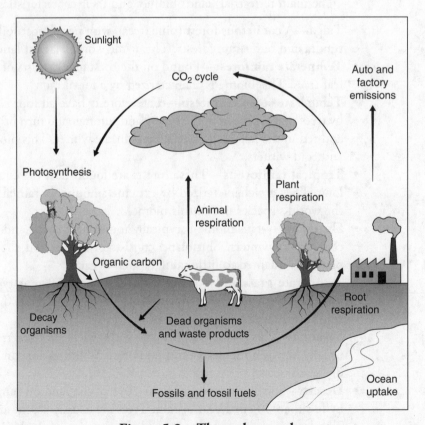

**Figure 5.2   The carbon cycle.**

forest fires, respiration, and burning of fossil fuels. As carbon moves through the carbon cycle it moves between sources and sinks, which can take very long periods of time or be rather quick.

Photosynthesis and cellular respiration are how carbon cycles in living things and is known as short-term cycling. When living organisms die and get buried deep underground, we see the long-term cycling and storage of carbon. This long-term storage has been interrupted by humans with the burning of fossil fuels. This takes carbon that has been stored for millions of years and puts it back into the atmosphere.

## Nitrogen Cycle

Like carbon, nitrogen cycles between sources and sinks (Figure 5.3). Seventy-eight percent of our atmosphere is composed of nitrogen, which makes it the primary sink, but other sinks include living organisms, sedimentary rocks, and sediments. Denitrifying microorganisms are fixers of nitrogen, making them a major source of nitrogen because they push nitrogen back into the atmosphere. This form of nitrogen is unusable by plants. Another type of microorganism, known as nitrifying microorganisms, fix nitrogen into a useable form for plants. The steps of the nitrogen cycle can be easily memorized by a mnemonic device known as FixNAAD ANPAN. Let's put this into a chart so this will make more sense (Table 5.1).

As you can see from the chart, the nitrogen cycle relies heavily on bacteria to cycle it between land, water, and the atmosphere. It is a relatively fast cycle.

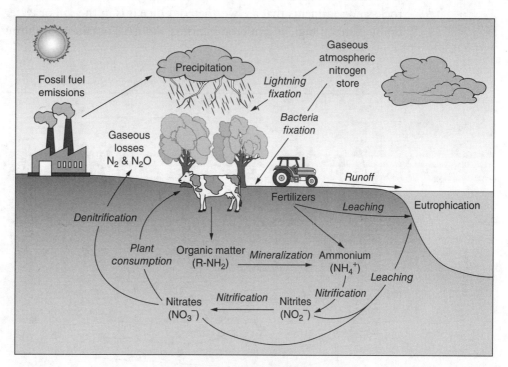

**Figure 5.3   The nitrogen cycle.**

**Table 5.1    The Steps of the Nitrogen Cycle**

| PROCESS | PRODUCT | EXPLANATION |
|---------|---------|-------------|
| **Fix**—Nitrogen Fixation | **A**—Ammonia | During nitrogen fixation, $N_2$ from the atmosphere is converted by nitrogen-fixing microorganisms into ammonia. |
| **N**—Nitrification | **N**—Nitrites/Nitrates | During nitrification, bacteria convert ammonia into nitrites and then nitrates. |
| **A**—Assimilation | **P**—Proteins (DNA/Amino Acids) | During assimilation, nitrates are then converted into plant proteins, and nucleic acids that animals can then get from the plant tissues. |
| **A**—Ammonification | **A**—Ammonia | Ammonification is the process where decomposers take plant and animal cells and return the nitrogen back to the soil in the form of ammonia. |
| **D**—Denitrification | **N**—Nitrogen Gas | Bacteria convert nitrogen in the soil back to an atmospheric form. |

# Phosphorus Cycle

The phosphorus cycle is a slow cycle and it does not have an atmospheric form; phosphorus is only found on the land and in the water (Figure 5.4). The major sinks for phosphorus are rocks and sediments that are weathered. Once it is in the soil or water it can be easily taken up by plants, fungi, and microorganisms. Animals obtain phosphorus by eating plants and

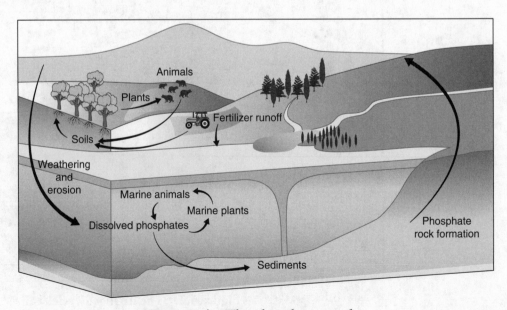

**Figure 5.4    The phosphorus cycle.**

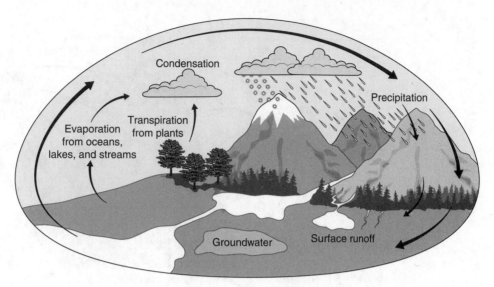

**Figure 5.5    The water cycle.**

it is returned to the soil or water when they die. Phosphorus is used as a building block for DNA, RNA, and ATP. Phosphorus is often considered a limiting factor in the environment because there is very little available and because it is not very water soluble.

## Hydrologic Cycle (Water)

The water cycle is the process in which water moves from the atmosphere to the oceans/lakes/rivers to the land (Figure 5.5). The major steps include evaporation, condensation, runoff, precipitation, transpiration, and infiltration. Water on our planet is found in three phases: solid (ice or snow), liquid (rainfall or water in lakes), and gas (in the atmosphere). The majority of water on our planet is found in the oceans, which cover approximately 70% of Earth.

## Primary Productivity

**Primary productivity** is the rate at which food energy is generated by photosynthesis. It is measured in units of energy per unit area per unit time. Since energy cannot be created or destroyed, and since the sun is the source of energy for our planet, we can study the two parts of primary productivity (gross productivity and net productivity) to see how productive a particular area is. In some areas productivity changes with the seasons, like the wet and dry seasons of the tropics or the spring or fall seasons in the United States. We also consider the primary productivity of bodies of water by looking at the photosynthesizers found there. The primary productivity in water is dependent on how clear the water is and how deep the red and blue light can penetrate. Primary productivity is important because it is the process that forms the foundation of food webs in most ecosystems.

**Gross productivity** is the total rate of photosynthesis in an area, or the full amount of food produced by the producers.

**Net productivity** is the difference between gross productivity and the energy lost by producers for respiration.

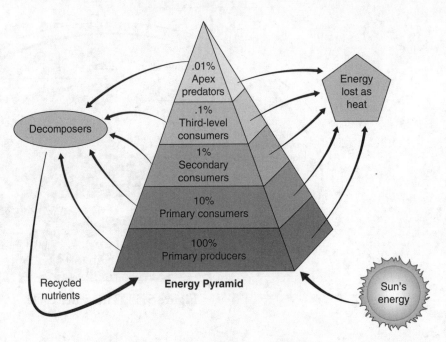

Figure 5.6    Trophic levels and energy.

# Trophic Levels

Once again, all energy comes from the sun but it can be converted from one form to another. Plants take energy from the sun in the process of photosynthesis and convert that energy into usable forms (Figure 5.6). Animals eat that plant or another animal and get their energy from the food they eat. The cycles we studied earlier are how matter moves around the planet. These cycles demonstrate the law of conservation of matter.

The **first trophic level** are the plants, or primary producers. These are then eaten by primary consumers (the second trophic level) and so forth up the pyramid.

# Energy Flow and the 10 Percent Rule

**The 10 percent rule** is the idea that as usable energy moves up the pyramid much of it is "lost." The first law of thermodynamics states that energy cannot be created or destroyed, but the second law states that it can be transferred or transformed. So according to the 10 percent rule, a plant or primary producer will only transfer 10 percent of the energy to the primary consumer that eats it, let's say a rabbit. This rabbit then goes about its day hopping around, heating its body, etc., and it uses up 90 percent of the energy it received from the plant. Next, when a coyote comes around and eats the rabbit, we assume the coyote only gets about 10 percent of the energy from the rabbit because the rabbit "used up" 90 percent doing what rabbits do. This also explains why the shape is a pyramid because energy is "lost" as it goes up to each higher level.

# Food Chains and Food Webs

A food chain is a visual representation of how organisms depend on one another for a source of food with arrows pointing from the organism that is being eaten to the organism that eats it and receives the energy from it (Figure 5.7).

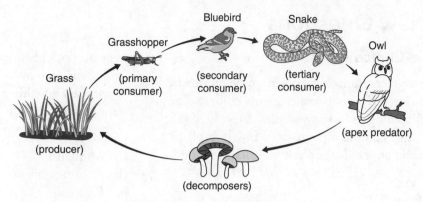

**Figure 5.7    Food chain.**

A food web is a visual representation of many food chains put together and is more like real life because it shows the complexity of feeding relationships in the system (Figure 5.8). In other words, most animals don't have just one thing they eat, but rather multiple options for any given meal.

The important thing as you look at a diagram of a food chain or food web is to understand the relationships that occur and be able to predict what might happen if a particular animal or plant were to be removed from the food web/chain.

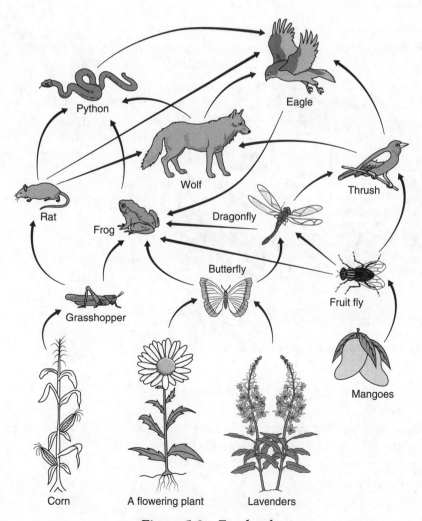

**Figure 5.8    Food web.**

# › Review Questions

## Multiple-Choice Questions

1. An evergreen plant is found in an environment with extremely cold winter temperatures. The plant has long, thin waxy needles that it keeps all year long. The soil is permafrost. In which of the following biomes is the plant most likely found?

   (A) Taiga
   (B) Desert
   (C) Tundra
   (D) Grassland

2. What is the process where bacteria take nitrogen from the atmosphere and convert it to a form that is usable by plants (primarily ammonia)?

   (A) Nitrogen fixation
   (B) Nitrification
   (C) Ammonification
   (D) Denitrification

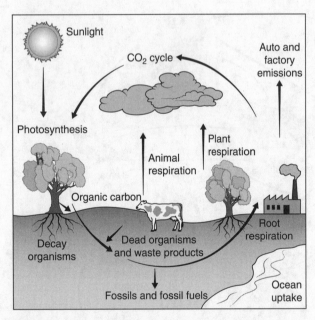

3. Which of the following is true and seen in the image above?

   (A) Carbon does not have an atmospheric component.
   (B) The majority of our atmosphere is carbon.
   (C) Carbon is found only anthropogenically.
   (D) Carbon cycles between photosynthesis and cellular respiration.

4. The burdock plant produces spiny seeds that cling to the fur of animals or clothing of humans. The plants rely on this method of seed dispersal for reproduction, while the animals are unaffected. Which of the following is this an example of?

   (A) Mutualism
   (B) Commensalism
   (C) Parasitism
   (D) Predator-prey

5. If the producers in an ecosystem convert 15,000 kCal of energy stored in organic compounds, which of the following would most likely be the amount of energy available to the tertiary consumers?

   (A) 15,000
   (B) 1,500
   (C) 150
   (D) 15

**6.** According to the graph below, what best describes the relationship between what is happening in 1885 with the lynx and hare?

(A) The lynx numbers are higher than the hare numbers because of predation.

(B) The environment experienced a severe drought limiting the number of plants the hares were able to graze on.

(C) There is a mutualistic relationship between hare and lynx.

(D) There were more hares in the area than lynx because of healthy predator-prey relationships.

**7.** Which of the following changes would most likely occur if the wolf were removed from the food web below?

**A Food Web**

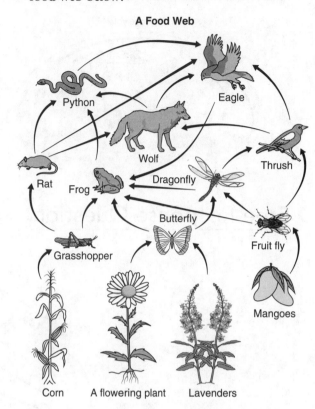

| (A) | increase in eagles | increase in pythons |
|-----|-------------------|---------------------|
| (B) | increase in frogs | decrease in eagles |
| (C) | decrease in eagles | increase in thrushes |
| (D) | increase in lavenders | decrease in corn |

**8.** Which of the following is true of gross primary productivity?

(A) Gross primary productivity is the total rate of photosynthesis in an area, or the full amount of food produced by the producers.

(B) Gross primary productivity is the difference between net productivity and the energy lost by producers for respiration.

(C) Gross primary productivity is the energy captured by producers added to the energy used by primary and secondary consumers over time.

(D) Gross primary productivity is the total amount of energy lost by both producers and consumers through respiration over time.

**9.** Which letter correctly identifies the process of the water cycle that would most be impacted by a city with asphalt parking lots and buildings?

(A) A
(B) B
(C) C
(D) D

**Water Cycle**

## › Free-Response Question

**A Food Web**

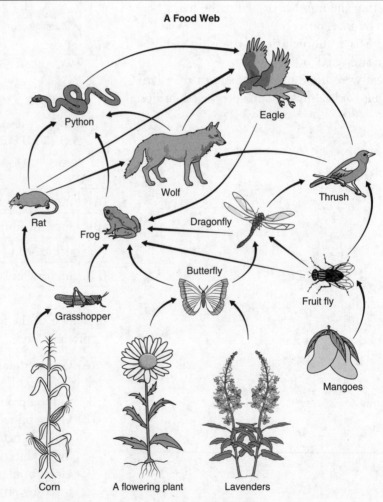

**10.** Refer to the diagram above to answer all parts of the question.

(A) **Identify** one primary producer in the food web above.

(B) **Identify** one primary consumer in the food web above.

(C) **Identify** one predator-prey relationship in the food web above.

(D) If the corn plant has 12,000 kCal available, **identify** the kCal available for the grasshopper, the rat, and the python and then **explain** why these organisms would have the amount you identified.

## › Answers and Explanations

**1. A**—The taiga is a coniferous forest (pine trees), with permafrost soil, usually found between the tundra and temperate forests. It is also the world's largest land biome.

**2. A**—During nitrogen fixation, $N_2$ from the atmosphere is converted by nitrogen-fixing microorganisms into ammonia.

**3. D**—Photosynthesis and cellular respiration are how carbon cycles in living things and is known as short-term cycling.

**4. B**—Commensalism is a relationship between species where one organism benefits and the other neither benefits nor is harmed. In this case the burdock plant has its seeds dispersed for reproduction but the animal is not affected.

**5. D**—According to the 10 percent rule, a plant (which in this case has 15,000 kCal) will be eaten by a primary consumer, giving the primary consumer 1,500 kCal. When a secondary consumer eats the primary consumer, it only gets 10 percent of that energy (or in this case 150 kCal). Finally when a tertiary consumer eats the secondary consumer, it gets 10 percent or 15 kCal.

**6. D**—The graph shows the relationship between the lynx and the hare. The lynx would not survive without its food source, the hare. However, the lynx keeps the hare numbers in check so they don't reach high numbers and begin to starve for lack of food resources for the hare. A healthy predator-prey relationship is important in the environment.

**7. C**—If the wolf were removed, the eagle would decrease because the eagle preys on the wolf and some of the eagle's food source would be removed. At the same time, there would be an increase in thrush birds since the wolves prey on thrush birds and without wolves their numbers would go up.

**8. A**—Gross productivity is the total rate of photosynthesis in an area, or the full amount of food produced by the producers.

**9. D**—If you built a city with parking lots and buildings, less water would be able to infiltrate into the ground and more would run off since asphalt and concrete are impermeable.

**10. (A)** One point for identifying either corn, flowering plant, lavenders, or mangoes.
**(B)** One point for identifying either grasshopper, butterfly, or fruit fly.
**(C)** One point for identifying a predator-prey relationship in the food web. There are many but some are python and rat, python and frog, eagle and wolf, eagle and frog, etc.
**(D)** One point for identifying the grasshopper as 1,200 kCal, one point for identifying the rat as 120 kCal, and one point for identifying that the python would get 12 kCal. Then one point for explaining that according to the 10 percent rule:

A plant or primary producer has 100 percent of the energy from the sun. But once a primary consumer eats that plant, it only gets 10 percent of the original energy from the producer so, in this case, the grasshopper will get 1,200 kcal. Then as the grasshopper goes about its day hopping around, heating its body, etc., it uses up 90 percent of the energy it received from the plant, leaving only 120 kCal for the rat. Next the python will only get 12 kCal because it only gets 10 percent of the energy from the rat.

## › Rapid Review

- Predator-prey—One eats, one gets eaten.
- Mutualism—Both species benefit by being in the relationship. Example: clownfish and anemone.
- Commensalism—One species benefits and the other is unaffected. Example: remora and shark.
- Parasitism—One species benefits and one species is harmed. Example: fleas on a dog.

- Competition—Two species competing for the same resources. There are two types:
  - Intraspecific competition is competition between members of the same species.
  - Interspecific competition is competition between members of different species.
- Biome—Major communities of plants and animals.
- Ecosystem—Living and nonliving parts of an environment.
- Taiga—Lengthy cold, wet winters with lots of coniferous trees.
- Temperate rainforest—Coniferous and broadleaf trees with lots of rain.
- Temperate seasonal forests—Four seasons with warm, wet summers and cold winters.
- Tropical rainforests—Greatest diversity of species with rain all year and warm all year.
- Shrubland—Hot, dry summers and cool, moist winters; found near coasts with short trees and grasses.
- Temperate grassland—Lots of grasses, low rainfall.
- Savanna—Grassland with a wet season and a dry season; wildfires are common.
- Desert—Dry with little vegetation.
- Tundra—Extremely cold, no trees, little rain.
- Freshwater biomes—Examples: rivers, lakes, streams, ponds.
- Saltwater biomes—Examples: oceans, coral reefs, kelp forests, marshlands, estuaries, mangrove forests, tidepools.
- Carbon cycle—How carbon cycles in the environment. It includes both photosynthesis and cellular respiration, which is how carbon is stored in the short term. Also included are dead organisms buried for millions of years, which is long-term storage of carbon.
- Nitrogen cycle—Nitrogen makes up 78 percent of our atmosphere. Bacteria are important in the nitrogen cycle. FixNAAD/ANPAN is a mnemonic to remember the steps (see chart in this chapter).
- Phosphorus cycle—Phosphorus cycles in the environment but it is a slow cycle with no atmospheric form. It is found in rocks and sediments.
- Hydrologic cycle—Otherwise known as the water cycle and includes evaporation, condensation, runoff, precipitation, and transpiration.
- Primary productivity—The rate at which food energy is generated by photosynthesis. It is measured in units of energy per unit area per unit time.
- Gross productivity—The total rate of photosynthesis in an area, or the full amount of food produced by the producers.
- Net productivity—The difference between gross productivity and the energy lost by producers for respiration.
- Trophic levels—Made up of producers, primary consumers, secondary consumers, and decomposers and shows that each level has less energy available.
- The 10 percent rule—90 percent of energy is used by the organism and only 10 percent moves up the pyramid because the organism below it used up the energy to heat its body and move, etc. The shape is a pyramid because energy is "lost" as it goes up to each higher level.
- Food chains—Visual representation of how one organism is food source for another.
- Food webs—Visual representation that is more like real life with multiple food source options for each animal.

# CHAPTER 6

# The Living World: Biodiversity

**IN THIS CHAPTER**

**Summary:** Biodiversity is all the variety of life on Earth. If we lose one part of the biodiversity on our planet, other species and entire ecosystems can be affected. Each species, no matter how large or how small, has an important role to play and species depend on each other for their own survival. There are both natural and human causes that can impact eco-systems and organisms must adapt to these causes.

**Key Idea**

✪ Ecosystems have structure and diversity that change over time.

**Key Terms**

- Adaptations
- Climax community
- Cultural service
- Ecological tolerance
- Generalists
- Genetic diversity
- Habitat diversity
- Indicator species
- Island biogeography
- Keystone species

- Pioneer members
- Population bottleneck
- Primary succession
- Provisioning service
- Regulating service
- Secondary succession
- Specialists
- Species diversity
- Species richness
- Supporting service

This chapter will be 6 to 8 percent of your AP Environmental Science exam, or about 5 to 6 questions out of the 80 multiple-choice questions. We will focus on biodiversity, things the environment does for humans, island biogeography, tolerance, impacts on ecosystems, how organisms adapt to their environment, and how environments change over time.

# Introduction to Biodiversity

There are three types of biodiversity: genetic, species, and habitat.

- **Genetic diversity** refers to the diversity within a species. Think of humans. Unless you are an identical twin, you are different from every other person on the planet. Each person has unique features such as eye color, skin color, hair color, height, and so on. These genetic differences also contribute to different environmental pressures, which affect organisms in different ways. Some organisms can withstand a particular environmental pressure while others will die. Genetic diversity is important because it helps maintain the health of a population.
- **Species diversity** is the number of species and abundance of each species that live in a particular community. Species diversity helps to contribute to the health of an ecosystem because each species has an important role in this health.
- **Habitat diversity** is the different habitats found in a certain region. Since a habitat is a home to plants and animals, how diverse a habitat is can tell us about the health of the area.

Genetic diversity is a way for populations to adapt to changing environments and allows for the population to better respond to environmental stress. With more **variation**, it is more likely that some individuals in a population will possess variations of alleles that are suited for the environment and it is more likely that these individuals will survive and reproduce.

A population that has been reduced for a generation or more, usually due to an environmental event like a drought or flood, is a **population bottleneck.** This reduces genetic variation and can lead to a loss of biodiversity. Ecosystems with many different species are more likely to recover from an environmental event than ecosystems with fewer species.

**Specialists** are organisms that require particular habitats, food, and so on. An example of a specialist species would be a koala, who can only eat eucalyptus. If the habitat where koalas live is damaged and their specific food source is gone, this could be particularly devastating to the population of koalas.

**Generalists** are the opposite. They can live in many different places and eat many different things. Generalists are less likely to be impacted by an environmental event. For example, think of a cockroach, who can live almost anywhere and eat almost anything.

**Species richness** is the number of species per sample. The more species present in a sample, the "richer" the sample. It is a count of the species, not the abundance or number of individuals of each species present. It gives as much weight to those species that have very few individuals as to those that have many individuals. Thus, one cactus has as much influence on the richness of an area as 1,000 dandelions.

# Ecosystem Services

Think about the many different ways that you as a human benefit from healthy ecosystems. These are tangible items like food, money, medicine, and more. Human activities can damage these services both economically and ecologically.

Scientists break these services into four categories:

- Provisioning—Services like food and clean water.
- Regulating—Services like plants cleaning the air, bees pollinating flowers, plants holding soil in place to prevent erosion, or the regulation of climate by natural processes.
- Cultural—Services that are not tangible things that benefit us but rather interactions with nature, such as taking a walk and enjoying what you see or art that comes from looking at nature, and so on.
- Supporting—These are harder to understand but are the ecosystem services that support all other others, such as producing oxygen, water cycling, and so on.

# Island Biogeography

Figure 6.1 is an example of a mainland with several small islands located different distances away from the mainland. You can see that each island is a different size. Island biogeography is the study of the species and distribution that would occur on each of these islands. The theory states that islands closer to the mainland (where the animals/plants have moved from) and/or larger islands will have more species than islands farther away or smaller. The size of the island in theory matters because larger islands can support more and different species while smaller ones would be more limited.

Consider an activity where masking tape is used to tape "islands" of different sizes on the floor, and they're different distances from a taped area called the "mainland." In this simulation, you're given lots of different supplies such as cotton balls, toothpicks, paper clips, rubber balls, rubber bands, etc. Your task would be to stand on the "mainland" and try to get as many objects to land (by throwing them) onto the "islands." Picturing this, obviously you discover that the islands that are smaller and farther away will have fewer items land on them than larger or closer islands. This helps to explain island biogeography. A real-life example would be why are there more birds on the island of New Guinea than the island of Bali? Well, New Guinea is 50 times the size of Bali!

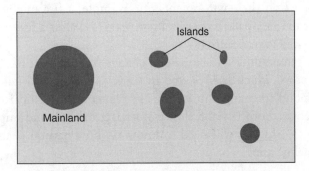

**Figure 6.1   Island biogeography.**

The other thing you will be tested on is how island biogeography has impacted evolution. Because an island is a special kind of environment, isolated and where species can't move easily, species on islands react to environmental pressures differently than species on continents. Islands have limited resources like food and habitats. Islands also often have specialists living on them. These species have adapted to become a specialist because of the unique characteristics on islands such as limited food or habitat resources. Because specialists are more likely to be impacted by human and/or natural events, such as the introduction of a nonnative (invasive) species, they could become threatened.

# Ecological Tolerance

All organisms have a range of conditions that they can survive in. Consider a goldfish in a bowl. If you put that bowl out in the sun in Texas in the middle of the summer, it will not only be cruel, but will result in a dead goldfish. Why? Well, because a goldfish has an ecological tolerance for temperature and the water temperature in the bowl has gone above that.

Other ecological tolerances in addition to temperature are salinity, sunlight, flow rate, and availability of water. These tolerances can apply to species or to individuals.

So far, everything you have seen will be tested as either a concept explanation or a visual representation. In other words, you will either have to read the question and be asked to explain an environmental concept, process, or model or analyze a visual like a food web or biogeochemical cycle.

On the exam, any questions relating to ecological tolerance will be in a text-analysis form where you will read a short passage, answer questions regarding the passage, and identify the author's claim.

In the next section, natural disruptions to ecosystems, adaptation, and ecological succession will all be tested as some sort of data analysis. This might involve reading a graph, data table, or chart or perhaps looking at a picture or map and explaining what is seen and so on. Make sure you can look for patterns, trends, or relationships and draw conclusions.

# Natural Disruptions to Ecosystems

Ecosystems can be impacted by natural factors such as fire, climate change, sea level rising, and more. These disruptions may be short/fast as in a fire, or slow/long over thousands or millions of years such as natural impacts of climate change. This factor will determine the impact on the environment. For example, a fire might have a large impact immediately, but the area will recover in a few years and after a few decades you might not even know a fire had even occurred.

An example of a slow/long change is climate. It has changed many times over millions of years, which has resulted in sea levels rising and falling over this time span. Sea levels respond to changes in ice on our planet and as land ice melts sea levels rise. All of these changes, both fast and slow can impact habitats and impact wildlife.

Terms you will need to know on how natural changes have occurred during Earth's timeline are:

- Periodic—This is a change that occurs at regular intervals, for example, the tides that come in every day at a predictable time.

- Episodic—This means it happens in irregular intervals. It repeats but irregularly, for example, El Niño and La Niña.
- Random—This is something that is totally random and can't be guaranteed to repeat. It might happen once or multiple times, for example, a meteor striking Earth.

## Adaptations

We have discussed both short- and long-term changes as well as both natural and human-caused changes. In order for organisms to survive these changes they have to be able to adapt. This is done by incremental changes at the population level.

The different ways organisms can adapt are biological (structural) adaptation and behavioral adaptation. Keep in mind these genetic adaptations do not happen over a lifetime or even over a few generations but rather take thousands of years and multiple generations before they are found in a species. Organisms that can't adapt to both short- and long-term environmental changes may not survive.

## Ecological Succession

There are two ways that habitats or communities change over time. One is primary succession and the other is secondary succession.

**Primary succession** occurs when an area has barren rock with no soil; for example, a new volcanic island (Figure 6.2). First, lichens will come in and begin to break down the rock. After small amounts of soil are formed, small annual plants followed by grasses and perennial plants will arrive. More soil will now form because these "pioneer" plants break down the rock and form soil. Larger plants, grasses, and fast-growing trees like conifers will then grow. Finally, after hundreds of years hardwood trees will be established in the area.

**Secondary succession** is a much faster process and occurs after a disturbance of some kind (Figure 6.3). This could be a fire, flood, or human activity like farming. Because soil is already well established, plants can return faster than without soil.

**Figure 6.2   Primary succession.**

**Figure 6.3 Secondary succession.**

You will also be tested on the following terms, so make sure you know what each is describing:

- Keystone species—Species that many other species depend on. If this species is removed the ecosystem would be drastically impacted. Some common examples of keystone species are otters, prairie dogs, and bison.
- Indicator species—A species that "indicates" an environmental condition and is used to diagnose the health of the ecosystem. Some common examples of indicator species are plants, lichens, and many amphibians like frogs.
- Pioneer species—The first species into a disturbed area undergoing succession.

## › Review Questions

### Multiple-Choice Questions

1. A family goes to a protected National Park for a hike. They take in the beauty of the surroundings and are inspired by what they see. Which of the following ecosystem services is the family enjoying?

    (A) Provisioning
    (B) Regulating
    (C) Cultural
    (D) Supporting

2. One island is 50 km away from the mainland and another is 10 km away. Both are virtually the same size. Which of the following would be correct about the number of species living on the islands?

    (A) The numbers would be generally the same and would include species from the mainland.
    (B) There would be fewer species on the island farther away and more species on the island closer to the mainland.
    (C) There would be more species on the island farther away and fewer species on the island closer to the mainland.
    (D) The numbers would be generally the same but neither island would have species from the mainland.

**3.** Oftentimes, in the hot summer temperatures, lakes and rivers will become so warm and the dissolved oxygen levels fall so low that there are major fish deaths. This usually occurs to large fish and will often be seen in the morning after oxygen levels plummet overnight. Large fish are more susceptible to low oxygen turnovers than small fish and small fish are often seen at the surface of the water gulping for air.

Which of the following best identifies the author's claim?

(A) The author claims that the kills of large fish are from not enough dissolved oxygen in the water.
(B) The author claims that large fish are unable to breathe air from the surface.
(C) The author claims that small fish consume the excess dissolved oxygen.
(D) The author claims that small fish don't require oxygen to survive but large fish do.

**4.** The picture below shows where climate change is impacting coastal communities. Which of the following would be best supported by the map?

(A) Wildlife near coastal areas will be impacted.
(B) Iceland will have extensive habitat loss.
(C) Invasive species will become a larger concern in Asia.
(D) Island nations will need to switch to renewable energy.

**5.** Looking at the graph below you can see that many plant species move into an area over time. Which of the following claims would be best supported by the graph?

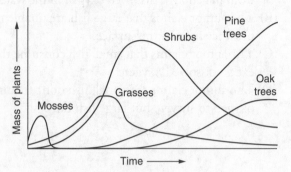

(A) Shrubs are pioneer plants and arrive first into a disturbed ecosystem.
(B) Oak trees are pioneer species.
(C) Mosses are known as climax species.
(D) Mosses are pioneers and trees are climax communities.

**6.** The raccoon is an animal who lives in all areas of the United States. They eat a wide variety of food sources, including human garbage. Which of the following best describes a raccoon?

(A) Raccoons are predators.
(B) Raccoons are generalists.
(C) Raccoons are specialists.
(D) Raccoons are keystone species.

## ❯ Free-Response Question

**7.** (A) **Identify** one regulating service provided by ecosystems and for that service **describe** how this benefits humans.
(B) **Define** a keystone species and **describe** how a lion could be considered a keystone species.
(C) **Define** primary succession and **explain** how primary succession can lead to soil formation on a newly formed volcanic landscape.

## ❯ Answers and Explanations

**1. C**—Cultural ecosystem services are not "things" we benefit from but rather interactions with nature, such as taking a walk and enjoying what you see or art that comes from looking at nature, and so on.

**2. B**—The theory states that islands closer to the mainland (where the animals/plants have moved from) and/or larger islands will have more species than islands farther away or smaller. The size of the island in theory matters because larger islands can support more and different species while smaller ones would be more limited.

**3. A**—The author is stating that large fish need greater amounts of oxygen and during the summer months will die because of less oxygen due to heat.

**4. A**—The graph shows that coastal communities are being affected by climate change, so any wildlife near the coasts could be impacted.

**5. D**—Pioneer species are the first species into a disturbed area undergoing succession and climax communities are the last. According to the graph, the first things that moved into the area were the mosses and over time came the trees, or climax community.

6. **B**—Generalists are animals who can eat anything and live in many different places.

7. **(A)** One point for identifying it is a regulating service and one point for describing how this benefits humans. Things like plants cleaning the air, bees pollinating flowers, plants holding soil in place to prevent erosion, or the regulation of climate by natural processes are regulating services. Describing how this benefits humans will depend on what you choose to write about. For example, bees pollinating plants and flowers provides food and beauty to humans.

**(B)** One point for defining a keystone species and one point for explaining why the lion can be considered a keystone species. A keystone species is a species that many other species depend on. If this species is removed the ecosystem would be drastically impacted. Lions help balance large ecosystems by consuming a wide variety of prey species.

**(C)** One point for defining primary succession and one point for explaining how primary succession works. Primary succession occurs in an area that has barren rock with no soil, a new volcanic island for example. First, lichens take hold and begin to break down the rock. After small amounts of soil are formed, small annual plants followed by grasses and perennial plants arrive. More soil is created because these "pioneer" plants break down the rock and form soil. When enough soil has been created, larger plants, grasses, and fast-growing trees like conifers will grow. Finally, after hundreds of years, a climax community of hardwood trees will be established in the area.

## › Rapid Review

- Genetic diversity—Diversity within a species. Example: unless you are a twin you look different than all other humans on the planet.

- Species diversity—Number of species and abundance in a community. Example: the bears, rabbits, toads, ferns, and oak trees in an area.

- Habitat diversity—How many different habitats are in a region. Example: tropical rainforest, tropical dry forest, grasslands.

- Population bottleneck—A population that has been reduced because of an environmental event. Ecosystems with many different species are more likely to recover from an environmental event than ecosystems with fewer species.

- Species richness—The number of species per sample. The more species present in a sample, the "richer" the sample.

- Provisioning service—Ecosystem services that give humans what they need to survive, like food and clean water.

- Regulating service—Ecosystem services that indirectly benefit humans, such as plants cleaning the air and bees pollinating plants.

- Cultural service—Ecosystem services that provide humans beauty, art, and enjoyment.

- Supporting service—Ecosystem services such as producing oxygen, water cycling, and other services that support human life.

- Island biogeography—Study of the species and distribution that would occur on islands. There are usually more species on islands closer to the mainland (more migration from the mainland) and larger islands that can hold more species.

- Specialists—Organisms that require specific habitats, food, etc., like a koala.

- Generalists—Organisms that can live in many places and eat many things, like a cockroach.

- Ecological tolerance—The total range of conditions organisms can live in. Each species has its own ecological tolerance before it dies.

- Adaptations—Biological and behavioral ways organisms adapt over time to survive.

- Primary succession—Bare rock, such as after a volcanic eruption, over time becomes a climax community. Moss or lichen usually inhabit first, break down rock to make soil, and afterward larger and larger plants move in. This is a slow process.

- Secondary succession—After a fire or flood destroys the habitat, but the soil remains. Over time it becomes a climax community as new plants begin move in. This is faster than primary succession.

- Keystone species—Species that many other species depend on.

- Indicator species—Species that indicate an environmental problem.

- Pioneer members—First members into an area after a fire, etc.

- Climax community—The stable stage of the environment after a disruption.

# CHAPTER 7

# Populations

## IN THIS CHAPTER

**Summary:** Populations in ecosystems change over time in response to factors in their environment and populations are limited by availability of resources and space. This chapter is all about populations, both populations in nature and human populations.

### Key Ideas

○ Populations change over time in reaction to a variety of factors.
○ Human populations change in reaction to a variety of factors, including social and cultural factors.

### Key Terms

- Age-structure diagrams
- Biotic potential
- Carrying capacity
- Demographic transition
- Density-dependent factors
- Density-independent factors
- Generalist
- Infant mortality rate
- K-selected species

- Population overshoot
- R-selected species
- Rule of 70
- Specialist
- Total fertility rate
- Type I survivorship curve
- Type II survivorship curve
- Type III survivorship curve

> This subject will account for about 10 to 12 percent of your AP Environmental Science exam, or about 8 to 10 questions out of the 80 multiple-choice questions. Make sure you can discuss trends in population data and can read and interpret different population graphs.

# Generalist and Specialist Species

Generalists, defined in Chapter 6, are going to be able to survive in habitats that change often. If the food availability of the area changes, a generalist can just change its diet and will most likely survive. Generalist species are more adaptable than specialist species.

A specialist species will have a difficult time with changing habitat conditions. In fact, a specialist will likely become endangered in an area if habitat conditions change because specialists are less likely to adapt to the new environment. They require very specific conditions and specific food requirements to survive and when these conditions or requirements change they suffer or die.

# k-Selected and r-Selected Species

For some students, this might be easy to remember: For "k" just remember kangaroo and for "r" remember roach. If you can remember that, you can answer any questions about this. However, keep in mind this topic will be assessed as a data analysis question, so you will have to describe patterns or trends in data.

What do we know about kangaroos? Well, they are large animals, they have a pouch, they hop around carrying their baby for 11 to 18 months . . . that's huge parental care! Usually a kangaroo only has one baby at a time, or maybe twins, and they don't have a baby until they are a few years old. They are herbivores who live in only one place in the world (Australia) and can live 12 to 18 years on average.

What are the characteristics of **k-selected species**?

- Large size
- Few offspring per year
- Live in stable environments in certain places
- Specialized diets
- Spend a lot of time and energy caring for their offspring
- Long life spans
- Reproduce more than once in their lifetime
- Can be impacted by invasive species or environmental changes

What about roaches? Roaches are small and live only a few months. They lay lots of eggs (sometimes 16 at a time), they can lay eggs about 14 times during their life, and they can lay eggs when they are only three to five months old. When a cockroach lays eggs they leave them and never return to care for the young. They can live almost anywhere on the planet and eat almost anything, but they only live about six months.

What are the characteristics of **r-selected species**?

- Small
- Many offspring
- Don't take care of their offspring (or very little care)
- Mature early
- Short life spans
- Live almost anywhere

- Eat almost anything
- Not as impacted by invasive species or environmental changes

Now, can you see how just remembering "r" for roach and "k" for kangaroo helps remember the characteristics of r-selected and k-selected species? It is an easy way to remember these two concepts!

**Biotic potential** is the maximum number of offspring a species could have if conditions were perfect. If we think about the roach and kangaroo examples from above, the roaches would have a high biotic potential and the kangaroos would have a low biotic potential. In other words, if conditions for a roach were perfect, one could produce a lot of babies before it died. On the other hand, a kangaroo, even under perfect conditions, would only produce a few babies in its lifetime.

When you plot biotic potential on a graph, it would look like the letter J and is known as exponential growth (Figure 7.1). Below is an example of exponential growth on a graph. This section will be tested using data analysis so make sure you can recognize different graphs like the ones below.

# Survivorship Curves

Figure 7.2 demonstrates the three **survivorship curves**.

Humans are the example most often used for Type I. If you look at Type I, you can see that almost 100 percent of humans survive childhood and most humans survive many years. Type I are often k-selected species.

Songbirds are an example of a Type II. In other words, the death rate for this species is constant during their entire lifetime. Some die young, others in middle age, and some live a long time. Type II are often k-selected species.

**Figure 7.1   Exponential growth.**

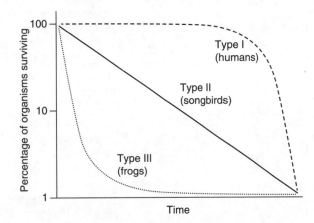

**Figure 7.2   Survivorship curves.**

The final type, Type III, can be characterized by frogs. Very few frogs make it to adulthood. Think of frog eggs—most get eaten, dry out and never mature, or never hatch at all. Then, tadpoles are also a major food source for many species so lots of young frogs are also killed. However, a few make it to old age and become adult frogs. Type III are often r-selected species.

## Carrying Capacity

**Carrying capacity** is the number of organisms an ecosystem can support over time. This is often shown in a graph depicted in Figure 7.3. The dotted line shows the carrying capacity and the solid line shows the growth of a particular species. As the species increases in number, it will sometimes overshoot the carrying capacity. This is usually because the species has continued to reproduce beyond what the area can support. However, there can be a lag before we begin to see the die-off because it takes a while before the species begins to starve, is impacted by disease, and so on. A reproductive time lag is the time it takes for the birth rates to decline and the death rates to increase in response to the amount of resources in the area.

The population could crash completely if the ecosystem can't recover. But usually, there will be small die-off and then the population will hover around the carrying capacity.

## Population Growth and Resource Availability

Populations are limited by the amount of resources available. When resources, things like food and shelter, are available and plentiful, populations can grow. When resources are scarce, populations will exhibit a dieback and decrease in size. This dieback is due to species dying or species being unable to reproduce or having a decreased rate of reproduction.

One way you might be tested on population growth and resource availability, other than carrying capacity, is by a formula that you will have to solve. This will usually involve calculating the percent change. The formula for percent change is shown below.

$$\text{Percent change} = \frac{\text{New value} - \text{Old value}}{\text{Old value}} \times 100$$

If the result is positive, it is an increase.
If the result is negative, it is a decrease.

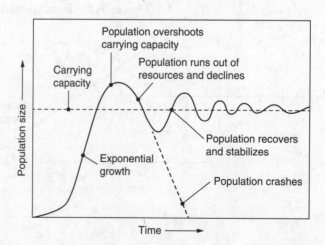

**Figure 7.3 Population changes and carrying capacity.**

Let's look at a money example. Let's say you had $100 and spent $50. What is the percent change of your money?

You would solve it like this:

$$\frac{\$50 - \$100}{\$100} \times 100 = -50\%$$

Your answer is negative 50 percent, or in other words, you have 50% less than what you started with. However, in an AP Environmental Science class you might be asked about the percent change of a population of cacti or blackbirds, etc. Regardless, you solve it the same way.

# Age-Structure Diagrams

You will be asked to look at an age-structure diagram like the four shown in Figure 7.4 and answer questions about it. Let's look at each one separately, but first let's see how we read one.

The size of the population (in either total numbers or percentage) is along the x-axis. Males are on the left side and females on the right and infants/children are along the bottom of the pyramid while elderly are on the top. Each age group is represented by a bar that is usually five years each.

Rapid growth countries: These are countries with a lot of infants, babies, and children. These countries grow very quickly because these children will grow up and have even more children since they are close to reproductive age. Some examples of countries with an age structure like this are Kenya, Nigeria, and Saudi Arabia. See Figure 7.4A.

Slow growth countries: These are countries with more a more column-shaped pyramid with steeper sides. There are more older people in this population than in a rapid growth country because conditions in this country (health care, food, etc.) are usually more advanced. There are still more children than adults but not as great a difference as in a rapidly growing country. See Figure 7.4B.

Zero/stable growth countries: These countries have about the same number of middle-aged people as children so they are considered stable or having a zero growth rate. In other words, for example, a family would have two children and when mom and dad die, the two children replace mom and dad and the population remains stable. This would be like Japan, Italy, and Greece. See Figure 7.4C.

Declining/negative-growth countries: Countries like Germany, Bulgaria, and Russia are considered negative or declining growth countries because there are fewer children than middle-aged adults. In these countries, mom and dad may only be having one child so when mom and dad die, the family (and country) gets smaller. See Figure 7.4D.

**Figure 7.4 Age-structure diagrams.**

Sometimes the AP exam will only have three pyramids, essentially combining slow and zero into the same one. Don't let this confuse you. Just make sure you look at the pyramid structure and answer the questions accordingly.

# Total Fertility Rate

This is another topic that will be tested using data for you to interpret. This could be in the form of data tables or graphs. You will need to understand things like total fertility rate and replacement levels and then look at the data and answer questions.

The definition of **total fertility rate (TFR)** is the total number of children born, or likely to be born, to a woman in her lifetime if she were subject to the prevailing rate of age-specific fertility in the population. In other words, what is the age in the country that girls normally have their first child? Do they wait until they are in their 30s to start having kids? Or do they have them in their early teens? What educational opportunities are available in the country and specifically to the women in the country? Is there good, reliable birth control in the country and is it acceptable to use birth control? What impact does the government have in the country when it comes to women, family planning, etc.? All of these things can determine the total fertility rate of a country.

In a country that has a TFR of 2.0 or close to that, the country is considered in **replacement level fertility** because the two children will replace the parents when they die and the country has a population growth rate that is relatively stable.

**Infant mortality rates** are also important to understand when it comes to the country's total fertility rate. A country where there is not good health care and/or nutrition will have high infant mortality rates. Infant mortality rates are expressed as the number of infants that die before they reach their first birthday out of every 1,000 births in that country. This rate is often an indicator of the health of the country. In most cases, when infant mortality rates are high, the TFR is also usually high. I know this seems to contradict itself. You might be asking yourself, "If a lot of babies die, how can the total fertility rate be high?" Well, population scientists have discovered that in developing nations, when lots of babies die, moms have even more babies to ensure at least a few make it to adulthood. So, when lots of babies die, the population usually increases dramatically.

# Human Population Dynamics

Human populations can be growing or declining. There are many factors that can impact this, including:

- Birth rate
- Death rate
- Infant mortality rate
- Access to reliable birth control/family planning
- Nutrition and food availability
- Education, particularly for women and girls
- Age of marriage

Thomas Malthus wrote an essay in 1798 in which he stated that humans were growing exponentially, but that food on our planet grew in a linear fashion. He developed the Malthusian Theory of Population Growth in which he proposed that if left unchecked, populations (specifically the human population) will outgrow their resources, particularly food. In other words, humans will grow beyond the Earth's carrying capacity. Of course,

Malthus could not predict in the late 1700s that we would be able to grow food more efficiently and more abundantly with the invention of fertilizers and more. Nor could he have known that we would have the capability to ship food around the world to where it is needed. However, the question still exists of what is the carrying capacity for humans on Earth and could it ever be reached?

**Density-dependent factors** are things that affect a population as its density increases. For example, diseases are transmitted from human to human; if you live in a place with a lot of people you are more likely to get the disease (let's say the flu) than if you live in the middle of nowhere on a farm with very little interaction with other humans. Other density-dependent factors are air pollution and access to clean water.

**Density-independent factors** are things such as severe storms, droughts, heat waves, and fires that can influence populations regardless of their density. For example, a drought can hit a tiny town or a large city.

Finally, you will almost certainly be asked to solve a problem using the rule of 70. The formula is:

$$\text{number of years to double} = \frac{70}{\text{annual percentage growth rate}}$$

You might be given the annual percentage growth rate and asked to solve for how many years it takes for the population to double. Or you might be given the number of years it takes for the population to double and asked to determine the annual percentage growth rate. Regardless, just manipulate the formula algebraically and solve for the missing value. Do not change the number given to a decimal; use the percent as a whole number in the calculation. So, if you are told the annual percentage growth rate is 4 percent, then you just take 70 and divide it by 4, so it will take 17.5 years to double.

# Demographic Transition

The **demographic transition model** is another way to look at populations (Figure 7.5). Similar to age-structure diagrams, these are broken up into four stages: preindustrial, transitional, industrial, and postindustrial. The model demonstrates how countries change as they develop economically. Let's break down each.

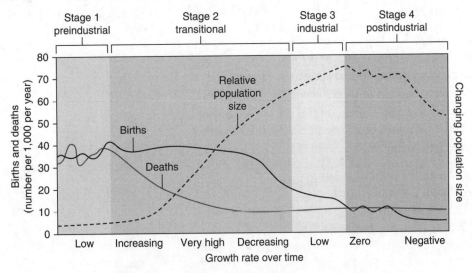

**Figure 7.5 The demographic transition.**

**Preindustrial** countries have high birth rates and high death rates so the country has a low growth rate. This stage applied to most of the world before the Industrial Revolution. Even though birth rates are very high, with death rates just as high the country is stable and not growing.

**Transitional** countries are the ones you will most likely be asked about on the exam because these are countries where birth rates stay high but death rates begin to drop due to increases in health, food availability, and medicine. Infants begin to survive into childhood but because there are still so many births the country's population begins to explode. In addition, because education and birth control for women is limited, the TFR will remain high and the population will grow exponentially. The least developed countries today are in the transitional stage of the demographic transition.

**Industrial** countries have birth rates that begin to drop due to access to reliable birth control, family planning, women having access to education and jobs and are similar to most developing countries today. With birth rates dropping, the population begins to slow, but not as quickly as you might think due to population momentum.

**Population momentum** is the idea that even though birth rates have fallen, since there are already so many people in reproductive ages, it takes many decades for the population to finally stabilize.

In **postindustrial** countries economies are strong, citizens are highly educated, medical care is advanced, and women have access to many employment opportunities. In this final stage, both birth rates and death rates continue to fall until death rates exceed birth rates and thus the population begins to decrease.

# › Review Questions

## Multiple-Choice Questions

1. A country has a growth rate of 4%. How many years will it take for the population to double?

   (A) 17.5 years
   (B) 1,750 years
   (C) 175 years
   (D) 280 years

2. A country has begun to get access to health care for women and children and there is better access to food resources and clean water. However, it is still very expensive to get access to reliable birth control so most women do not use it. What stage of the demographic transition is this country most likely in?

   (A) Stage 1—preindustrial
   (B) Stage 2—transitional
   (C) Stage 3—industrial
   (D) Stage 4—postindustrial

3. Which of the following would be an r-selected species with very little parental care?

   (A) Fish with 9,000 eggs per season
   (B) Bird with five eggs per clutch
   (C) Bat with one pup per season
   (D) Dog with eight pups per year

4. Which of the following characteristics is most closely associated with the age-structure diagram below?

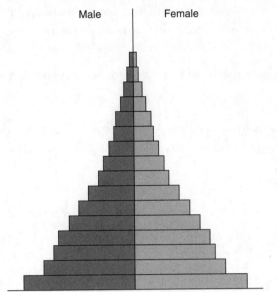

Male          Female

(A) People in this country have access to good, reliable birth control.
(B) People in this country have high levels of education
(C) People in this country have one child or fewer per couple
(D) People in this country have a high total fertility rate

5. Sparrows are a type of small passerine bird that shows a roughly constant mortality rate for the species through its entire life. This means that the individual's chance of dying is independent of their age. Which of the following best characterizes this type of animal?

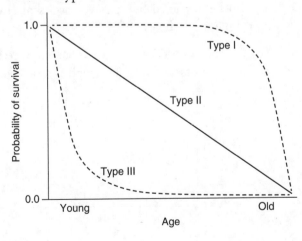

(A) Sparrows are k-selected species, displaying a Type III survivorship curve.
(B) Sparrows are r-selected species, displaying a Type I survivorship curve.
(C) Sparrows are k-selected species, displaying a Type II survivorship curve.
(D) Sparrows are r-selected species, displaying a Type III survivorship curve.

6. The idea that the carrying capacity for humans is fixed and the size of the human population will outgrow Earth's carrying capacity is best described by which of the following economic arguments?

(A) Malthusian Theory
(B) Keynesian Theory
(C) Hayek Theory
(D) Marshall Theory

7. A country had a population of 150,000 in 1980 and 210,000 in 2010. What is the percent change of the population in this country from 1980 to 2010?

(A) 4%
(B) 40%
(C) 1.33%
(D) 2,000%

# › Free-Response Question

8. A population of elephants lives in sub-Saharan Africa. A female elephant will bear approximately 12 calves in her lifetime of almost 70 years and usually only one calf at a time. Elephants are herbivores who eat grasses, herbs, fruits, plants, and trees.

   (A) **Identify** the type of species the elephant would be, either r-selected or k-selected, and **explain** why you chose this as your answer.
   (B) **Draw** a survivorship curve that best describes an elephant.
   (C) In the early part of the twentieth century, there were as many as 5 million African elephants, but now there are approximately 415,000. **Calculate** the percent change in African elephants during this time span.

# › Answers and Explanations

1. **A**—70/4 = 17.5 years

2. **B**—Countries in the transitional phase are the ones you will most likely be asked about on the exam because these are countries where birth rates stay high but death rates begin to drop due to improvements in health, food availability, and medicine. Infants begin to survive into childhood but because there are still so many births, the country's population begins to explode. The least developed countries today are in the transitional stage of the demographic transition.

3. **A**—Characteristics of r-selected species? They are small, mature early, and have short life spans. They have many offspring but don't take care of their offspring (or very little care). They can live almost anywhere and eat almost anything. They're not as impacted by invasive species or environmental changes.

4. **D**—Rapid growth countries: These are countries with a lot of infants, babies, and children. They grow very quickly because these children will grow up and have even more children because they are close to reproductive age. Some examples of countries with an age structure like this are Kenya, Nigeria, and Saudi Arabia.

5. **C**—Songbirds are an example of a Type II. In other words, the death rate for this species is constant during their entire lifetime. Some die young, others in middle age, and some live a long time. These are often k-selected species.

6. **A**—The Malthusian Theory of Population Growth proposed that if left unchecked populations (specifically the human population) will outgrow their resources, particularly food. In other words, humans will grow beyond the Earth's carrying capacity.

7. **B** $\dfrac{210,000 - 150,000}{150,000} \times 100\% = 40\%$

8. **(A)** One point for identifying that it would be a k-selected species and one point for explaining why from the list of characteristics below.

   K-selected species because the characteristics of k-selected species are:

   - Large size
   - Few offspring per year
   - Live in stable environments in certain places
   - Specialized diets
   - Spend a lot of time and energy caring for their offspring
   - Long life spans
   - Reproduce more than once in their lifetime
   - Can be impacted by invasive species or environmental changes

   **(B)** One point for the x- and y-axes labeled correctly and one point for a correct line graph as seen below.

   **(C)** Two points possible: one point for correct setup and one point for correct answer.

$$\frac{415,000 - 5,000,000}{5,000,000} \times 100 = -91.7\%$$

# ⟩ Rapid Review

- Generalist—A species that can eat almost anything and live almost anywhere, like a cockroach.

- Specialist—A species that only eats a specific item or lives in only one place/habitat, like a koala.

- K-selected species, like a kangaroo
  - Large size
  - Few offspring per year
  - Live in stable environments in certain places
  - Specialized diets
  - Spend a lot of time and energy caring for their offspring
  - Long life spans
  - Reproduce more than once in their lifetime
  - Can be impacted by invasive species or environmental changes

- R-selected species, like a roach
  - Small
  - Many offspring
  - Don't take care of their offspring (or very little care)
  - Mature early
  - Short life spans
  - Live almost anywhere
  - Eat almost anything
  - Not as impacted by invasive species or environmental changes

- Biotic potential—Maximum reproductive rate of a population if conditions were ideal. In other words, if there was plenty of room, plenty of food, no predators, and so on, then how many of a particular species could live in the area.

- Type of Survivorship Curves
  - Type I survivorship curve—Long life, not many die young. Example: humans.
  - Type II survivorship curve—Die at all stages of lifetime. Example: birds.
  - Type III survivorship curve—Almost all die young and only a few live to maturity. Example: fish.

- Carrying capacity—The number of organisms an ecosystem can support over time. This is often shown in a graph.

- Population overshoot—When a population exceeds its carrying capacity and there is a dieback.

- Age-structure diagrams—Pyramid-shaped graphs showing the number of female and males in each age group. See pictures of differently shaped pyramids in the chapter.

- Total fertility rate—The total number of children born, or likely to be born, to a woman in her lifetime if she were subject to the prevailing rate of age-specific fertility in the population.

- Infant mortality rate—The number of infants that die before their first birthday out of 1,000 births.

- Density-dependent factors—Things that become worse as the density of the population is larger. Infectious disease is an example of this since the more humans there are, the faster the disease can spread.

- Density-independent factors—Things such as severe storms, droughts, heat waves, and fires that can influence populations regardless of their density. For example, a tornado doesn't hit a city more than a rural area; where people live doesn't matter to a tornado.

- Rule of 70—This is a calculation to solve for how many years it will take for a population to double. 70/growth rate = doubling time. If you are given the doubling time, then rearrange the formula to solve for the growth rate.

- Demographic transition—The demographic transition model is another way to look at populations. Similar to age-structure diagrams, these are broken up into four stages: pre-industrial, transitional, industrial, and postindustrial. It demonstrates how countries change as they develop.

# CHAPTER 8

# Earth Systems and Resources

IN THIS CHAPTER

**Summary:** This chapter is all about the nonliving part of our planet that supports our living systems. We will focus on how energy is transferred from the sun to different parts of Earth and how different parts of our planet interact with one another. We will cover geological concepts like plate tectonics, soil formation and composition, the atmosphere and wind, watersheds, and climate topics.

**Key Ideas**

✪ Earth's systems interact, resulting in a state of balance over time.
✪ Most of the Earth's atmospheric processes are driven by input of energy from the sun.

**Key Terms**

- Convergent boundaries
- Coriolis effect
- Divergent boundaries
- Earthquakes
- El Niño
- Erosion
- Exosphere
- Hot spot volcanism
- Island arcs
- La Niña
- Mesosphere

- Permeability
- Porosity
- Rain shadow effect
- Soil horizons
- Soil texture triangle
- Stratosphere
- Thermosphere
- Transform boundaries
- Troposphere
- Volcanoes
- Watershed

These topics will cover about 10 to 12 percent of your AP Environmental Science exam, or about 8 to 10 questions out of the 80 multiple-choice questions. Unless you have taken an Earth Science class, some of topics may be new to you and you might need to review this chapter several times.

## Plate Tectonics

Once again, this will be a topic that will be tested using a visual representation. In other words, you will be given a diagram and will need to answer questions based on the picture. Let's look at some of the diagrams.

The Earth's lithosphere, which includes the crust and upper mantle, is made up of a series of pieces, or tectonic plates, that move slowly over time (Figure 8.1).

The first way plates move is away from each other at **divergent plate boundaries**. When plates move apart we get seafloor spreading, rift valleys, volcanoes, and earthquakes. Along these boundaries, earthquakes are common and magma (molten rock) rises from the Earth's mantle to the surface (Figure 8.2). Once this magma solidifies we get new oceanic crust. The most common example of a divergent plate boundary is the Mid-Atlantic Ridge found in the middle of the Atlantic Ocean on the bottom of the seafloor.

The second way plates move is together at **convergent plate boundaries**. When two land (continental) plates come together, the land buckles and mountain ranges are formed. The Himalayan Mountains are an example of this. When a land plate and a sea (oceanic) plate collide, we get deep seafloor trenches with lines of volcanoes and earthquakes near them. The reason you will get a lot of volcanoes is seen in Figure 8.3.

As the ocean plate subducts, or is forced below the continental plate, the ocean plate melts and rises. Have you ever watched a lava lamp work? The wax (lava) is down on the bottom of the lamp where the heat source (light bulb) is found. As the heat melts the wax, the wax begins to rise up through the liquid to the top; this is like what is happening on our planet. As the ocean plate melts because of the heat in our Earth, it begins to rise forming a volcano.

**Figure 8.1    Plate tectonics.**

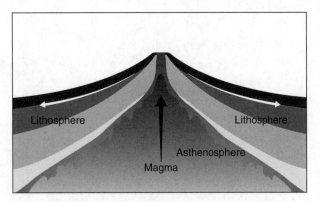

**Figure 8.2    Divergent plate boundary.**

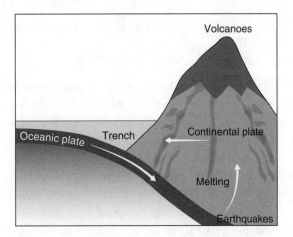

**Figure 8.3    Convergent plate boundary.**

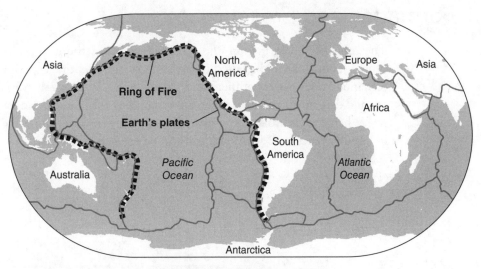

**Figure 8.4    The Ring of Fire.**

The **Ring of Fire** (see Figure 8.4) is an area around the Pacific Plate where a "ring" of volcanoes and earthquakes can be found because of convergent plate boundaries.

**Island arcs** are a chain of volcanic islands found on subduction zones and there are often earthquakes associated with these. Examples of island arcs are the Japanese islands, Kuril Islands, and the Aleutian Islands of Alaska.

**Figure 8.5   Transform plate boundary.**

The final way plates move is at **transform boundaries** (Figure 8.5) where two plates moving in opposite directions slide by one another. The most common example you may be familiar with is California's San Andreas fault. Earthquakes are common along these faults as the plates move past each other and stored energy becomes released as energy of motion.

**Hot spots** are areas where the magma from the mantle rises through the lithosphere creating a volcano (Figure 8.6). If the lithosphere is moving over a stationary hot spot, you can get a line of volcanic islands. The Hawaiian Islands are an example of a hot spot volcanism.

Remember, these will be visual representations so make sure you can identify on a map the locations of volcanoes, island arcs, earthquakes, and so on.

## Soil Formation and Erosion

The topic of soil formation and erosion, as well as the next section on composition and properties of soil, will be tested in the context of a scientific experiment. You will be given a scenario of a science experiment and asked a question about the variables. Review independent and dependent variables if you aren't familiar with these topics before you take the exam.

When rock is broken down (weathered) by rain, wind, snow, ice, and so on, and carried to another place and deposited, soil can be formed.

**Figure 8.6   Hot spot volcanism.**

**Figure 8.7   Soil profile.**

Soil is broken down into many horizons as shown in Figure 8.7. The top layer is the "O" horizon, or organic layer, where freshly dead leaves and other organic matter are found. Lots of decomposition is happening here.

The second layer, the "A" horizon or surface layer, is often called topsoil and is rich in organic matter. The "B" horizon, or subsoil, often has a lot of clay from above layers. The "C" horizon, or substratum, is mostly weathered rock from the bedrock below.

Soil erosion can be caused from water and wind taking soil away. It is very important to stop soil erosion because of the importance of soil for plants, the ability soil has to clean and filter water, and the concern that when soil erodes it can damage the local waterways.

## Soil Composition and Properties

Different types of soils allow water through at different rates, or not at all. For example, water goes easily through sand since the water is smaller than the particles of sand. Water can go through silt slower, because silt particles are smaller. Water can't go through clay at all because the particles of clay are so small that water can't squeeze between them (Figure 8.8).

**Figure 8.8   Infiltration by soil texture.**

The type of soil determines how much water the soil can hold, or the soil's water holding capacity. Think of it like this: clay is used to make things like pots and bowls. Why? Well, because clay has a high water-holding capacity. It can hold water for days. Would you make a cup out of sand? Of course not—the water would go right through the sand because sand has a low water-holding capacity. How much water the soil can hold can also determine how fertile the soil is and how productive the land might be.

Here are some terms you should know, including knowing how these affect the fertility of the soil:

**Porosity**—Having small spaces between the particles. The finer the particle size, the more porosity. This might seem backward but clay has tiny holes and very fine particle sizes so clay has the highest porosity.

**Permeability**—The ability of a material to allow liquid to flow through it. Sand has a high permeability since water flows easily through it.

You may be asked to read a soil triangle and determine the type of soil based on the percentage of sand, silt, and clay. A soil triangle looks like Figure 8.9.

You may be given information such as: a soil has 40 percent sand, 40 percent silt, and 20 percent clay. You would be asked to determine the type of soil texture using the soil pyramid.

To do this, you start with the sand and find the percentage along the bottom of the triangle, in this case 40 percent, and follow the line that goes up and to the left for sand. Then, you move to the right side of the triangle and find the line for silt, in this case also 40 percent. Follow this line down and to the left until it hits the line you had drawn for sand. They should cross. Then, where they cross, if you draw a straight line to the left, where you find clay, you should be at the 20 percent line, which is your percentage of clay. Where these three lines intersected is the type of soil you have; in this case, loam. You might want to use a ruler or a straight edge when drawing the three lines to make sure you are accurate.

**Figure 8.9   Soil triangle.**

**Figure 8.10  Layers of the earth's atmosphere.**

# Earth's Atmosphere

The Earth's atmosphere is mostly made of nitrogen gas. In fact, 78 percent of the atmosphere is nitrogen. The next highest is oxygen, making up 21 percent, followed by argon, which is 0.9 percent. The rest of the atmosphere is made up of what are known as trace gases, including carbon dioxide, methane, nitrous oxides, and ozone.

The Earth's atmosphere has layers as you move away from the land; the layers are seen in Figure 8.10. The layer we live in is called the troposphere, where all weather occurs. The layer that is farthest away is the exosphere. You can see the temperature line going up through each layer. As you move up through the troposphere, the temperature gets colder. Once you hit the stratosphere, the temperatures begin to go in the other direction, heating up. This back-and-forth continues as you move up through each layer. The thermosphere (*thermo* means "heat") has temperatures that reach hundreds to thousands of degrees! But, the air is so thin it would feel freezing cold to us if we went there. Don't be surprised if you see a picture just like this one on the exam since this section will be tested with a visual representation.

# Global Wind Patterns

Another visual representation you will be tested on shows the global wind patterns.

Look at Figure 8.11. Earth is tilted at a 30-degree angle. Because of this, the sun's radiation hits Earth with different intensities. It hits the equator most directly since it is directly overhead most of the year. Remember that warm air rises and cooler air sinks because warm air is less dense than cold air. So, if you look at the 0-degree equator, you see rising, moist air that goes off in both directions and sinks at 30 degrees north and south.

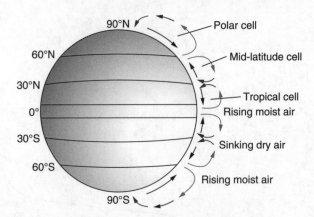

**Figure 8.11   Global wind patterns.**

This sinking, dry air is where the Earth's major deserts are found. Air is also rising at the 60-degree line (both north and south) going off in both directions and sinking again at 30 degrees or at 90 degrees. These different cells are responsible for the climate patterns that define our biomes.

**Coriolis effect**—Because Earth is spinning on its axis, winds and water veer to the right, and storms like hurricanes spin counterclockwise in the Northern Hemisphere and veer to the left and spin clockwise in the Southern Hemisphere (Figure 8.12).

# Watersheds

A watershed is a land area that directs water or snow to a river, creek, or stream and eventually to the ocean. Some watersheds are very large, like the Mississippi River watershed that covers about 40 percent of the United States. Watershed characteristics such as size, slope, shape, drainage density, land use/land cover, geology, soils, and vegetation are important factors of watersheds. Things that can affect a watershed would be a dam and housing developments.

# Solar Radiation and Earth's Seasons

Earth is tilted 23.5 degrees and solar radiation hits the planet at different intensities depending on the season and latitude. So, let's look at the visual representation shown in Figure 8.13.

**Due to the Earth's Rotation**

Objects deflect to the right
in the Northern Hemisphere

Northern Hemisphere

Southern Hemisphere

Objects deflect to the left
in the Southern Hemisphere

**Figure 8.12   The coriolis effect.**

**Figure 8.13    Solar radiation.**

The diagram on the left is Earth in December. Do you see how the Tropic of Capricorn is receiving the most direct (straight) sunlight in December? Now, look at the diagram on the right; this is Earth in June. Where is the most direct sunlight now? Is it the Tropic of Capricorn? No, it is the Tropic of Cancer. The amount of sunlight varies seasonally. In addition, the equator gets direct sun year-round and as you move up or down to the poles the sunlight becomes less and less direct. The fact that Earth is tilted and rotates around the sun accounts for the Earth's seasons.

# Earth's Geography and Climate

Figure 8.14 shows the rain shadow effect. Our planet's weather and climate are impacted by other things in addition to the tilt of Earth and the amount of sunlight. Weather and climate can be impacted by things like tall mountains. In the picture, the ocean is on the left, which provides a lot of moisture to the area. As the moisture evaporates and clouds are formed, there is a lot of rain on the windward side of the mountain. However, because the mountain is so tall, the rain clouds don't go over the mountain and it is very dry on the other side.

# El Niño and La Niña

Every three to seven years on average, the Pacific Ocean has climate shifts with warmer surface waters known as the El Niño–Southern Oscillation (ENSO). Upwellings from the seabed occur in normal years that bring nutrients up for the plankton to feed on. Plankton are food for the marine life up the food chain. In an El Niño year, that upwelling does not occur so the plankton decrease and, in turn, so do the fish stocks.

**Figure 8.14    The rain shadow effect.**

La Niña is essentially the opposite of El Niño. With La Niña, the trade winds are particularly strong in carrying warmer water westward across the Pacific leading to colder than average temperatures in the east and warmer than average temperatures in the west. The result is that plankton increase in the areas where the temperature is cooler, leading to an increase in fish stocks.

The impacts of El Niño and La Niña are changes to rainfall, wind, and ocean circulation patterns. It is particularly rainy during an El Niño year on the West Coast of the United States and South America.

# › Review Questions

## Multiple-Choice Questions

1. The graph below shows the difference in temperature in each layer of the atmosphere.

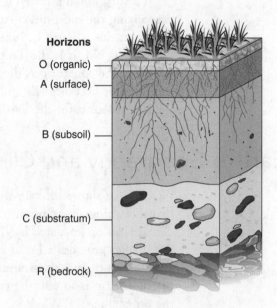

Which of the following correctly describes the Earth's atmosphere?

(A) The mesosphere is where temperatures get warmer.
(B) The troposphere is where the ozone layer is found.
(C) The troposphere is where all weather is found.
(D) The stratosphere contains most of the oxygen in our atmosphere.

2. According to the diagram above, which layer would have the most organic material?

(A) O
(B) A
(C) B
(D) C

**3.** Which of the following would be found at the plate boundary seen below?

(A) Mountain formation, due to plates colliding together

(B) Deep ocean trenches

(C) Earthquakes, due to stored energy being released

(D) New crust being formed as magma rises

**4.** An experiment is done where water is poured through a soil sample as shown below.

100 ml of water is added and after one hour, 2 ml is found in the bottom of the jar. Which type of soil is likely in the funnel?

(A) Sand

(B) Silt

(C) Loam

(D) Clay

**5.** Around December, fisherman off the coast of South America would discover that the normal numbers of fish they would catch would diminish every three to seven years. Which of the following is the best explanation of why this was happening?

(A) Warmer waters were causing the fish to move to colder waters.

(B) Overfishing was occurring in the region.

(C) Large predators such as sharks were frequenting the region.

(D) Fallout from local coal-burning power plants was generating acid rain.

**6.** What type of biome would you expect to find on the leeward side of the mountain?

(A) Tropical rainforest

(B) Desert

(C) Temperate forest

(D) Grassland

## ❭ Free-Response Question

7. The Ring of Fire is a ring of volcanoes around the Pacific Ocean that result from subduction of oceanic plates beneath lighter continental plates. Most of the Earth's volcanoes are located around the Pacific Ring of Fire because that is the location of most of the Earth's subduction zones.

(A) **Explain** what happens when two plates collide along a subduction zone.
(B) Another common phenomenon around the equatorial Pacific Ocean is known as El Niño. **Describe** what an El Niño is and what impact it would have on the environment.

## ❭ Answers and Explanations

1. **C**—The troposphere is where we live and where all weather is found.

2. **A**—The top layer is the organic layer where dead and decaying leaves are found.

3. **C**—The diagram is a transform boundary where plates are sliding past one another. Earthquakes are common along these faults.

4. **D**—Clay, because clay has a high water-holding capacity. It has the highest porosity but it is not very permeable.

5. **A**—Every three to seven years on average, the Pacific Ocean has climate shifts with warmer surface waters known as the El Niño–Southern Oscillation (ENSO). Upwellings from the seabed occur in normal years that bring nutrients up to the plankton to feed on. The plankton are food for the marine life up the food chain. In an El Niño year, that upwelling does not occur so the plankton are reduced and, in turn, so are the fish stocks.

6. **B**—You would find a desert. The prevailing wind coming off the ocean brings a lot of rain to the windward side of the mountain. However, because the mountain is so tall, the rain clouds don't go over the mountain and it is very dry on the other side.

7. **(A)** One point for explaining that one plate is pushed beneath another and a trench may form.
**(B)** One point for describing an El Niño. Every three to seven years on average, the Pacific Ocean has climate shifts with warmer surface waters known as the El Niño–Southern Oscillation (ENSO). Upwellings from the seabed occur in normal years that bring nutrients up to the plankton to feed on. The plankton are food for the marine life up the food chain. In an El Niño year, that upwelling does not occur so the plankton decrease, and in turn, so do the fish stocks. One point for describing the impact of El Niño. The impact on the environment from El Niño is fewer fish on the West Coast of South America and increased rainfall on the western coasts of both North and South America.

# › Rapid Review

- Convergent boundaries—Where two tectonic plates are colliding together.

- Divergent boundaries—Where two tectonic plates are moving apart.

- Transform boundaries—Where two tectonic plates moving in opposite directions are sliding by one another.

- Hot spot volcanism—A volcano created by the magma from the mantle rises through the lithosphere. If the lithosphere is moving over a stationary hot spot, you can get a line of volcanic islands.

- Island arcs—A chain of volcanic islands found on subduction zones. There are usually earthquakes associated with these.

- Erosion—Soil moving from one area to another caused by wind or water.

- Soil horizons—Layers of soil that include O, A, B, C, and bedrock. The top layer is the "O," or organic layer, where freshly dead leaves and other organic matter is found. Lots of decomposition is happening here. The second horizon, "A," or surface layer, is often called topsoil and is rich in organic matter. The "B" layer, or subsoil, often has a lot of clay from above layers. The "C" horizon is mostly weathered rock from the bedrock below.

- Porosity—Having small spaces between the particles. The finer the particle size, the more porosity. This might seem backward but clay has tiny holes and very fine particle sizes so clay has the highest porosity.

- Permeability—The ability of a material to allow liquid to flow through it. Sand has a high permeability, since water flows easily through it.

- Soil texture triangle—A way to determine the type of soil based on the percentage of clay, silt, and sand.

- The layers of the atmosphere—Troposphere, stratosphere, mesosphere, thermosphere, and exosphere. The temperature changes with each layer.

- Coriolis effect—Because Earth is spinning on its axis, winds and water veer to the right, and storms like hurricanes spin counterclockwise in the Northern Hemisphere and clockwise in the Southern Hemisphere.

- Watershed—A watershed is a land area that directs precipitation to a particular creek, stream, or river and eventually to the ocean.

- Rain shadow effect—Where it rains on the side of the mountain with the ocean and is very dry on the other side of the mountain.

- El Niño and La Niña—Are opposite phases of what is known as the *El Niño–Southern Oscillation* (ENSO) cycle. The ENSO are the fluctuations in temperature in the ocean and atmosphere in the east-central Equatorial Pacific.

# CHAPTER 9

# Land and Water Use

## IN THIS CHAPTER

**Summary:** This chapter explains that humans are doing things to the environment that are both positive and negative and gives examples of ways we can reduce the negative impacts humans are causing.

### Key Ideas

✪ When humans use natural resources, they alter natural systems.

✪ Humans can mitigate their impact on land and water resources through sustainable use.

### Key Terms

- Aquaculture
- Aquifers
- Biocontrol
- Clear-cutting
- Concentrated animal feeding operations (CAFOs)
- Contour plowing
- Crop rotation
- Desertification
- Drip irrigation
- Ecological footprint
- Flood irrigation
- Free-range grazing
- Fungicides

- Furrow irrigation
- Genetically modified organisms (GMOs)
- Green Revolution
- Herbicides
- Impervious surfaces
- Infiltration
- Insecticides
- Integrated pest management
- Intercropping
- No-till agriculture
- Overburden
- Overfishing
- Overgrazing

- Permeable surfaces
- Perennial crops
- Pesticides
- Prescribed burns
- Reforestation
- Rodenticides
- Rotational grazing
- Salinization
- Saltwater intrusion
- Slag and tailings
- Slash-and-burn farming
- Spray irrigation
- Strip cropping

- Strip mining
- Subsurface mining
- Surface mining
- Sustainability
- Terracing
- Tilling
- Tragedy of the commons
- Urban runoff
- Urban sprawl
- Urbanization
- Waterlogging
- Windbreaks

This chapter about land and water use will cover about 10 to 15 percent of your AP Environmental Science exam, or about 8 to 12 out of the 80 multiple-choice questions. The topics of irrigation, pest control, mining, urbanization, integrated pest management, sustainable agriculture, aquaculture, and sustainable forestry are all going to be tested on your ability to come up with the best environmental solution. So, make sure when you read the question you are thinking pro-environment and choose the best solution from the answer choices.

# The Tragedy of the Commons

The **tragedy of the commons** holds that individuals tend to overexploit shared resources until the resource becomes unavailable to all. Garrett Hardin originally explained this concept using an analogy of ranchers taking their animals to a common field. Hardin said that when there are just a few animals feeding off the common area there is no problem. However, when many ranchers come and add more and more animals, and there are no rules as to how many or how long the animals can graze, with the rancher caring only about their own profits, soon the area will be decimated and unusable to anyone. This concept can be extended to many areas of environmental science (for example, polluting the air or water and overfishing our oceans).

# Clear-Cutting

Forests are an important resource, both for the environment and for human use. The trees in forests are huge carbon sinks, meaning they are able to absorb large amounts of carbon dioxide from our atmosphere (carbon dioxide is a leading contributor to climate change that we will discuss in a future chapter). When we cut and burn the trees to make room for housing or agriculture, we release the carbon stored in the trees into the environment, leading to increased carbon dioxide levels and climate change. Forests also remove pollutants both from the atmosphere and from the water and soil.

**Clear-cutting** is a method of harvesting trees in the forest for human use. These uses can be for building materials, fuel for fires, paper, and so on. A cheap and easy method of harvesting these trees is to cut them all down at one time in large areas. This method is called clear-cutting (Figure 9.1).

**Figure 9.1   Clear-cutting.**

Clear-cutting has many environmental consequences even though from an economic standpoint it is a benefit since it is cheaper than other methods. Since trees have roots that hold the soil, when we clear cut large areas of land we expose this soil, leaving it vulnerable to erosion and/or flooding. This soil may end up in a river, lake, or stream leading to problems there. Trees also provide shade, so when we cut them down, the temperature in these areas is increased because the sun hits the ground directly.

## The Green Revolution

In Mexico and India in the 1940s and beyond, the **Green Revolution** brought new disease-resistant varieties of plants like wheat and rice, new technologies for mechanized harvesting, and new chemical fertilizers, irrigation practices, and pesticides. The Green Revolution has allowed us to feed more people, to make larger profits, to create tastier and more nutritious food, and to use less pesticide and water, but there are some consequences to these practices. Increased mechanization has led to a greater use of fossil fuels, leading to climate change.

**Genetically modified organisms (GMOs)** are organisms (plants, animals, and microorganisms) that have had their DNA modified in some way through genetic engineering. GMOs are often developed to increase food's flavor or to make the plant resistant to disease and drought. Some people are concerned that GMOs have increased allergic reactions in some individuals.

This topic will be tested using text analysis. This means that you will be given a short passage to read and will be asked questions based on that passage.

## Impact of Agricultural Practices

Providing food for a growing human population is important and we are doing this in better and better ways. However, there are environmental impacts of many of the practices we use. For example, **tilling** the soil is how farmers dig, stir, and turn the soil over so they can plant new crops. This helps to aerate the soil and allows for the seedlings to get established.

However, when we till the soil it leaves the soil vulnerable to erosion, which we discussed as an environmental concern in a prior chapter. Also, many farmers use a technique called **slash-and-burn farming**, where they take wild or forested land and convert this to farmland. This devastates habitats and species, causes deforestation, and can lead to climate change. Fertilizers and pesticides also have large environmental problems. Fertilizers can run off the land and end up in the water causing a problem called eutrophication that we will discuss in a future chapter. Pesticides can contaminate the soil and water and be toxic to organisms that they were not intended to harm such as birds, fish, "good" insects, and plants.

# Irrigation Methods

Seventy percent of all water used by humans is to irrigate crops. One reason for the large use is the wasteful way we water those crops. You will need to know the pros and cons of the different methods.

**Drip irrigation**—This method saves water because only about 5 percent of the water is lost to evaporation, but it is pretty expensive. You might have seen this at your house or in businesses. This method uses hoses with small holes where water seeps out slowly, getting the water down to the roots (Figure 9.2). Using this on a large scale for mass food production is costly, but it helps prevent erosion and nutrient runoff and discourages weeds since the water is targeted.

**Flood irrigation**—In flood irrigation the farmer floods an entire field with water (Figure 9.3). The benefits of this include the ability to produce more food (therefore increasing profits for the farmer) and incur less loss of crops from drought. However, the cons of this are that a lot of water is lost to evaporation and it can increase salinization of the soil. **Soil salinization** results when salt in the water is left on crops after the water evaporates. While water can evaporate, salt will not. After time, so much salt can be left on the soil that plants can't grow.

Drip emitter

PVC pipe

**Figure 9.2   Drip irrigation.**

**Figure 9.3  Flood irrigation.**

**Figure 9.4  Furrow irrigation.**

**Furrow irrigation**—This method is similar to flood irrigation except that trenches are dug between rows of crops and that area is flooded with water. This allows the farmer to flow water down these trenches and the water is absorbed by the roots of the plants (Figure 9.4). The advantages and disadvantages are similar to flood irrigation with about 35 percent being lost to evaporation.

**Spray irrigation**—This method is the one you are probably most familiar with. You see this on lawns all the time with sprinklers, but on a large scale this is done on crops (Figure 9.5). This method loses less water than either flood or furrow but is more expensive.

There are several more terms relating to irrigation that you need to know for the exam. **Waterlogging** happens when so much water is left on the soil it is saturated. The water affects plants by lowering the levels of oxygen to the roots and impacting the germination of seeds and young plants. **Aquifers** are underground layers of water that can be tapped for irrigation and other uses. However, if too many wells are drilled, the water can be severely depleted depending on the type of aquifer and the demand for the water. In fact, the Ogallala Aquifer in the middle of the United States, where much of our food is grown, is being severely depleted due to massive overuse in the past century.

**Figure 9.5    Spray irrigation.**

# Pest Control Methods

Pests such as insects, fungus, rodents and weeds are a common problem for our land use. To combat these pests, farmers, homeowners, and ranchers have used many different types of pest control methods. Make sure you are familiar with the different terms when it comes to pest control. **Pesticide** is a generic term that includes the others. The other terms are: **herbicides** that get rid of unwanted plants such as weeds; **fungicides** that get rid of fungal organisms; **rodenticides** that kill rodents including mice and rats; and **insecticides** that are designed to kill insects. There are many different types and they all kill in different ways.

One problem with many of these pesticides is that the organism that the pesticide is designed to kill builds up resistance over time. Pesticides are designed to prevent crop damage and increase crop profits, but if pesticide resistance becomes a problem, the pesticide will no longer work (or will not work as well). The farmer/homeowner will have to either use more pesticide or stronger doses, or switch to a new type, and this can impact both the profits and the environment. The **pesticide treadmill** is a term used for when a farmer continues to add more and more pesticides or switches from one to another as they become ineffective.

One method to help stop this is by genetically engineering crops so the pests don't or can't harm them. This has pros and cons. A pro is that there is less need for pesticides, which is good for the environment since pesticides can often harm other organisms that they weren't designed to harm. Other pros are increased profits for farmers and helping keep the cost of food affordable. However, on the negative side is the loss of diversity in the crop.

# Meat Production Methods

You will be asked to look at various types of data and answer questions when it comes to meat production. Remember, this could be in the form of a graph or data table.

**Concentrated animal feeding operations (CAFOs)**, also known as feedlots, are defined as a feeding operation involving more than 1,000 animal units (defined as 1,000 pounds of animal weight) held for more than 45 days, or any size feeding operation that discharges manure or wastewater into a natural or man-made ditch, stream, or other waterway. The pros of CAFOs are profits because you can get a lot of animals ready for slaughter very quickly and cheaply, which means increased profits for ranchers and lower priced food for consumers. The cons of CAFOs are many. Animals are usually packed into small enclosures with thousands of animals crowded into one CAFO, they are often fed a man-made feed rather than grass, and many times the animals are given large doses of antibiotics to prevent disease. Because of the number of animals crowded together, large amounts of waste are generated, which can pollute local rivers, streams, lakes, and land areas.

**Free-range grazing** is what it sounds like—animals are allowed to roam free and graze as needed on open land. The pros of this method are animals are free to roam, fewer or no antibiotics are given, and because there are fewer animals, the manure is less concentrated, leading to the waste being a beneficial fertilizer and not a problem. However, this is a more expensive choice for ranchers and large amounts of land are needed.

Farmers must be careful to not overgraze the land. **Overgrazing** happens when farmers/ranchers put too many animals on an area and the area begins to lose all plants. Any area that has low rainfall in general and then loses all plants is said to have undergone **desertification**. Overgrazing can also lead to soil erosion; the plants' roots hold the soil in place and when the plants are gone the soil can easily be eroded by wind or water.

Eating less meat has some big environmental advantages. First, it takes almost 20 times less land to get the same number of calories from growing plants. Animals also produce a lot of methane and carbon dioxide, two things we will discuss in detail in the chapter relating to climate change. Finally, if we don't eat as much meat, we lower the use of antibiotics and growth hormone, use less water, and prevent erosion of soil caused by overgrazing.

# Impact of Overfishing

**Overfishing** is commercial fishing in which large quantities of fish are caught faster than the species can breed and replace itself. Since many people depend on fish for their food supply, overfishing can be very dangerous and can impact aquatic ecosystems by disrupting the food chain. When too many fish are taken out of the ocean, it can destroy food webs, lead to a loss of marine life, and can have a large socioeconomic impact on humans who rely on fishing for their livelihood and food needs.

# Impact of Mining

There are many minerals found on Earth's surface and underground that we need for human purposes, for example, coal. When the mineral resource is found on the surface of Earth and we extract this mineral resource, it is called **surface mining** (Figure 9.6). When the resource is found deep underground, it is called **subsurface mining**, which is more expensive (Figure 9.7).

There are many methods of surface mining, such as strip mining, open-pit mining, and mountaintop removal. Each of these has its own set of environmental impacts. In order to get to these resources, miners must first remove the soil, plants, and rock known as **overburden**. After mining, the wastes from mining, called **slag and tailings**, are left behind to be dealt with. Mining removes plant life, opens the soil up to erosion and runoff, harms habitats, can contaminate aquifers, releases methane from the soil, and causes fine particles of dust to be released.

**Figure 9.6   Surface mining.**

**Figure 9.7   Subsurface mining.**

# Impact of Urbanization

**Urbanization** occurs as people move from rural areas and into cities, usually in search of job opportunities. Urbanization has many benefits such as increased job opportunities and access to basic needs like clean water and electricity. However, as more people live together there are some costs to the environment. For example, as we pave land to build roads, houses, and parking lots, water can't seep into the soil and refill aquifers. This can also cause increased runoff and flooding since the water runs off the pavement and doesn't **infiltrate** into the soil. In addition, as more people move to cities and gain access to electricity, we mine and burn more coal, oil, or natural gas. This can lead to an increase of carbon dioxide or land damaged from mining.

There are a couple more terms relating to irrigation that you need to be familiar with for the exam:

**Saltwater intrusion**—If there are too many people putting a demand on fresh water, and the city is located near the ocean, we can overdraw the aquifer allowing the saltwater to move into the freshwater aquifer. This can destroy aquifers.

**Urban sprawl**—The expansion of urban areas into rural areas. It can cause water and air pollution and destroy habitats.

## Ecological Footprints

Each person or society has an ecological footprint, and it is measured by the amount of land (in hectares) needed by the person or society to support their way of life. To calculate the ecological footprint, you would take the person's or society's demands such as timber, electricity, food, gas, and so on, and assign a number to that need. For example, a person in the United States, who lives in a home that is heated by oil, drives a car using gas, has clothing and food needs, and produces carbon emissions would have a much greater ecological footprint than a person living in a poor country possibly living in a hut with no electricity, no car, and growing their own food or living off the land.

## Introduction to Sustainability

Everyone needs access to a healthy environment, clean air and water, and natural resources. Sustainability is the access to each of these for human use without depleting them. There are many things we can do as humans to help, such as limiting our use of resources, reducing, reusing, and recycling, green building, and employing sustainable agriculture. As long as we stick to a sustainable yield, or not taking more than can be regrown, replenished, or reused, we can live on this planet for many years to come.

## Methods to Reduce Urban Runoff

As we discussed earlier in this chapter, as we pave surfaces, build buildings, and put in roads, we stop allowing water to permeate the soil and we increase the amount of water that runs off. There are many ways to reduce this runoff. For example, if a company wanted to build a parking lot, they could add areas throughout the parking lot with plants and trees and soil. This way, although there are less actual parking spaces, when it rains the water can soak into the natural areas and the runoff will not be that bad. You can also plant trees around the parking lot that will absorb water and reduce runoff.

**Impervious surfaces** like concrete or asphalt don't allow for water to infiltrate into the ground. Using pavers instead of asphalt or concrete in a parking lot will allow water to seep into the ground between the pavers and not run off. These types of **permeable surfaces,** shown in Figure 9.8, allow water to seep into the ground and replenish aquifers or water plants. This topic will be given to you as a scientific experiment that you will need to read and come up with the best answer.

## Integrated Pest Management

Pests are a huge problem for humans for many reasons. They eat our crops, make us sick, destroy our building structures, and can be nuisances in our lives. We often try to kill these pests using pesticides, herbicides, and fungicides. But, as mentioned earlier in this chapter, these can have devastating effects on the environment. Humans can mitigate this problem a little by implementing **integrated pest management (IPM)**, which is a method of killing

**Figure 9.8  Permeable surfaces.**

or preventing the bugs without using as much pesticide. So, we might step on the cockroach rather than grabbing the can of insecticide.

But, on a larger scale for crops, we need other methods. These can include biological methods like predator bugs that a farmer buys to eat the pests (**biocontrol**), or rotating crops to plant ones that naturally are resistant to the pest. We can also use intercropping, a method of planting rows of crops that are different; one row is a crop that repels the insect while another row is the crop the farmer wants to harvest. These methods are all better for the environment than the chemical pesticides that have historically been used. The problem with IPM for farmers is the expense it incurs.

## Sustainable Agriculture

Our agricultural practices have environmental impacts. For instance, if we overgraze, we cause soil to erode, and we reduce soil fertility and its ability to sustain plant life. However, many farmers and ranchers are looking at ways to reduce this and still produce food for humans. The methods to make agriculture more sustainable are many. For example, ranchers can make sure to not overgraze by rotating their animals to different pastures, allowing the grass to regrow and recover. This is called **rotational grazing**. We can prevent soil from losing valuable nutrients by rotating the places we plant these crops or by adding manure to increase nutrient values and limestone to balance acidity to protect soil health.

We can prevent soil from eroding by each of the following techniques:

**Contour plowing**—Planting crops along the contours of the land as shown in Figure 9.9.

**Windbreaks**—Planting trees or shrubs to limit erosion as shown in Figure 9.10.

**Perennial crops**—Planting crops that don't need to be replanted each year and can be harvested multiple times during the year. After harvest, they automatically grow back. By eliminating replanting each year, perennial cropping can reduce soil erosion.

**Terracing**—Similar to contour plowing but when an area is very hilly or mountainous. The farmer will make step-like rows and plant the crops on these rows. This helps to reduce soil erosion. Figure 9.11 shows how the steep mountain was made into steps and crops were planted on the top of each step.

**Figure 9.9    Contour plowing.**

**Figure 9.10    Windbreaks.**

**Figure 9.11    Terracing.**

**No-till agriculture**—This method is what it sounds like, planting crops but without tilling the soil before planting. This reduces soil erosion because when we turn the soil over (tilling), it is vulnerable to wind and water erosion.

**Figure 9.12  Strip cropping.**

**Strip cropping**—Planting a strip of one crop, then a strip of another, alternating throughout the field. This prevents soil erosion because one row might have crops with deep roots, while the next one doesn't. The deep roots will hold in the soil for the plants that don't have deep roots. You can see an example of this in Figure 9.12.

## Aquaculture

**Aquaculture** is a method of farm raising fish, shellfish, or aquatic plants. A farmer can build large ponds and stock these ponds with large numbers of animals or plants, or use a natural river, lake, or ocean to do this with nets and holding pens. The benefits of aquaculture are that it doesn't deplete our natural supplies of these organisms, it feeds a large number of people, it uses less water, it increases profits, and it uses very little fuel.

However, there are environmental problems; large numbers of fish, for example, can produce huge quantities of waste (fish poop, excess fish food, etc.), which can pollute the river, lake, or ocean. These fish might escape their enclosures and if they are not a natural species can outcompete natural species or breed with wild species. In addition, when we put large numbers of animals together in one area, disease can spread very quickly and these diseases might spread to wild populations.

## Sustainable Forestry

Humans have a large need for resources made from forests. These include building materials, paper, medicine, and food. However, there are more sustainable ways to harvest forests so that humans can use them for many years and we don't harm the environment and the animal habitat as much. For example, we can replant trees after cutting them down (**reforestation**), we can do **prescribed burns** to clear out the brush, which can prevent larger "crown" fires. We can make sure to purchase wood that is grown on a tree farm rather than a natural forest. We can also reduce, reuse, and recycle wood products for future use. Using IPM to prevent trees from getting pests like fungi or bugs can also help sustain a forest for many years.

# › Review Questions

## Multiple-Choice Questions

1. A family of four realized their water bill was high and that a lot of water was being wasted in the shower. They replaced their 5-gallon-per-minute showerheads with ones that only use 3 gallons per minute. If each family member showers for 5 minutes per day and a typical month is 30 days long, how much water will the family save per month with the new showerheads?

   (A) 3,000 gallons
   (B) 1,800 gallons
   (C) 1,200 gallons
   (D) 9,000 gallons

2. A farmer is growing a crop that has historically been eaten by a particular insect. However, the farmer has noticed that each year they put the same amount of pesticide on and not as many insects are killed. The farmer has begun to add more and more amounts of the pesticide to kill the same number of insects. What is the best explanation of why this is happening?

   (A) The company that sells the pesticide has begun lowering the percentage of chemical in the bottles to save money.
   (B) The insects are becoming resistant to the pesticide.
   (C) The insects are flying away during the times the farmer is spraying their crops and then returning afterward.
   (D) The farmer doesn't realize that this is a different species of insect than they had in previous years.

3. A sustainable society would choose which of the following things to impress upon its people?

   (A) Use fossil fuels for their energy use.
   (B) Produce meat by using concentrated animal feeding operations (CAFOs).
   (C) Use commercial fishing methods that can capture thousands of fish at one time.
   (D) Use integrated pest management to mitigate their impact on the land.

4. Which of the following best describes an environmental problem associated with urbanization near coastal areas?

   (A) Saltwater intrusion from overdrawing of water can harm aquifers.
   (B) Cities generally have a lower transportation carbon footprint.
   (C) It is more expensive to live in cities than in rural areas.
   (D) People in cities use less electricity than people in rural areas.

5. Which of the following best describes an environmental solution using aquaculture?

   (A) Aquaculture can produce large amounts of fish that humans can purchase or sell.
   (B) Aquaculture prevents diseases in wild fish populations because of the antibiotics used.
   (C) Aquaculture uses a small amount of water and very little fuel.
   (D) Aquaculture prevents wastewater contamination because of the environmental methods that are employed.

6. Which of the following is the best example of an environmental problem from clear-cutting forests?

   (A) Soil erosion increases.
   (B) Stream temperatures fall.
   (C) Carbon dioxide levels fall.
   (D) Flooding decreases.

## › Free-Response Questions

**7. Identify** ONE method of mining that extracts natural resources from the earth and for the type you identified **describe** ONE environmental problem of this method.

**8. Describe** ONE ecological benefit that forests provide to Earth.

## › Answers and Explanations

**1. C**—1,200 gallons. Before: family of 4 × 5 gallons per minute × 5 minutes per day × 30 days per month = 3,000 gallons per month. Now: family of 4 × 3 gallons per minute × 5 minutes per day × 30 days per month = 1,800 gallons per month. 3,000 gallons per month − 1,800 gallons per month = 1,200 gallons per month.

**2. B**—One consequence of using common pesticides is the pests can develop a resistance to the pesticide.

**3. D**—Integrated pest management is a way to use less pesticides to minimize the harm done to the environment. A sustainable society would want to do this.

**4. A**—As more people put a demand for water in cities, those in coastal areas can have their aquifers impacted by saltwater intrusion, when saltwater from the oceans moves into freshwater aquifers.

**5. C**—Aquaculture uses little water and fuel.

**6. A**—The roots of trees help hold in the soil, so when a forest is clearcut, erosion of the soil will increase.

**7.** One point for the method and one point for the environmental problem of the method. The method must be linked to the correct problem.

| METHOD | ENVIRONMENTAL PROBLEM OF THE METHOD |
| --- | --- |
| Surface mining (strip mining, open-pit mining, and mountaintop removal) | In order to get to these resources, miners must first remove the soil, plants, and rock known as overburden. After mining the wastes from mining, called slag and tailings, are left behind to be dealt with. Mining removes plant life, opens the soil up to erosion and runoff, harms habitats, can contaminate aquifers, releases methane from the soil, and causes fine particles of dust to be released. |
| Subsurface mining | Subsurface mining is more expensive and can be dangerous. |

**8.** One point for describing how forests provide many benefits to Earth. They absorb pollutants, store carbon dioxide, prevent soil erosion, reduce flooding, and lower temperatures on the land and water around the forest.

# › Rapid Review

- Tragedy of the commons—A shared resource that no one owns and everyone can use is overexploited and eventually unavailable to all.

- Clear-cutting—An economically viable way of cutting down all the trees in an area of a forest for human use. This leads to erosion, flooding, and increased soil and water temperatures, and it removes the carbon sink that forests provide.

- Mechanization—Using mechanical means like tractors and farm equipment to harvest crops.

- Fertilization—Using man-made, chemical fertilizers on crops to help them grow better.

- Tilling—Turning the land over so you can plant crops, but this can lead to erosion of the soil from both water and wind.

- Slash-and-burn farming—This is an agricultural method for taking wild land such as a forest, and clearing it to grow crops. Usually this method involves slashing (cutting down) and burning the plants that were found there and planting a crop.

- Drip irrigation—Using hoses that slowly drip water onto the roots of plants. Pro: conserves water. Con: expensive.

- Flood irrigation—Flooding an entire crop with water. Pros: cheap and quick. Cons: uses large quantities of water and water is lost to evaporation.

- Furrow irrigation—Building rows between crops and flooding those rows with water. Pros: cheap and quick. Cons: uses large quantities of water and water is lost to evaporation.

- Spray irrigation—Using sprinkler-type devices to water crops. Pro: less water lost to evaporation. Con: expensive.

- Waterlogging—When soil gets so flooded with water, and the water then evaporates but the salt is left behind. After many years of this, the land is so salty that most plants can't grow.

- Salinization—Salt in the soil that limits plant growth.

- Aquifers—A layer of rock that is filled with water.

- Pesticides—A generic term to describe any herbicide, fungicide, rodenticide, or insecticide.

- Herbicides—A chemical that kills unwanted plants.

- Fungicides—A chemical that kills unwanted fungi.

- Rodenticides—A chemical that kills unwanted rodents such as mice and rats.

- Insecticides—A chemical that kills unwanted insects.

- Concentrated animal feeding operations (CAFOs)—Large feeding operations with many animals in a small area. Pro: increased profits. Cons: disease can spread, so large amounts of antibiotics are used. Additionally, manure and urine can run off into local waterways.

- Free-range grazing—Allowing animals to roam free and eat on grassy pastures.

- Overgrazing—When too many animals are allowed to eat in an area and the grass/plants can't recover. This often leads to desertification.

- Desertification—When an area is so overgrazed it can't recover and the area can become a desert.

- Overfishing—Taking too many fish at one time by commercial fishing and not allowing the breeding stock to reproduce and replenish.

- Surface mining—A type of mining where minerals are found near to the surface with only soil and small amounts of rock above it so it is inexpensive and relatively easy to obtain.

- Overburden—The rock and soil found above a mine that must be removed to get to the mineral resource.

- Slag and tailings—The waste from mining that must be dealt with and can be an environmental problem if it is not.

- Subsurface mining—Digging deep into the earth to get to the mineral resource. Pro: can get to a resource that is abundant deep within the earth. Con: expensive and sometimes dangerous.

- Urbanization—People moving from rural areas and into cities looking for jobs or other opportunities.

- Saltwater intrusion—Occurs when too many people living in cities close to the coastline draw on an aquifer for fresh water. The freshwater is removed and the salt water can move into the aquifer, destroying the aquifer.

- Impervious surfaces—Surfaces like concrete or asphalt that don't allow for water to infiltrate into the ground.

- Permeable surfaces—Surfaces that do allow water to seep into the ground and replenish aquifers or water plants.

- Urban sprawl—Term used to describe cities as they expand more and more into the surrounding ecosystems/habitats.

- Ecological footprint—The area of land (measured in hectares) that a person or society uses due to the pressures it puts on the environment. In other words, the amount of natural resources that it takes to support one person or one society. People living in developed nations have a greater ecological footprint than people living in developing nations.

- Urban runoff—Occurs when cities are so covered with concrete, asphalt, buildings, and so on, that water can't infiltrate into the land and runs off instead.

- Infiltration—The ability of water to move through the soil and perhaps into an aquifer.

- Integrated pest management—The method of killing pests without using as much pesticide; for example, using predator bugs and rotating crops.

- Biocontrol—A method of integrated pest management that uses predator bugs to control pest species.

- Intercropping—A method of integrated pest management where rows of crops that repel pests are planted next to the row of crops the farmer wants to sell.

- Crop rotation—A method of rotating crops to different fields so the soil has a chance to recover and minerals are not depleted.

- Contour plowing—Planting crops with the contour of the land to prevent erosion.

- Windbreaks—Planting trees or shrubs next to crops to prevent wind erosion.

- Perennial crops—Planting crops that don't need to be replanted each year but can be harvested multiple times throughout the year.

- Terracing—Creating flat terraces on mountainsides to plant crops and prevent erosion.

- No-till agriculture—Planting crops without tilling, or churning the soil, before you plant.

- Strip cropping—Planting crops in strips with one strip having a crop with deep, extensive roots and one that doesn't. The crop with roots will hold in the soil and prevent erosion that the other crop doesn't do.

- Rotational grazing—Moving animals around to various pastures to allow the grass to recover from grazing.

- Aquaculture—Farm raising fish, shellfish, or aquatic plants to sell. Pros: inexpensive and uses less water and energy. Cons: can cause disease and, if the farmed animal or plant escapes its enclosure, it could reproduce or outcompete with native species.

- Reforestation—Planting new trees after harvesting the mature ones.

- Prescribed burns—Intentionally starting a fire in a forest to allow the brush and dead trees to be burned and the larger trees to not be destroyed. This prevents a forest from having a larger "crown" fire that can destroy the entire forest.

# CHAPTER 10

# Energy Resources and Consumption

## IN THIS CHAPTER

**Summary:** Humans use both renewable and nonrenewable forms of energy and each has an impact on the environment. This chapter will examine each energy type, both renewable and nonrenewable, and provide benefits and costs of each.

### Key Idea

✪ Humans use energy from a variety of sources, resulting in positive and negative consequences.

---

### Key Terms

- Active solar systems
- Anthracite
- Biomass
- Bituminous
- Chernobyl
- Cogeneration
- Combustion
- Ethanol
- Fission
- Fossil fuels
- Fukushima
- Geothermal energy
- Half-life
- Hydroelectric power

- Hydrogen fuel cells
- Hydrologic fracturing (fracking)
- Kinetic energy
- Lignite
- Nonrenewable energy source
- Passive solar systems
- Peat
- Photovoltaic solar cell
- Radioactivity
- Renewable energy source
- Thermal pollution
- Three-Mile Island
- Turbine
- Uranium-235

This chapter is about both renewable and nonrenewable energy use and resources and will cover about 10 to 12 percent of your AP Environmental Science Exam, or about 8 to 10 out of the 80 multiple-choice questions. For the test you will have to know where energy sources are found and the environmental problems related to different types of energy. You will be asked to solve mathematical problems and propose environmental solutions to energy problems.

# Renewable and Nonrenewable Resources

**Renewable energy resources** are resources that can be replaced over a relatively short time scale. These include things like solar, wind, hydroelectric, geothermal, and biomass resources. **Nonrenewable energy resources** are not replaced quickly or they are not replaced at all. These include things like coal, oil, natural gas, and nuclear energy resources.

# Global Energy Consumption

This topic will be given to you as a math problem that you will need to solve. Remember, you can use a calculator so make sure you don't forget it. You might need to calculate a family's energy use or the energy use from a particular country and year. It should be simple math like addition, subtraction, multiplication, or division, but you should read carefully so you use the correct numbers in the correct way.

Developed countries use a lot more energy resources than developing countries, but as a country goes through the demographic transition and becomes more industrialized, they will begin to demand more and more energy. Currently, the major source of energy in the world comes from **fossil fuels** such as coal, oil, and natural gas. However, this depends on regional availability of other sources like geothermal, solar, and water or any government regulations that might influence the type of energy source a population uses or has access to.

# Fuel Types and Uses

We use many different types of fuel. This can be a family burning wood or charcoal to cook or heat their houses or using **peat**, partially decayed plant matter that is burned for cooking or heating in parts of Europe. Of course, fuel can also be coal, oil, and natural gas.

Let's talk first about coal. There are different types of coal such as lignite, bituminous, and anthracite (Figure 10.1). As we move from lignite to anthracite, the coal gets harder and burns hotter. **Anthracite** is the highest rank of coal. It has the highest amount of carbon

Increasing heat and carbon content

Increasing moisture content

| Heat Pressure | Heat Pressure | Heat Pressure |

Peat
(not a coal)

Lignite
(brown coal)

Bituminous
(soft coal)

Anthracite
(hard coal)

**Figure 10.1 Types of coal.**

and the lowest amount of volatile matter. **Lignite** is the lowest rank of coal with the least amount of carbon. **Bituminous** coal is the most abundant and extensively used.

Next, let's discuss oil. Oil or crude oil is made up of hydrogen and carbon with some other trace elements. It was formed millions of years ago as dead marine organisms sunk to the bottom of the ocean and under heat and pressure were changed to oil. We drill down to the oil reserves and pump it out. We can also find crude oil in tar sands, where a mixture of sand, clay, and water is saturated with petroleum known as bitumen. Oil is then burned for energy.

Natural gas is the fossil fuel that burns the cleanest and can be used for energy. It is made up mostly of methane but contains other things like carbon dioxide, nitrogen, and more. Natural gas can be used to create electricity, heat buildings, and fuel cars.

When an energy source is used to generate both heat and electricity, we say it is a combined heat and power (CHP) system or **cogeneration**.

## Distribution of Natural Energy Resources

If we look at Figure 10.2, we can see where oil and gas energy sources are found. You will be given a diagram similar to this on the test and asked to draw some conclusions. First, the oil is found in a layer below the gas. This is because gas bubbles up from the oil and floats on top. The rock reservoir is the layer that has the rich organic matter from millions of years ago. This has then been subjected to heat and pressure. The oil has risen up through the next permeable layer but stopped at the layer that is impermeable. We then drill down through the impermeable layer and get the gas and oil.

## Fossil Fuels

How do we actually get energy for electricity from a chunk of coal, or from a gallon of oil or natural gas? Well, since each of these energy items have stored energy, we can turn that stored energy into electrical energy. **Combustion** of these fossil fuels is burning the

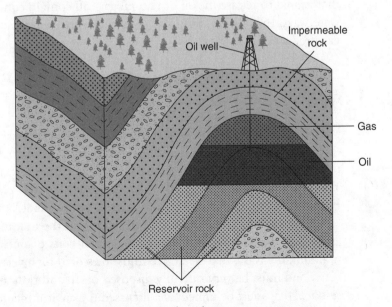

**Figure 10.2   Oil and gas energy sources.**

**Figure 10.3 Coal power plant.**

fossil fuel, which is a chemical reaction between fuel and oxygen, and turning it into carbon dioxide, water, and energy. Let's take coal as an example. First coal is pulverized into a very fine powder, which is then burned to make heat. This heat is used to boil water and produce steam. This steam is then pumped through a pipe at extremely high pressures and is focused on a giant **turbine**, causing the turbine to spin (similar to blowing on a pinwheel and causing it to spin). This turbine is connected to an electrical generator that generates electricity. The same is done when oil or natural gas is burned.

Figure 10.3 shows a typical coal energy generator.

When we burn fossil fuels we produce carbon dioxide and water. This carbon dioxide is a contributor to climate change that we will discuss in future chapters.

Another environmental problem of the use of fossil fuels for energy is caused when a method called **hydrologic fracturing,** commonly known as **fracking,** is used for extracting it. Fracking forces liquid at very high pressures down into the rock, which causes the oil or gas to be released. This can lead to groundwater contamination because the water that is used to release the oil or natural gas can contain contaminates that then run off into waterways. In addition, this process releases volatile organic compounds during the natural gas production process.

# Nuclear Power

We can also split atoms of **Uranium-235**, in a process known as **fission**, to produce extremely high heat. Similar to how electricity is generated from coal, oil, or natural gas, the heat is used to boil water to make steam to turn a turbine to generate electrical energy. You will be asked to look at a diagram of a nuclear power plant and answer some questions. Figure 10.4 is a picture of a typical nuclear power plant.

The uranium-235 is stored in fuel rods and the uranium atoms produce radioactivity as the isotopes lose energy. There are several cons of nuclear energy. First, when we use uranium, the waste that is left over must be stored for a very long time. This waste is radioactive and must be very carefully disposed of. In addition, uranium-235 is a nonrenewable resource that must be mined; we discussed the environmental problems with mining in the last chapter. Also, nuclear energy generation creates so much heat that it must be "dumped"

**Figure 10.4    Nuclear power plant.**

into a water source, which causes thermal pollution that we will discuss in a future chapter. However, the pro of nuclear energy is that because we aren't actually burning anything, no air pollution is produced and therefore this energy source does not cause climate change.

There have been three times in our history when a nuclear accident happened and radiation was released. The first was at **Three-Mile Island** in Pennsylvania, the second in **Chernobyl** in Ukraine, and the final one at **Fukushima**, Japan. In each of these cases radiation was released from the fuel rods and the environment was impacted, sometimes devastatingly.

**Half-life** is a term used to describe the amount of time it takes for a radioactive isotope to be half of its original value. We use this to calculate how long we must store the radioactive waste, and how radioactive the object is and for how long. For example, uranium-235 has a half-life of 700 million years! That's a long time to store radioactive waste and a lot of time for this waste to harm the environment.

# Energy from Biomass

People in developing nations may not have access to good, reliable energy to cook and heat their homes. In this case, many will burn different types of **biomass** because it is cheap and usually easy to get. This might be as simple as burning wood from trees. However, this practice, while inexpensive and abundant, can cause some human health and environmental problems. For example, openly burning wood in a closed home or hut produces carbon dioxide, carbon monoxide, nitrogen oxides, particulates, and volatile organic compounds. None of these is good to be breathing for long periods of time and many lead to climate change. In addition, if a country is doing this on a large scale there are problems of deforestation and habitat destruction.

Another type of biomass fuel comes from ethanol. **Ethanol** is made by fermenting things like corn, wheat, potatoes, and so on. Because it can be grown over and over, it is a renewable resource and is used as an alternative to gasoline. It has a 34 percent average reduction in greenhouse gases that lead to climate change over gasoline. However, ethanol doesn't have a very large return of energy on investment and if we are converting natural areas of forest and grassland into large farms to produce corn to make ethanol, we are contributing to a problem of habitat loss and greater pollution due to agriculture.

## Solar Energy

The sun is a huge, endless provider of free energy. We can capture this energy to create electricity or we can passively use this energy to heat our homes.

**Photovoltaic solar cells** capture and convert solar energy from the sun into electrical energy. The limitations of these cells are that they can only generate energy when the sun is out. However, we can use **active solar systems** to collect, store, and convert solar energy to electrical power. They do this by using heat from the sun to heat a liquid and store the energy. The pros of this system are that the energy is free and unlimited and that air pollution isn't generated because you aren't burning anything. However, these systems are often cost-prohibitive and if you build large solar "farms" with hundreds or thousands of large solar panels in a sunny place like a desert, you could be harming that fragile ecosystem.

**Passive solar systems** do not collect or store energy but can be used to heat or cool homes and other structures. An example is building a home with large windows that face where the sun shines the most. Then, the sun will come in through the windows and heat the home. During the summer the homeowner could put thick curtains on the windows to prevent the heat from coming in as well. Another option is planting shade trees to help keep a house cooler in summer.

## Hydroelectric Power

Another form of renewable energy is using the power of running water to create electricity. This can be done by building a dam across a river; the dam has a turbine that the water passes over as it goes downstream. This turbine turns and is connected to a generator that converts energy of motion into electrical energy. Another way to generate electricity is to use the movement of the tides to turn a turbine. The ocean tides come in and out every day; in some places this large movement of water is greater than in others. If the movement is large enough a turbine can be built and again it can be connected to a generator to generate electricity.

The pro of hydroelectric power is that it doesn't produce any air pollution since nothing is burned. The cons are that building dams is expensive, and when you build a dam you change the river ecosystem. You flood an area above the dam, which was once a land habitat. If some of the water is diverted to irrigation, you reduce the flow of water downstream, reducing the amount of nutrients available and changing the ecosystems. In some cases the flow is so reduced that the water never reaches the sea. This can damage habitats and cause loss of biodiversity.

## Geothermal Energy

Our planet has a huge amount of heat down in the subsurface of Earth. If we can access this heat we can create steam and, again, turn a turbine to create electrical energy with a generator. We can also use geothermal heat pumps to take that heat to the surface and heat buildings with it. The pros of **geothermal energy** are it is renewable and very efficient. The cons are it is expensive, can release hydrogen sulfide, requires a lot of water, and isn't readily available everywhere in the world.

# Hydrogen Fuel Cell

A **hydrogen fuel cell** is a device that converts potential energy into electrical energy. Fuel cells can be used in transportation and power. The cell uses hydrogen gas ($H_2$) and oxygen gas ($O_2$) and the products are water, heat, and electricity. Hydrogen is oxidized at the anode and flows to the cathode where oxygen reacts with hydrogen to make water.

The advantage of hydrogen fuel cells is they produce no carbon dioxide as they make electricity. The problems are they are still very expensive and, in order to create the hydrogen gas, a process called electrolysis is used, which requires energy possibly produced from nonrenewable sources such as coal.

# Wind Energy

Another way to generate free, renewable energy is to capture the energy from the wind to turn a turbine. Kinetic energy is energy of motion; if we allow the wind to turn a turbine and turn it into electrical energy, we can use that kinetic energy. This method is especially good off the coasts of continents where the wind blows stronger and more often than on land. The pro of this type of power is that it is clean, free, and can be used in areas where you are doing other things such as ranching or growing crops. A con is that migrating birds, butterflies, and bats have been known to get caught in the turbines and killed. This problem can be mitigated by slowing the turbines down or shutting them off during migration times but then an alternate energy source will be needed at those times.

# Energy Conservation

This is another topic where you will be asked to do some math to solve a problem. The calculation will involve ways to save energy. It might be in your home by lowering or raising the temperature on the thermostat, replacing an old appliance with a more energy efficient one, or conserving water. The question might also be about vehicles like hybrids, battery electric ones, or ones powered by hydrogen fuel cells. Regardless, read the question, do the math, and find the answer that best conserves energy or money.

# › Review Questions

## Multiple-Choice Questions

1. A family home uses five 80-watt lightbulbs every day for 10 hours a day. Approximately how many hours of electrical energy will the family consume in one year using these bulbs?

   (A) 1,460 kwh
   (B) 1,460,000 kwh
   (C) 120 kwh
   (D) 120,000 kwh

2. One way to decrease our dependence on fossil fuels is to use renewable energy resources. However, there are still environmental concerns from renewable energy. Which of the following correctly describes an environmental concern of getting energy from biomass?

   (A) Burning biomass is too expensive for people in developing countries.
   (B) Burning biomass reduces the emission of volatile organic compounds.
   (C) Burning biomass leads to deforestation.
   (D) Burning biomass releases large amounts of hydrogen sulfide.

**3.** The diagram below shows a typical nuclear power plant.

**Nuclear Power Plant**

At which of the following labels is water heated, causing thermal pollution, which can be an environmental problem?

(A) A
(B) B
(C) C
(D) D

**4.** Which of the following would be the best way to reduce the risk of wind farms to the environment?

(A) Slow down or stop the speed of the turbines during times of bird or bat migration.
(B) Don't build windfarms on ranches where cattle graze.
(C) Add orange flashing lights to alert animals.
(D) Plant trees around the windfarm to absorb the carbon emissions that are produced.

**5.** Which of the following is an example of an environmental disadvantage of geothermal energy?

(A) Geothermal energy is expensive.
(B) Geothermal energy generates carbon dioxide emissions that lead to climate change.
(C) Geothermal energy is dangerous to harvest.
(D) Geothermal energy releases hydrogen sulfide.

**6.** People that live in the northern part of the United States can reduce their energy cost by lowering their thermostat by 2 degrees in the winter. This reduces their energy costs by about 8 percent in many homes. If the family was paying $120 per month, how much will their bill be if they lower the thermostat by 2 degrees?

(A) $110.40
(B) $9.6
(C) $100.80
(D) $24

## ❯ Free-Response Questions

**7.** Identify ONE environmental benefit of wind energy.

**8.** Dams are built to provide electricity to towns with no air pollution or waste. However, there are environmental concerns of dams.

(A) **Identify** ONE environmental cost of a dam.
(B) **Explain** how electrical energy is made at a hydroelectric dam.

# ❯ Answers and Explanations

1. **A**—5 × .080 kw × 10 hours × 365 days a year = 1,460 kwh

2. **C**—Biomass can come from cutting down trees, which leads to deforestation if done at an unsustainable rate.

3. **D**—Thermal pollution is the heat produced that is then dumped into a local river or lake.

4. **A**—Wind farms can kill migrating birds and bats.

5. **D**—Geothermal energy can release hydrogen sulfide gas.

6. **A**—$120 × .08 = $9.60 less, so $120 − $9.60 = $110.40

7. One point for describing one environmental benefit of wind energy. The benefits: it's renewable and it's a clean energy source with no air pollution.

8. **(A)** One point for identifying one environmental cost of a dam. The environmental costs are change of habitats by flooding areas above the dam and, if water is extracted from the reservoir for irrigation or other purposes, lowering the water flow below the dam. Sometimes, if enough water is taken from the reservoir, the water flow below the dam is so decreased that no water reaches the sea; this destroys estuary habitats.

**(B)** One point for explaining how energy is generated at a dam. A turbine is placed in the water running through the dam; the rushing water turns the turbine. This generator then turns the energy of movement into electrical energy.

# ❯ Rapid Review

- Nonrenewable energy source—Coal, oil, natural gas, and nuclear energy resources that can't be renewed or regrown for thousands or millions of years.

- Renewable energy source—Wind, biomass, hydrogen, water, and solar energy resources that can be renewed or regrown rather quickly.

- Fossil fuels—Energy sources that come from organisms that lived millions of years ago. After being buried with heat and pressure, they have become coal, oil, or natural gas.

- Peat—Partially decayed plant matter that is used for cooking or heating in parts of Europe.

- Lignite—The least efficient type of coal that generates the least amount of heat and isn't very common.

- Bituminous—The type of coal used the most because it is very abundant and generates a lot of heat.

- Anthracite—The most efficient type of coal that generates the maximum amount of heat but isn't very common and is more expensive.

- Cogeneration—Creating electricity and heat from one energy source.

- Turbine—A giant fan-type structure that is turned by steam or water (hydroelectric power) and connected to a generator to make electrical energy.

- Hydrologic fracturing (fracking)—Forcing liquid at very high pressures down into the rock to cause the oil or gas to be released.

- Combustion—The burning of fuel to produce energy.

- Fission—The splitting atoms for energy.

- Uranium-235—The radioactive isotope used to create nuclear power.

- Radioactivity—The radiation emitted from a nuclear isotope.

- Thermal pollution—The heat that is produced by nuclear power generation that can be a pollutant to aquatic organisms.

- Three Mile Island—A nuclear power plant in Pennsylvania where a small nuclear accident occurred, releasing some radiation.

- Chernobyl—A nuclear power plant in the Ukraine where a large nuclear meltdown occurred, releasing a lot of radiation.

- Fukushima—A nuclear power plant in Japan where a tsunami and earthquake caused a release of radiation.

- Half-life—The time it takes for a nuclear isotope to lose half of its radioactivity.

- Biomass—Organic matter that can be used for heating or cooking or fuel. Example: wood from trees or ethanol from decaying plant matter.

- Ethanol—A substitute for gasoline that is made from decaying plant matter.

- Photovoltaic solar cell—A cell that captures light from the sun and converts it into electricity.

- Active solar energy—Turning solar energy into electricity or heat and can be stored.

- Passive solar energy—Using the sun to heat or blocking the sun to cool a house or building.

- Hydroelectric power—Using the power of a river or tides to turn a turbine to generate electricity.

- Geothermal energy—Using the heat below the surface of Earth to make steam to turn a turbine to generate electricity.

- Hydrogen fuel cells—Taking $H_2$ and $O_2$ and producing water, heat, and electricity.

- Kinetic energy—The energy of motion as in the turning of a turbine.

# Atmospheric Pollution

## IN THIS CHAPTER

**Summary:** Air pollution is a problem both inside and outdoors. This chapter will cover the sources and effects of both indoor and outdoor air pollution and the human activities that have caused these issues. Included will be topics such as photochemical smog, thermal inversions, atmospheric $CO_2$ and particulates, indoor air pollutants, how to reduce air pollution, acid rain, and noise pollution.

**Key Idea**

✪ Human activities have physical, chemical, and biological consequences for the atmosphere.

## Key Terms

- Acid deposition
- Acid rain
- Anthropogenic
- Carbon dioxide
- Carbon monoxide
- Catalytic converter
- Clean Air Act
- Electrostatic precipitators
- Formaldehyde
- Hydrocarbons

- Lead
- Nitric acid
- Nitrogen oxides
- Noise pollution
- Ozone
- Particulates
- Photochemical smog
- Primary air pollutants
- Radon-222
- Secondary air pollutants

- Sulfur dioxide
- Thermal inversion
- Toxic metals

- Vapor recovery nozzle
- Volatile organic hydrocarbons
- Wet and dry scrubbers

Atmospheric pollution will account for about 7 to 10 percent of your AP Environmental Science exam, or about 5 to 7 questions out of the 80 multiple-choice questions. This chapter is all about air pollution. You will need to be able to predict trends and data as well as draw conclusions from the data and/or graphs. You may also be asked to propose solutions to environmental problems and describe a research method to understand the problem.

# Introduction to Air Pollution

When coal combusts, or burns, carbon dioxide, sulfur dioxide, nitrogen oxides, toxic metals, and particulates are released. These go into the air and can result in both environmental and human health concerns. Let's go through each of these air pollutants, discuss what they do that is harmful, and consider how we can prevent this and still get the needed energy from these resources.

**Carbon dioxide ($CO_2$)** traps heat, leading to climate change, melting ice caps, rising sea levels, and coastal flooding. Carbon dioxide can be removed from the atmosphere through a few processes, but the main one is **carbon sequestration**. This is the process of capturing and storing atmospheric carbon dioxide in either rock formations or through terrestrial and aquatic ecosystems.

**Sulfur dioxide ($SO_2$)** can harm trees and plants by damaging leaves and decreasing growth when the $SO_2$ leads to acid rain. Human health is impacted by sulfur dioxide by making it difficult to breathe, particularly for people with asthma, or other respiratory health concerns. Sulfur dioxide can be removed by gas scrubbing or by using fluidized bed combustion from coal-fired power plants.

**Nitrogen oxides** come from a mixture of $NO_x$ and $NO_2$. They are colorless, acidic when combined with water, and highly corrosive. They contribute to the formation of photochemical smog (to be covered in the next section) and to the formation of tropospheric ozone, another component of photochemical smog. They can form a secondary pollutant, nitric acid, which contributes to acid deposition. Nitrogen oxides can be removed during burning of fossil fuels by catalytic converters in vehicles. In manufacturing plants, they can be removed by $H_2O_2$ or sodium hydroxide scrubbers. Catalytic converters remove pollutants using redox reactions that convert about 98 percent of the fumes from a car into less harmful gases and scrubbers remove it by spraying the gas through a liquid substance. Make sure you are familiar with pollution remediation strategies, as they can show up in many different question types.

There are many **toxic metals** that can be released from burning coal. These include things like lead, mercury, nickel, tin, cadmium, and arsenic. The type of toxic metal will determine the environmental and human health effects. We can limit the amount of toxic metals by using catalytic reduction, electrostatic precipitators, and other technologies to address these pollutants.

**Particulates** are simply small solid or liquid particles that are suspended in the air. These include things like dust, dirt, soot, and smoke. The size of the particle can determine the harm they can do to humans. They can get into the lungs and some are even small enough to get in the bloodstream. They can cause haze and, depending on what the particle is, can acidify lakes and streams, deplete the soil of nutrients, and damage materials. Particulates can be prevented by using baghouse filters or electrostatic precipitators.

In the United States, a law was passed called the **Clean Air Act** that has helped control air pollution. The Environmental Protection Agency, the enforcer of the Clean Air Act, has eliminated **lead** from gasoline, protecting us from lead poisoning. Lead poisoning can lead to permanent nerve damage, anemia, or mental retardation, and is particularly dangerous for children since their nervous system is still developing.

**Primary air pollutants** come directly from a source, such as your car. Primary pollutants include sulfur dioxide, carbon monoxide, nitrogen oxides, and particulate matter. **Secondary air pollutants** form when two or more primary air pollutants react in the atmosphere. Examples of secondary pollutants are photochemical smog, ozone, and secondary particulate matter.

# Photochemical Smog

**Photochemical smog** occurs in sunny places that have a lot of people, cars, factories, and power plants. It is formed when volatile organic hydrocarbons and nitrogen oxides, along with heat and sunlight, mix and pollution occurs. The major contributors are coal-burning power plants and cars. This is worse in the summer because of the long hours of sunlight. It usually forms in the morning as people are driving to work and can be affected by rainfall, wind, daily temperatures, and topography.

Photochemical smog can cause eye irritation and respiratory illness. In the morning, nitrogen oxide is high because of so many cars on the road; we discussed the problems with this in the prior section. In the afternoon when it gets hot and the sunlight is the most intense, ozone is produced. Ozone can cause a variety of health effects such as chest pain, throat irritation, coughing, and congestion. It is particularly dangerous to people with asthma, bronchitis, and emphysema.

**Volatile organic compounds (VOCs)** come from many things. They are up to 10 times higher inside than outside and can come from paints, fuels, formaldehyde, gasoline, varnishes, and wax. Trees can also be a natural source of these. They can cause eye, nose, and throat irritation as well as headaches and nausea. Symptoms depend on the exposure level and the health of the person. We can reduce photochemical smog by reducing VOCs and nitrogen oxide.

# Thermal Inversion

If you look at Figure 11.1, you can see what happens during a **thermal inversion**. This is a weather condition when warm, less dense air moves over dense, cold air. Because of

**Figure 11.1   Thermal inversion.**

the thermal inversion and the dense air, pollution, particularly smog and particulates, gets trapped near the ground and can't "escape" to upper atmosphere. Normally, the temperature would get colder as you go away from Earth.

Look at the first illustration; warm air rises and pollutants move upward and are dispersed into space. Look at the second illustration; cold air is dense and sinks, trapping the pollutants with it. Warm air above the polluted cold air traps the particles and creates poor air quality. This often occurs in regions surrounded by mountains.

# Atmospheric $CO_2$ and Particulates

There are many natural forms of $CO_2$ and particulates found on Earth. For example, every time you exhale, you exhale $CO_2$ and add it to the atmosphere. $CO_2$ is also formed as things decompose and when volcanoes erupt. $CO_2$ is measured in parts per million (ppm). Natural sources of particulates are things like dust, sea salt, pollen, and also things from volcanic eruptions. For the test, they will give you a scientific experiment and you will have to answer questions about atmospheric $CO_2$ and particulates from that experiment.

# Indoor Air Pollutants

This section will be tested by giving you questions on data in the form of a chart or graph. The indoor air pollutants that you might be asked about are carbon monoxide, particulates, asbestos, dust, smoke, radon, mold, dust, nitrogen oxides, sulfur dioxide, particulates, and tobacco smoke.

**Indoor air pollutants** come from natural sources; from man-made things like furniture, carpet, and paneling; or from burning things like wood or cigarettes.

Another natural source is **radon-222**, which comes from the decay of uranium that is found in the ground. This is a particularly dangerous indoor air pollutant because radon decays quickly and when it does tiny radioactive particles are released. When these are inhaled they can damage the lining of the lungs. Long-term exposure can lead to lung cancer. When we build homes, and particularly homes with basements where we dig down into the rock or soil, radon gas can work its way into the home via cracks. It can also enter homes through the groundwater from a local well.

# Reduction of Air Pollutants

We have already discussed most of the methods for reducing air pollutants in the topics above. But let's review and learn a few more:

**Catalytic converters** are used on automobiles, electrical generators, locomotives, and so on and they take pollutants like carbon monoxide, $NO_x$, and hydrocarbons and make them less harmful.

**Scrubbers** remove particulates so they don't get into the atmosphere.

**Vapor recovery nozzles** are put on gasoline pumps to capture the fumes that are produced.

**Electrostatic precipitators** remove fine particles like dust, smoke, soot, and ash before they leave the coal-burning smokestack.

# Acid Rain (Acid Deposition)

Coal-burning power plants, vehicles, manufacturing, and even volcanoes release nitrogen oxides ($NO_x$) and sulfur oxides ($SO_2$) into the atmosphere. When these chemicals go into the atmosphere and mix with atmospheric water like rain, snow, fog, hail, or dust, they can become **acid rain** and fall to Earth. This can be in wet or dry forms. Winds can then blow this far away from the source, so usually places downwind from the pollution have the biggest problems. Because acid rain comes from things that humans are doing such as burning coal and driving vehicles, acid rain is considered an anthropogenic pollutant. **Anthropogenic** means "caused by human activity."

When soil or water becomes acidified because of acid deposition there can be some environmental effects. For example, often you will see dead or dying trees in areas affected by acid rain. The soil may have higher levels of aluminum in it since acid rain can leach aluminum from the soil; this is toxic to plants and animals. In aquatic biomes acid rain can be harmful to fish and other wildlife. The aluminum that was leached from the soil on the land may run off into the water and lead to a loss of biodiversity.

The impact on the environment from acid rain depends on the type of soil and rock that is found in the area. For example, limestone and dolomite have a natural ability to neutralize acid because of their high amounts of calcium carbonate. Calcium carbonate helps to maintain a constant pH as the minerals react with the acid rain. One way to remediate the problem is to add limestone (lime) to the soil; lime is a base that counters the effects of the acidic soils.

# Noise Pollution

This topic will be tested by giving you a short text about noise pollution; you will be asked to answer questions about the text. Make sure you read the text carefully and answer with evidence from the text.

The definition of noise pollution is "harmful or annoying levels of noise, as from airplanes, industry, etc." Noise pollution can be high enough to cause damage to people's hearing and can cause anxiety, poor concentration, loss of productivity, difficulty communicating, lack of sleep, and stress. It can also cause problems to animals by altering their behavior, making them relocate to quieter places, and impacting migration routes. It can also impair their ability to navigate, communicate, and reproduce. In marine ecosystems, animals can be impacted because of boats, sonar, and oil and gas drilling.

# › Review Questions

## Multiple-Choice Questions

1. A coal-burning power plant is located on a lake. The citizens of the town are concerned that the power plant might be doing harm to the organisms living in the lake by increasing acid levels in the lake. Which of the following would be the best way to test and see if the citizen's concerns are valid?

   (A) Take the temperature of the water in the morning, mid day, and evening and see if the temperature changes over time.
   (B) Test the water for radon-222 to see the levels of this in the lake.
   (C) Take blood samples from fish in the lake to see if they have elevated levels of mercury and lead in their bloodstream.
   (D) Test the pH levels in the lake to see if it is elevated.

2. An electricity company wants to lower the amount of fine particles like dust, smoke, soot, and ash before the particles leave the smokestack. Which of the following would be the best addition to the power plant to accomplish this?

   (A) Install electrostatic precipitators.
   (B) Install catalytic converters.
   (C) Install vapor recovery nozzles.
   (D) Install fluidized-bed combustion devices.

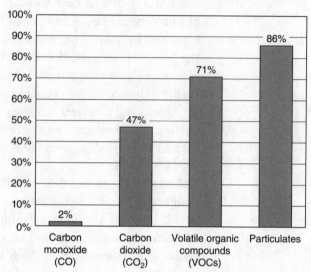

**AirAdvice 2004 IAQ Findings: Problem Type and Occurrence**

3. The percentages of homes that tested positive for certain pollutants is shown above according to a study in 2004. Which of the following would most likely help solve the problems with indoor air pollutants as seen in the graph?

   (A) Vent all combustion appliances outdoors and install and use exhaust fans vented to the outside when cooking.
   (B) Use fireplaces with wood to heat homes rather than electrical heat.
   (C) Open windows to allow fresh air to enter the home.
   (D) Install asbestos siding in homes to prevent fires.

**4.** "When we start to add artificial, unfamiliar noises to natural soundscapes, it can alter the acoustic environment of these marine and terrestrial habitats. This can cause a range of problems. It can affect an animal's ability to hear or make it difficult for it to find food, locate mates and avoid predators. It can also impair its ability to navigate, communicate, reproduce and participate in normal behaviors. Interest in the way sound affects wildlife has intensified over the last decade as more and more studies begin to explore how these changes in behavior could have flow-on effects for not only individual animals and their populations, but for whole ecosystems."

—Reprinted with permission from the Australian Academy of Science, "Noise Pollution and the Environment." (https://www.science.org.au/curious/earth -environment/noise-pollution-and-environment)

Which of the following best describes the author's claim about noise pollution?

(A) Noise pollution can cause physiological stress and hearing loss in humans.
(B) Switching from burning fossil fuels to wind energy would lower the concern about noise pollution.
(C) Noise pollution has affected wildlife in many ways and is now being studied more.
(D) Noise pollution is worse in industrialized countries than in developing countries.

**5.** Based on the diagram below, which of the following best describes why pollution tends to be trapped near the ground during a thermal inversion?

(A) A cold front has moved into the area and caused heavy rainfall.
(B) Warm, less dense air moves over dense, cold air over a city and traps the pollution near the ground.
(C) Warm air rises pushing the denser pollutants toward the ground.
(D) Cold air pushes its way through the warm air, which has a greater pollutant load than cold air has.

## › Free-Response Question

**6.** Air pollution, both indoors and outside, can have large environmental and human health effects.

(A) **Identify** ONE way that particulates are commonly introduced into the atmosphere.
(B) **Describe** ONE way to reduce the number of particulates in the atmosphere.

## › Answers and Explanations

**1. D**—pH is a measure of hydrogen ion concentration that determines the amount of acid in a solution.

**2. A**—Electrostatic precipitators remove fine particles like dust, smoke, soot, and ash before they leave the smokestack.

**3. A**—Indoor particulate matter can be generated through cooking, combustion activities (including burning of candles, use of fireplaces, use of unvented space heaters or kerosene heaters, or cigarette smoking).

**4. C**—Only choice C correctly states the author's claim.

**5. B**—A thermal inversion occurs when warm, less dense air moves over dense, cold air over a city and pollutants are unable to escape to space.

**6. (A)** One point for identifying one way particulates are commonly introduced into the atmosphere. Some answers include: fossil fuel combustion, dust, tobacco smoke, pollen, burning wood.

**(B)** One point for describing one way to reduce the amount of particulates in the atmosphere. Some answers include scrubbers, electrostatic precipitators, not burning wood inside, closing windows to stop dust and pollen from getting in.

## 〉 Rapid Review

| POLLUTANT | HUMAN HEALTH EFFECT | ENVIRONMENTAL EFFECT | WAYS TO PREVENT |
|---|---|---|---|
| Carbon dioxide | Not applicable except in high quantities | Traps heat leading to melting ice caps, rising sea levels, and coastal flooding; causes climate change | Carbon sequestration |
| Sulfur dioxide | Makes it difficult to breathe, particularly for people with asthma | Harms trees and plants by damaging leaves and decreasing growth; leads to acid rain | Gas scrubbing or by using fluidized bed combustion |
| Nitrogen oxides | Photochemical smog because of the formation of ozone molecules; cause acid rain | Chronic lung disease and damage to the respiratory system | Catalytic converters in vehicles; $H_2O_2$ or sodium hydroxide scrubbers in manufacturing plants |
| Toxic metals | The type of toxic metal will determine the environmental and human health effects | The type of toxic metal will determine the environmental and human health effects | Catalytic reduction, electrostatic precipitators, and other technologies |
| Particulates | Can get into the lungs; some are even small enough to get into the bloodstream | Cause haze and, depending on what the particle is, can acidify lakes and streams, deplete the soil of nutrients, and damage materials | Baghouse filters or electrostatic precipitators |

- Ozone—Photochemical smog can cause ground-level ozone to occur particularly in the afternoon when it gets hot. Ozone can cause a variety of health effects such as chest pain, throat irritation, coughing, and congestion. It is particularly dangerous to people with asthma, bronchitis, and emphysema.

- Photochemical smog—This type of smog occurs in warm places that have a lot of people, cars, factories, power plants, etc. It is formed when volatile organic hydrocarbons, nitrogen oxides, heat, and sunlight mix. Photochemical smog can cause eye irritation and respiratory illness; ground-level ozone is produced.

- Acid rain (acid deposition)—When nitrogen oxides ($NO_x$) and sulfur oxides ($SO_2$) in the atmosphere mix with rain, snow, fog, hail, or dust, they can become acid rain and fall to Earth. This can be in wet or dry forms.

- Clean Air Act—American law that regulated the use of lead in fuels and the atmosphere.

- Lead—Leads to permanent nerve damage, anemia, or mental retardation.

- Volatile organic hydrocarbons—When they mix with nitrogen oxides and heat they can form photochemical smog.

- Thermal inversion—Occurs when pollution gets trapped near the Earth's surface because of warm air trapping cooler, denser air near Earth.

- Radon-222—A gas that comes from uranium decay and is the second leading cause of cancer in America.

- Catalytic converter—A device that converts pollutants into less dangerous things.

- Vapor recovery nozzle—A device added to gasoline fuel pumps that traps the vapors before they can be released to the atmosphere.

- Wet and dry scrubbers—Air pollution devices that remove particulates so they don't get into the atmosphere.

- Electrostatic precipitators—Remove fine particles like dust, smoke, soot, and ash before they leave the smokestack.

- Anthropogenic—Caused by humans.

- Noise pollution—Sound that is loud and long enough to cause harm to humans and animals.

# CHAPTER 12

# Aquatic and Terrestrial Pollution

## IN THIS CHAPTER

**Summary:** Pollution is a major problem that has been caused by humans and impacts ecosystems as well as human health. While we have laws that have helped in the United States, there are global concerns for the animals and plants on our planet from the pollution that we have created.

### Key Ideas

✪ Human activities, including the use of resources, have physical, chemical, and biological consequences for ecosystems.

✪ Pollutants can have both direct and indirect impacts on the health of organisms, including humans.

### Key Terms

- Bioaccumulation
- Biomagnification
- Cholera
- Composting
- Dead zones
- Dose-response curve
- Dysentery
- E-waste
- Endocrine disruptors
- Eutrophication
- Hypoxic

- Lethal Dose 50% ($LD_{50}$)
- Malaria
- Middle East respiratory syndrome (MERS)
- Nonpoint source
- Oligotrophic
- Oxygen sag curve
- Pathogens
- Persistent organic pollutants (POPs)
- Plague

- Point source
- Primary sewage treatment
- Recycling
- Sanitary municipal landfill
- Secondary sewage treatment
- Severe acute respiratory syndrome (SARS)

- Tertiary sewage treatment
- Tuberculosis
- West Nile virus
- Wetland
- Zika

Aquatic and terrestrial pollution will cover about 7 to 10 percent of your AP Environmental Science Exam, or about 5 to 8 questions out of the 80 multiple-choice questions. This chapter all about pollution is usually not familiar to students since a lot of the concepts are not covered in prior science courses. You will be asked to propose solutions to environmental problems and do some calculations around environmental problems.

# Sources of Pollution

**Point source** is pollution you can point to and say, "There it is." For example, a pipe that is dumping waste into a river, or a smokestack that is spewing out soot and smoke: you can literally point to it. On the flip side is **nonpoint source** pollution. You can't point to any particular thing, like cars on the road. You can't point with your finger to all the cars on the road, or farmers spraying pesticide on all the crops in an area. As you read the question think about it like this: is that a single thing or a bunch of things? If it is a single thing, it is most likely point source. Many things are most likely nonpoint source pollution.

# Human Impacts on Ecosystems

This topic is broad, covering many ways that humans impact aquatic ecosystems. It will be tested using mathematical routines, so you need to know the information on how humans impact ecosystems but also be able to take a word problem and do some math. Let's look at the topics you could be asked.

Organisms have specific ranges of tolerance that they can live within, known as a species range of tolerance. Think of yourself. If you go outside without any protection in below-freezing weather, you could survive for a while but pretty quickly you would begin to shiver, get frostbite, and if you couldn't protect yourself, you might even die from the cold. Other organisms have similar ranges of tolerance and humans are putting stresses, particularly pollutant stresses, on them. That can have many different impacts, depending on the organism and the pollutant. For example, many aquatic organisms would die if the salinity were to exceed the species range of tolerance.

One example is coral reefs. Corals are very delicate animals that live in shallow, warm waters where they can get lots of sunlight and food. When corals die they turn white because their exoskeletons are white and the coral animal, which can be many beautiful colors, is no longer alive. Humans are doing harm to corals through global climate change, which has caused water temperatures to rise past the range of tolerance for coral animals to live. We are also causing erosion on the land, which runs off into the water and clouds the water so the coral animals can't get sunlight. There are also fishing techniques that are harming the corals when fisherman drag nets across them or drop anchors down on top of the coral reefs.

Oil spills are another way humans are harming the oceans. Oil that spills from drilling platforms, pipes, and ships can cause damage to animals that live on the surface of the water such as birds and mammals, where the oil gets in their feathers or fur and they lose their ability to fly or stay warm. Some oil components sink to the ocean floor where they can do damage to organisms like oysters and clams that live on the ocean floor. In addition, some of the oil might end up on the beach or in the estuaries and cause damage to organisms that live there.

**Dead zones** are being formed in the ocean where there is low oxygen (hypoxic) caused by too many nutrients coming from the land. For example, the Gulf of Mexico has a huge "dead zone" that varies in size but can be 6,000 to 8,000 square miles large. This is because of the fertilizers that are coming from the Mississippi River watershed. The map in Figure 12.1 shows the Mississippi River watershed.

Since a lot of the area in the watershed is farmland and very dense urban populations that use a lot of fertilizer, this amount adds up to millions of tons of nitrogen and phosphorus fertilizers in the Gulf. The Gulf of Mexico is just one example; there are ocean dead zones all over the world.

An **oxygen sag curve** is a graph of discharged pollutant and the distance from the discharge. It is usually sewage pollution but can be other things.

Figure 12.2 shows a graphical view of a river. The point of discharge is where the sewage is being dumped into the river. The dissolved oxygen begins to drop because sewage contains millions of organisms, like fungi and bacteria, that need oxygen. This increases the **biological oxygen demand (BOD)** on the oxygen in the river and lowers the amount of dissolved oxygen. Usually there are very few organisms that can live in the area where the dissolved oxygen is at the lowest. However, since this is a river and the pollutant will eventually get diluted, the dissolved oxygen goes up again as you get farther downstream

**Figure 12.1  Mississippi watershed.**

**Figure 12.2    Biological oxygen demand.**

from the pollutant. One great way to remember this is "dilution is the solution to pollution." This helps you remember that time and space disperse pollutants!

Other things that can harm aquatic ecosystems are litter, heavy metals from industry, and mercury that is released into the air from coal-burning power plant smokestacks, among other sources. The bacteria in the water can take the mercury and convert it to an extremely toxic form called methylmercury. Another concern with mercury is Minamata disease, which is a neurological syndrome caused by severe mercury poisoning.

## Endocrine Disruptors

**Endocrine disruptors** are chemicals that can mimic hormones in organisms; they can come from a variety of things, like pesticides, food, and pharmaceuticals. These can cause birth defects and have been linked to developmental, reproductive, neural, immune, and other problems in animals. The endocrine disruptor can block the receptor protein so that the cell can't receive a hormone signal. This can also lead to fertility problems.

## Human Impacts on Wetlands and Mangroves

Swamps, marshes, and bogs are the three main types of **wetlands** that have a huge ecological importance. They do things like clean the water naturally, protect from floods, and provide habitats to many plants and animals. This ecosystem service helps humans and has ecological importance as well for animals. Mangroves are trees and shrubs found near the coastal zone that protect the coast from erosion and flooding and provide habitat to many organisms. These are being harmed by humans when we drain and build on the areas and pollute with trash and chemical waste.

## Eutrophication

**Eutrophication** occurs when a body of water has so many nutrients (fertilizers like nitrogen and phosphorus) that have run off from the land that the nutrients "fertilize" the algae that live in the water. This comes from agriculture runoff, mainly from fertilizers and waste water runoff from concentrated animal feeding operations (CAFOs). This can cause the water to become so thick and green with algae that no light can penetrate it. The water can literally look like pea soup. Then, when the algae die, microbes like bacteria and fungi that live in the water eat the algae and in doing so take up a lot of oxygen. As with an oxygen sag curve, when there isn't enough oxygen, it results in large die-offs of fish and other aquatic organisms that need oxygen to survive. When a body of water has little to no oxygen it is known as **hypoxic**.

On the flip side, we have waters that have very few nutrients in them. These are known as **oligotrophic** (*oligo* meaning "few") and they have normal-to-low algae levels, high amounts of oxygen, and very few nutrients. The water is usually very clear and often very deep.

# Thermal Pollution

**Thermal pollution** is often from a nuclear power plant where large amounts of heated water are being dumped into a body of water. The heated water doesn't have to have any pollutants in it, but just being warm can cause problems. This is because warm water can't hold as much oxygen as cold water. The oxygen diffuses out of the water and into the air. If an organism such as fish that need dissolved oxygen in the water can't get it, they might die. In addition, the higher temperatures may exceed an organism's range of temperature tolerance.

# Persistent Organic Pollutants (POPs)

There are 12 key **persistent organic pollutants (POPs)** that were targeted in the 2001 Stockholm Convention to be reduced or eliminated. You are probably most familiar with DDT (dichlorodiphenyltrichloroethane), a synthetic organic chemical used as an insecticide, and PCBs (polychlorinated biphenyls), used as dielectric and coolant fluids in electrical equipment. POPs do not break down in the environment very quickly and can build up in the tissues and the fat of animals. This accumulation of POPs in an organism's tissues can be toxic. In addition, because they are persistent (they don't break down quickly), because animals migrate long distances, and because these chemicals can travel in wind and water very far distances, we have POPs in almost all parts of our planet.

# Bioaccumulation and Biomagnification

As mentioned above, chemicals like the pesticide DDT can build up in the fatty tissues of animals because they don't break down but accumulate there. This is referred to as **bioaccumulation**. In addition, because animals eat other animals, these chemicals can magnify up the food chain; this is referred to as **biomagnification.** It occurs because top predators eat many different prey; each prey may have eaten many different organisms as well. Figure 12.3 is an illustration of how things magnify up the food chain.

As you can see in the illustration, the water has only a small amount of DDT, but as the zooplankton pick this up it gets a little more, then because the small fish eat many zooplankton, it gets even more. Then, when large fish eat many small fish, the amount of DDT greatly increases and finally when we get to the birds, it is at the highest. This amount of DDT is now high enough to cause major problems to the birds that might not have happened to the organisms down the food chain.

**Figure 12.3   Biomagnification.**

Persistent chemicals like DDT, PCBs, and mercury can have environmental and human health effects. For example, when DDT made its way up to predatory birds like bald eagles, the chemical interfered with the ability of the bird to make strong eggshells. The shells were so soft that they often broke during incubation and the baby birds died. It went on for many generations with the bald eagle population, and we had entire species on the brink of extinction due to this problem. In humans, persistent chemicals can damage the reproductive, nervous, and circulatory systems.

# Solid Waste Disposal

Humans generate large amounts of solid waste. This can be normal household trash; e-waste from electronics like computers, televisions, and cell phones; or waste from industrial and agricultural processes.

Most waste in the United States is sent to a landfill. A landfill must be carefully maintained and monitored or the waste can leach out and contaminate groundwater. As the waste decomposes it can produce methane and carbon dioxide, which can lead to climate change.

**Sanitary municipal landfills** have been designed to control the disposal of solid waste so that our water and air is protected. Look at Figure 12.4. There is a clay and plastic lining to prevent leaks, a leachate pump to collect the liquid that passed through the trash, and, in addition, there are pipes to collect the methane gases produced as a result of decomposition. The methane is either used to create electricity or burned off safely. There are also ways to collect large amounts of storm water so it doesn't end up in the landfill.

How quickly the trash decomposes depends on many things. For example, what is the trash consisting of? Where is the landfill located? What is the temperature? How much rainfall is there? All of these factors can determine how fast items decompose.

In addition to putting trash into a landfill, we can also burn the trash at high temperatures. It is important that this is done carefully as air pollutants can be released. But, as a result of burning, the volume of the trash is greatly reduced and the concern of water pollution goes way down.

Other concerns about solid waste are people illegally dumping it into our oceans and people putting things into landfills that are not allowed.

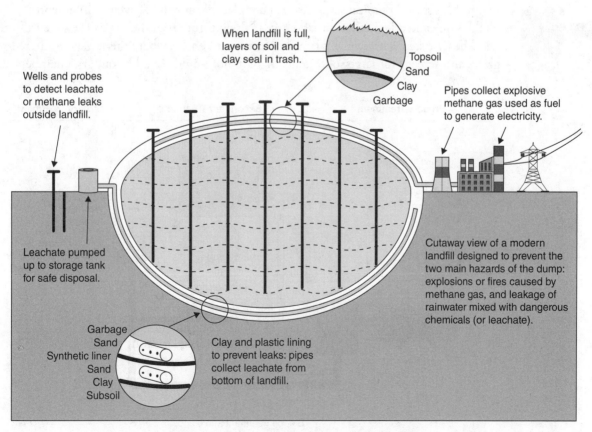

**Figure 12.4    Sanitary municipal landfills.**

# Waste Reduction Methods

We know that solid waste is going to be a problem because of the numbers of people on Earth. However, there are other ways to reduce the amount of waste or to recycle the waste. **Recycling** is taking something like plastic and turning it into something new. This does a few things: first, it means that new oil doesn't have to be pumped to make more plastic, and it also means that the plastic doesn't end up in the landfill or the ocean. However, recycling can be expensive and require a lot of energy.

Another way to reduce the waste that is generated is to compost it. **Composting** works well for food waste, paper waste, and yard trimmings. Rather than throwing these products into the landfill, we can put them in composting piles, and after they decompose, we can use it for fertilizer. Some people don't like composting because it can attract rodents and can have a pungent odor. However, it produces some of the best fertilizer and is chemical free.

Computers, TVs, cell phones, and other **e-waste** can also be recycled for their parts and turned into new items. Like the example above, this avoids having to mine new metals and prevents the items from ending up in a landfill.

Another way to lessen the impact of landfills can be done after they are full. If we cap them and plant trees and other plants to restore habitats or use as city parks, we can help lower the impact they have on the environment.

Finally, the methane and $CO_2$ gas from a landfill can be captured. Then it can be burned to heat water, produce steam, and turn a turbine to generate electrical energy.

# Sewage Treatment

Figure 12.5 shows a typical sewage treatment plant. You will be given a visual representation like this one and asked questions about it. Let's go through all the steps of sewage treatment.

The first step is known as **primary treatment**. This is where the sewage is filtered with grates and screens for large solid items that are not liquid. In addition, grit chambers allow

**Figure 12.5 Sewage treatment plant.**

the sewage to slow down so things like ground-up eggshells and coffee grounds that also are not liquid can sink to the floor and be disposed of in a landfill.

Now, only liquid waste is going to move into the next stage, **secondary treatment**. The bacteria found in the sewage is given lots of air so it can begin to consume the waste and break it down into carbon dioxide and inorganic sludge. The sludge sinks to the bottom of the tank and is disposed of as well.

Finally, we move to the last stage known as **tertiary treatment**, where either chemicals like chlorine and ozone gas or water disinfectants like UV light kill any bacteria that remain. Then the water is released to a river or lake.

## Lethal Dose 50% (LD$_{50}$)

**Lethal Dose 50%** is a term used in toxicology to say the amount of a toxin that kills 50 percent of the organisms that are being tested. This can be any animal but usually refers to test rats and mice in a laboratory. This concept is useful for toxicology because it can help us determine the relative short-term toxicity of a substance. For example, the LD$_{50}$ of nicotine is 50 milligrams per kilogram for a rat; for table salt it is 3,000 milligrams per kilogram for a rat. This is commonly used to measure the toxicity of a chemical's active ingredient and is a way to measure the short-term poisoning potential of a substance.

## Dose-Response Curve

The **dose-response curve** (or dose-response relationship) is a curve plotting the relationship between the dose of a drug administered and its pharmacological effect. This is usually graphed with the dose on the *x*-axis and the effect on the *y*-axis. You will be given a graph or chart to read and you will need to explain what the graph says about an environmental issue.

A dose-response curve is usually shaped like the letter "S." This is because usually small doses are not toxic and as you increase the dose, the individuals show a response to that dose. Look at the example of a dose-response curve in Figure 12.6; the sharp increase in the graph of the line shows that there are increasingly higher risks of toxic response as the dose amount increases until almost 100 percent of the organisms are experiencing toxicity.

**Figure 12.6   Dose-response curve.**

# Pollution and Human Health

Humans are exposed to many different chemicals every day. This can be in what we eat, what we breathe, where we live, and so on. Therefore, it is hard to directly say if a particular chemical causes a particular human health issue. However, there are a few that can be significantly linked to particular things.

For example, **dysentery** is an infection of the intestines resulting in severe diarrhea with blood and mucus in the feces. This comes from untreated sewage in streams and rivers that become drinking water or food contaminates. Another is asbestos, a building material that was used because it was flame resistant. That seemed like a good idea—build homes that couldn't catch on fire! What we didn't know at the time was that when these panels, floor boards, or ceiling tiles began to break down, tiny fibers would be released into the air that people breathed in. This led to various serious lung conditions such as lung cancer. Also, as tropospheric ozone from the chemical reaction between $NO_x$ and VOCs is formed and we breathe it in we can get respiratory problems like asthma, emphysema, and COPD.

# Pathogens and Infectious Disease

A **pathogen** is a bacterium, virus, or other microorganism that can cause disease. This disease can be transmitted from human to human or animal to human. You could be asked about a number of pathogens and how they are transferred. Let's look at Table 12.1 with the pathogens you need to know:

**Table 12.1**

| PATHOGEN | INFORMATION ABOUT |
|---|---|
| Plague | A bacterial infection transmitted by fleas, famous for killing millions in Europe in the Middle Ages. Modern antibiotics are effective in treating this. |
| Tuberculosis (TB) | A bacterial infection that usually attacks the lungs and is spread from one person to another. TB can be treated by taking several drugs for six to nine months. |
| Malaria | A parasitic disease transmitted by mosquitos. People get fever, chills, and flu-like illness. However, if left untreated it can be deadly. Nearly half a million people die each year, mostly in the African region. |
| West Nile virus | A mosquito-transmitted virus and most people show no signs or symptoms. However, fever, a mild headache, and inflammation of the spinal cord or brain can occur. |
| Severe acute respiratory syndrome (SARS) | SARS is a viral respiratory illness that was first reported in 2003 but there haven't been any known cases since 2004. It is spread easily by coughing and sneezing, touching contaminated surfaces, skin-to-skin contact, or kissing. |
| Middle East respiratory syndrome (MERS) | A viral respiratory illness that was first reported in 2012. This causes fever, coughing, and shortness of breath. It is transferred from animal to human. |
| Zika | Zika is a virus from infected mosquitoes, sexual contact, blood transfusions, or from a pregnant woman to her fetus. There is no vaccine or medicine for Zika. It causes fever, rash, headache, and joint/muscle pain. |
| Cholera | A bacterial disease that causes severe diarrhea and dehydration and is spread in water. Rehydration and antibiotics are the treatment for this disease. |

As our climate is changing and Earth is getting warmer, diseases from insects like West Nile and malaria are spreading to areas that they were not in before. In addition, many of these diseases are spread in areas that are poor and lack sanitation or clean water.

# › Review Questions

## Multiple-Choice Questions

1. The graph below shows the dose-response curves for three common pesticides.

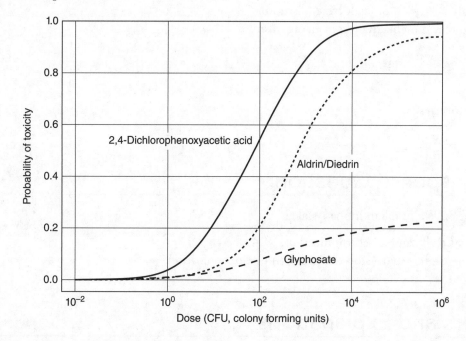

All three of these pesticides are used to kill pests such as rodents, insects, or plants. Which of the three would have the greatest dose response according to the graph?

(A) 2,4-Dichlorophenoxyacetic Acid
(B) Aldrin/Dieldrin
(C) Glyphosate
(D) DDT

2. A scientist is trying to discover why large amounts of lake trout are dying in a particular area. The scientist discovers that the temperature in the water is much warmer than it would be naturally. The scientist explores the area and discovers what they think is causing the problem. Which of the following would most likely be what is killing the lake trout?

(A) Pesticides are raising the temperature in the lake, killing the lake trout.
(B) Electricity from a local power plant is shocking the lake trout.
(C) Persistent organic pollutants (POPs) are being dumped into the lake from a local pesticide plant.
(D) Heated water from a nuclear power plant is being dumped into the lake.

3. The $LD_{50}$ for caffeine in humans is approximately 180 mg/kg. If a person weighs 150 lbs and 1 kg = 2.2 lbs, how many grams of caffeine would it take to reach the $LD_{50}$ for a human?

(A) 12.27 grams
(B) 12,272 grams
(C) 2.64 grams
(D) 2,640 grams

4. Which of the following is true about persistent organic pollutants (POPs)?

(A) POPs are only a concern in areas where they were used, particularly developed nations.
(B) The Montreal Protocol was written to stop the problem of POPs.
(C) POPs pose the biggest problem to producers.
(D) POPs are soluble in fat and they can accumulate in organisms' fatty tissues.

5. Dioxins, PCBs, pesticides, and perfluorinated chemicals are all types of endocrine disruptors. What would they most likely affect in an organism?

(A) Nervous system
(B) Hormones
(C) Skin
(D) Circulatory system

6. Which of the following is a point source pollutant that might affect the oysters and clams living at the bottom of the ocean floor?

(A) $CO_2$ from the cars in a large city near the ocean
(B) Fertilizer runoff from local farms and feedlots
(C) Oil spilling from a tanker with a leak
(D) Pesticides sprayed on the estuary system to prevent disease from mosquitoes

## › Free-Response Question

7. Eutrophication is a problem in many lakes.

(A) **Identify** ONE cause of eutrophication.
(B) **Describe** ONE way to stop the problem of eutrophication.

## › Answers and Explanations

1. **A**—2,4-Dichlorophenoxyacetic acid has the highest probability of toxicity.

2. **D**—Thermal pollution is what is lowering the dissolved oxygen and this is most likely coming from a nuclear power plant, which generates a lot of heat.

3. **A**—$\dfrac{150 \text{ lb} \times 1 \text{ kg} \times 180 \text{ mg} \times 1 \text{ g}}{2.2 \text{ lb} \times 1 \text{ kg} \times 1{,}000 \text{ mg}} = 12.27$ grams

4. **D**—POPs do not break down in the environment very quickly and can build up in the tissues and fat of animals. This bioaccumulation of POPs in organisms' tissues can be toxic.

5. **B**—Endocrine disruptors are chemicals that can mimic hormones in organisms and can come from a variety of things, like pesticides, food, pharmaceuticals, etc. These can cause birth defects and have been linked to developmental, reproductive, neural, immune, and other problems in animals.

6. **C**—Point source pollution is pollution you can point to and say, "There it is." In this example, the oil tanker with the leak.

7. **(A)** One point for stating one cause of eutrophication. Eutrophication is the term used to describe a body of water that has many nutrients (fertilizers like nitrogen and phosphorus) that have run off from the land and these nutrients have "fertilized" the algae that live in the water.
**(B)** One point for describing one way to stop eutrophication. Possible answers include plant vegetation around farms or streambeds to slow erosion and absorb fertilizer; construct barriers; control the application, amount, and timing of fertilizers; use no-phosphorus fertilizer on lawns and gardens; use better drainage systems; remove pet waste.

# › Rapid Review

- Point source—A pollutant that you can see and point to. Usually a single source.

- Nonpoint source—A pollutant that comes from many sources such as pollution from cars in a city. You can't point to one particular place or thing.

- Dead zones—Formed in the ocean where there is low oxygen (hypoxic) caused by too many nutrients coming from the land.

- Oxygen sag curve—A graph of discharged pollutant and the distance from the discharge. It is usually sewage pollution but can be other things.

- Endocrine disruptors—Chemicals that can mimic hormones in organisms and can cause birth defects and have been linked to developmental, reproductive, neural, immune, and other problems in animals.

- Wetland—Land consisting of marshes, swamps, or bogs; saturated land.

- Eutrophication—A body of water that has so many nutrients (fertilizers like nitrogen and phosphorus) that have run off from the land that the nutrients have "fertilized" the algae that live in the water.

- Hypoxic—A body of water with little to no oxygen in the water.

- Oligotrophic—A body of water with normal to low algae levels, high amounts of oxygen, and very few nutrients.

- Thermal pollution—Occurs when warm water is pumped into a lake or river, lowering the oxygen levels and harming biodiversity.

- Persistent organic pollutants (POPs)—POPs do not break down in the environment very quickly and can build up in the tissues and fat of animals.

- Bioaccumulation—POPs, like the pesticide DDT, can accumulate in the fatty tissues of animals; this is referred to as bioaccumulation.

- Biomagnification—When animals eat other animals and the prey have POPs that have bioaccumulated in their tissues, the POPs can magnify up the food chain. This biomagnification occurs because top predators eat many different prey.

- E-waste—Electronic waste like TVs, computers, phones, etc.

- Sanitary municipal landfill—Where solid waste from homes, businesses, and more is stored. It has a clay or plastic liner, leachate detection systems, a way for the gas to be collected or burned, and a way to make sure storm water doesn't enter the landfill.

- Recycling—Taking solid waste and turning it into something new rather than throwing it away.

- Composting—Taking food, yard, or other organic waste and letting it decompose to form good soil.

- Primary sewage treatment—The first stage of sewage treatment in which the sewage is filtered in grates and screens for items that are not liquid. In addition, the sewage is slowed down so things like eggshells and coffee grounds that also are not liquid can sink to the bottom and be disposed of in a landfill.

- Secondary sewage treatment—The second stage of sewage treatment where lots of air is added so the bacteria found in the sewage can begin to consume the waste and break it down into carbon dioxide and inorganic sludge. The sludge sinks to the bottom of the tank and is disposed of as well.

- Tertiary sewage treatment—The stage of sewage treatment where either chemicals like chlorine and ozone gas or UV light kills any remaining bacteria. Then the water is released to a river or lake.

- Lethal Dose 50% ($LD_{50}$)—A term used in toxicology to indicate the amount of a toxin that kills 50 percent of the organisms that are being tested.

- Dose-response curve—A curve plotting the relationship between the dose of a drug administered and its pharmacological effect. This is usually graphed with the dose on the $x$-axis and the effect on the $y$-axis.

# CHAPTER 13

# Global Change

## IN THIS CHAPTER

**Summary:** Global climate change, ozone depletion, ocean warming, and endangered species are just a few of the ways humans have affected Earth. This chapter focuses on environmental solutions to environmental problems that are caused by humans. You will need to look at global changes and be able to explain the causes and consequences of these. Make sure you can look at data and use this data to propose solutions or legislation to global problems. One of the most important aspects that students confuse is the difference between global climate change and ozone depletion. You need to be experts on these two concepts and make sure you can differentiate between them before you take the AP Environmental Science Exam.

### Key Ideas

✪ Local and regional human activities can have impacts at the global level.
✪ The health of a species is closely tied to its ecosystem, and minor environmental changes can have a large impact.

**Key Terms**

- Chlorofluorocarbons (CFCs)
- Coral bleaching
- Endangered species
- Habitat fragmentation
- Hydrofluorocarbons (HFCs)

- Invasive species
- Ocean acidification
- Ozone depletion
- Positive feedback loop
- Stratospheric ozone layer

Global change will account for 15 to 20 percent of your AP Environmental Science exam, or about 12 to 16 questions out of the 80 multiple-choice questions. That means that you *must* know this chapter to be successful on this exam. This chapter contains by far the most covered topics on the exam and therefore is the most important. This chapter is all about global changes that humans have made on the environment. You will learn all about global climate change and ozone depletion. You will be asked multiple questions about these two concepts and must be sure you know the difference! In addition, other important topics you need to know are ocean acidification and ocean warming, as well as invasive and endangered species.

# Stratospheric Ozone Depletion

The **stratospheric ozone layer** is a shield around Earth that absorbs most of the sun's ultraviolet radiation (UV). This layer of our atmosphere contains ozone ($O_3$). It is the ozone ($O_3$) and oxygen molecules ($O_2$) in this layer that absorb the UV light. The stratosphere is above the troposphere, which is the layer closest to the Earth's surface; it extends from 10 km (6 miles) to about 50 km (31 miles) into space.

Because of the stratosphere's ability to absorb the sun's UV light, this dangerous radiation is prevented from passing to the Earth's surface. Without this stratospheric ozone layer life on Earth as we know it would not be possible.

Ozone is produced naturally in the stratosphere when the sun's UV rays split $O_2$ molecules into single oxygen atoms. These oxygen atoms then combine with $O_2$ to form $O_3$ molecules, which are very good at absorbing UV light.

However, human-produced chemicals, such as **chlorofluorocarbons (CFCs)**, although they are heavier than air, have been carried into the stratosphere by the air currents and mixing processes of the atmosphere. These CFC molecules are hit by the sun's UV energy and break up, releasing chlorine atoms. The chlorine atoms then react with the $O_3$ molecules, breaking up the $O_3$ by taking one oxygen atom to form chlorine monoxide and $O_2$. The chemical equation, which you need to know and memorize, looks like this:

$$Cl + O_3 \rightarrow ClO + O_2$$

Next, if the ClO molecule finds a free oxygen atom, the oxygen atom will steal the O from the ClO to become $O_2$, which releases the Cl atom back into the stratosphere to destroy more ozone. The second equation looks like this:

$$ClO + O \rightarrow Cl + O_2$$

Now the Cl can repeat the process again, taking another ozone molecule and breaking it down as in the first equation. A single CFC molecule can destroy 100,000 ozone molecules and it is thought that chlorine can remain in the stratosphere for 50 years or so.

UV light naturally breaks $O_3$ down, and $O_3$ is still formed naturally, but chlorine accelerates this process and puts the cycle out of balance.

One example of **ozone depletion** is the "hole" over Antarctica. This isn't really a "hole" but rather very low levels of ozone over this area during the Antarctic spring. However, the South Pole isn't the only place with very low levels of ozone.

The result of all this chemistry is more UV light is able to get through the stratosphere and to the surface of Earth. UV light is dangerous because it damages the DNA in skin cells and leads to skin cancer, eye damage such as cataracts, and premature aging. It can also suppress the immune system. In plants it can affect their growth and has been shown to cause problems for marine phytoplankton, the foundation of the marine food web.

## Reducing Ozone Depletion

The main way we have tried to stop the problem of ozone depletion is to stop using ozone-depleting substances. The Montreal Protocol (1987) and the Vienna Convention (1985) were treaties to control the release of these substances. The main ozone-depleting substances are chlorofluorocarbons (CFCs), hydrochlorofluorocarbons, and halons. Using things like hydrofluorocarbons can be a helpful replacement, but some are very potent greenhouse gases. CFCs may also be reduced by inspecting and maintaining air conditioners and refrigeration appliances to prevent leaks.

## The Greenhouse Effect

The greenhouse effect is shown in Figure 13.1. As you can see, solar radiation (infrared) from the sun is absorbed by Earth's surface, warming the surface, and some is reflected back to space. This is important because without the greenhouse effect, it would be too cold on Earth for life.

The main gases that are in our atmosphere that absorb the solar radiation are carbon dioxide, methane, water vapor, nitrous oxide, and chlorofluorocarbons. Each of these has a different amount of global warming potential (GWP). Let's look at each in Table 13.1.

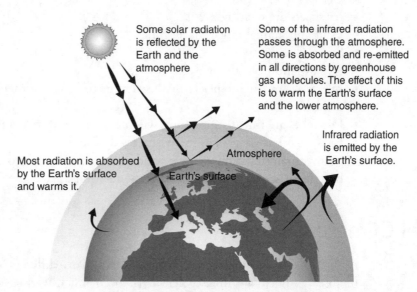

**Figure 13.1   The greenhouse effect.**

**Table 13.1**

| GAS | SOURCES | GWP | ATMOSPHERIC LIFETIME |
|---|---|---|---|
| Carbon dioxide | Decomposition, respiration, burning fossil fuels, deforestation | 1 | 50–200 years |
| Methane | Burning of fossil fuels, livestock, landfills, decomposition, burning biomass, natural wetlands | 21 | 12 years |
| Nitrous oxide | Soils, livestock manure, biomass or fossil fuel combustion, wastewater management | 310 | 120 years |
| Chlorofluorocarbons | Refrigerants, aerosols, aircraft halons, solvents | 12,000–16,000 | 20–100 years |

Water vapor's GWP is unknown but not of great concern since the water cycle cycles relatively quickly.

# Increases in the Greenhouse Gases

There are many things that have increased the amount of greenhouse gases in the troposphere. For this topic, you will be given an image and asked questions about that image. You will need to know the things responsible for increasing the amount of greenhouse gases: transportation, electricity production, industry, businesses and homes, agriculture, and reduction of forested land.

Some results of increased greenhouse gases that have impacted either the environment or harmed humans are:

- Glaciers have shrunk.
- Ice sheets are melting.
- Plant and animal ranges have shifted.
- Sea levels are rising.
- Seas expand from thermal expansion.
- Insects are moving to places that used to be too cold for them, and these insects can carry disease.
- Droughts are threatening crops, wildlife, and freshwater supplies.
- Biodiversity is affected as many species depend on ice for food and for a place to live.
- Many organisms cannot move or adapt quickly enough to survive, so population numbers decrease, particularly specialist populations.

# Global Climate Change

As you can see in Figure 13.2, Earth has had many different changes in temperature over its history. There are times when it has been much warmer and times when it has been much colder. Currently, we are in a warming trend, which as mentioned in the topic above,

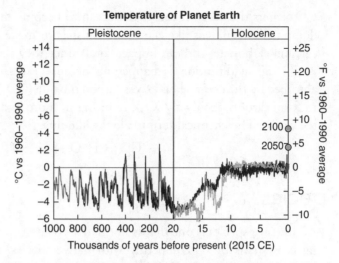

**Figure 13.2  Historical data of temperatures on Earth.**

has led to many impacts on the environment and human health. Let's look at a few other impacts, both positive and negative, of a warmer Earth:

- Sea levels are rising, which can flood coastal communities, impact ocean organisms that are now too deep to photosynthesize, and may create new habitats for other organisms.
- Weather patterns are changing due to changes in the circulation of winds in the atmosphere.
- Ocean currents, which push tropical heat toward the poles, are changing and weakening the oceans' global conveyor belt as warm freshwater melts into the sea, which stops the sinking of cold, salty water. This is changing climates across the globe.
- Soil can be impacted if we have droughts and increased soil erosion from wind and water.
- There is a positive feedback loop in the polar regions, where normally the ice reflects the sun's rays back (albedo effect). With a warmer planet we have more melting of the ice and less sunlight being reflected back to space. This then increases the temperatures on Earth even more, causing more melting. A **positive feedback loop** is when one thing gets worse and worse, as in this example. In addition, as ice and permafrost areas melt, methane is released; this a global warming gas mentioned above. This is another example of a positive feedback loop.

# Ocean Warming

As our oceans get warmer because of climate change from greenhouse gases, there is a negative impact to ocean biodiversity. For example, corals need zooxanthellae, an algae that lives in the tissues of coral and captures sunlight and converts this into energy for the coral animals. When the temperature of the ocean is too warm, the zooxanthellae come under stress and can die or leave their coral host, causing the coral to die and turn white, a process known as coral bleaching. A warmer ocean also can lead to loss of habitat to marine organisms.

# Ocean Acidification

The ocean absorbs carbon dioxide from the atmosphere and the carbon dioxide reacts with the ocean water creating carbonic acid. The oceans absorb almost a quarter of global $CO_2$ emissions we create from burning fossil fuels and deforestation. As the

$CO_2$ enters the ocean it causes the ocean to become more acidic (lower pH). This acidity doesn't allow animals like clams and mussels to make protective shells, due to the loss of calcium carbonate, and can impact corals since they also make protective shells.

Ocean acidification is happening because excess $CO_2$ in the atmosphere is being absorbed by the ocean. This excess carbon dioxide ($CO_2$) reacts with water molecules ($H_2O$) to form carbonic acid ($H_2CO_3$), resulting in more hydrogen ions and lowering the pH of the ocean. The chemical formula looks like this:

$$CO_2 + H_2O \rightarrow H^+ + HCO_3^-$$

# Invasive Species

An invasive species is one that is not native to an area. Invasive species can harm the natural ecosystems by outcompeting with native species, reducing biodiversity, and altering habitats, sometimes leading to extinctions of native plants and animals. Invasive species tend to be generalists and r-selected species, and they become invasive because of a lack of competition, no predators, and/or abundant resources.

The three main ways to control invasive species are:

- Biological—Using natural enemies to control the pest species. This can work but sometimes the biological control backfires and the new species becomes a problem.
- Mechanical—Mowing, hoeing, hand pulling, and more to control the pest species. This is expensive and time consuming.
- Chemical—Using pesticides (such as herbicides, insecticides, and rodenticides). This can lead to the problems discussed earlier in this book on pesticides.

Many species are introduced to environments by human transport, either with the global trade of species (for example, exotic pets) or with humans traveling and intentionally or unintentionally bringing the species back with them.

# Endangered Species

An endangered species is any animal or plant that is considered at risk of extinction. A species can be listed as endangered at the international, national, or state level. The Endangered Species Act has the endangered species listed on it and it is managed federally and allows the United States to enforce the international treaty known as CITES.

A species may become endangered for many reasons. Habitat loss, invasive species, poaching, climate change, taking too many of a species in hunting and fishing, pollution, if the animal is highly specialized (lives in a certain place, eats a certain thing), competition within or with other species, and selective pressures on the species are all reasons animals and plants might become endangered. If the species can't adapt or move it might be in danger.

Humans can help prevent and can combat species becoming endangered by protecting the habitats where they live and protecting the species itself.

# Human Impacts on Biodiversity

A way to remember how we harm biodiversity is the mnemonic device HIPPCO. Let's look at each letter:

H—Habitat loss
I—Invasive species

P—Population growth

P—Pollution (but always name a chemical if you want to use this one—just "pollution" is too general)

C—Climate change, which leads to droughts, floods, sea level rising, and so on

O—Overharvesting (overfishing, overhunting)

So, if asked to give a solution to a problem, you can think of each of these reasons and come up with a way to stop this loss to biodiversity.

Of all these reasons for loss of biodiversity, the greatest one is habitat loss. We harm habitats by cutting down forests, by building roads, by building human habitation in areas where there used to be large areas of land (habitat fragmentation), and so on.

We can prevent this loss of habitat by protecting large tracts of land so it can't be developed, creating and enforcing legislation to protect biodiversity, preventing importation of nonnative species, creating habitat corridors so animals can move between native areas, preventing deforestation, using sustainable farming and ranching practices, and helping to restore areas that have been harmed by human or natural disasters.

# ❯ Review Questions

## Multiple-Choice Questions

1. Which of the following correctly describes the problem of coral bleaching?

   (A) Factories are dumping chemicals into the ocean water that cause corals to fade in color.
   (B) Sewage that is dumped into the ocean smothers the coral causing it to turn white.
   (C) Parrot fish, a main predator on the reefs, are voraciously eating coral animals.
   (D) The algae that lives in the tissues of the coral die and, as a result, the coral animals die and turn white.

2. Use the graph below to answer the question.

**Global Average Temperature**

Which of the following can you conclude from the data above?

   (A) Earth was warmer in 1920 than in 1980.
   (B) The temperature lines go up and down each year because people drive cars more in the winter than in the summer.
   (C) The average global temperature fluctuates, but the average for the last five years was hotter than at any time previously.
   (D) Temperature data on the graph is correlated with soil erosion rates.

**3.** The graph below shows the total number of species that are listed under the Endangered Species Act.

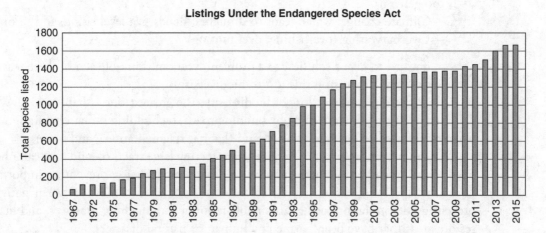

Which of the following conclusions is the correct solution to the problem shown above in the graph?

(A) Protecting the habitat of the species would help to lower the number of species listed each year.

(B) Removing fishing regulations would help lower the number of species listed each year.

(C) Invasive species have little effect on the total number of species listed each year.

(D) Decriminalizing poaching would help lower the number of species listed each year.

**4.** Which of the following best describes the environmental disadvantage of habitat fragmentation?

(A) Profits decrease when you build homes in forested areas.

(B) Habitat fragmentation has negative impacts on many species in the ecosystem.

(C) Building habitat corridors prevents animals from migrating from one area to another.

(D) Habitat fragmentation lessens the impact from invasive species.

**5.** Which of the following best describes why the stratospheric ozone layer is so important to life on Earth?

(A) The stratospheric ozone layer absorbs most of the UV rays that come from the sun.

(B) The stratospheric ozone layer traps the infrared rays from the sun and keeps Earth warm.

(C) The stratospheric ozone layer is replaced annually by an interaction between CFC molecules and $O_3$ molecules.

(D) Greenhouse gases are destroying the ability of the stratospheric ozone layer to reflect the sun's energy back to space.

**6.** Which of the following is correct about the ability of greenhouse gases to trap infrared heat from the sun?

(A) Carbon dioxide has the greatest global warming potential of any greenhouse gas.

(B) Because water vapor remains in the atmosphere for many years at a time, it has the greatest global warming potential of any greenhouse gas.

(C) Chlorofluorocarbons have the greatest global warming potential of any greenhouse gas.

(D) Ozone depletion in the stratosphere is increasing Earth's ability to absorb the sun's infrared heat.

**7.** Ocean acidification would be increased by which of the following activities?

(A) Switching to solar power for homes and businesses

(B) Stopping the deforestation of national forests

(C) Increasing fishing practices in coastal waters

(D) Burning coal, oil, and natural gas as energy sources

## 〉 Free-Response Question

8. (A) As cities expand habitat destruction can occur. **Identify** ONE activity that occurs as cities are built that can destroy habitats.
(B) For the activity you identified in Part (A), **describe** TWO ways to reduce this effect on biodiversity.

## 〉 Answers and Explanations

1. **D**—When the temperature of the ocean is too warm, the zooxanthellae come under stress and can die or leave their coral host, causing the coral to die and turn white, a process known as coral bleaching.

2. **C**—The last five years have been the hottest in history as shown on the graph.

3. **A**—Habitat protection is the best way to protect species.

4. **B**—When we take large natural areas and break them up into smaller areas with roads and buildings in the middle, we get loss of biodiversity.

5. **A**—Because of the stratosphere's ability to absorb the sun's UV light, the dangerous radiation is prevented from passing to Earth's surface. Without this stratospheric ozone layer life on Earth as we know it would not be possible.

6. **C**—Chlorofluorocarbons have a GWP of 12,000–16,000.

7. **D**—Burning of fossil fuels increases $CO_2$ concentrations, which leads to a lower pH of oceans and ocean acidification.

8. **(A)** One point for correctly identifying an activity that occurs as cities are built that can destroy habitats. Possible answers include hunting, loss of habitat to homes, roads, businesses, pipelines, climate change, introduction of invasive species, etc.
**(B)** Two points, one for each correct description of a way to reduce the effect on biodiversity. Possible answers include building wildlife habitat corridors, promoting sustainable land use practices, remediating habitat that has been destroyed, switching to renewable energy resources, etc.

## › Rapid Review

- Stratospheric ozone layer—The protected layer of our atmosphere that absorbs UV light.
- Chlorofluorocarbons (CFCs)—A man-made chemical that works its way through the troposphere and into the stratosphere where it can destroy ozone molecules.
- Ozone depletion—$Cl + O_3 \rightarrow ClO + O_2$ and $ClO + O \rightarrow Cl + O_2$ are the chemical formulas for ozone depletion. This is caused by chemicals like CFCs breaking down ozone in the stratosphere. This means less natural ozone to absorb UV light coming to Earth.
- Greenhouse effect—The natural ability of Earth to absorb heat from the sun (infrared) and keep our planet warm enough to live on.
- Global climate change—As more and more greenhouse gases are emitted into the atmosphere, we are trapping more heat from the sun and the temperature of Earth is getting warmer. Sea levels are rising, estuaries are getting deeper, storms get stronger, insects are moving farther away from the equator, ice caps are melting, and permafrost is melting.
- Positive feedback loop—When one thing causes something else to get progressively worse. An example is as Earth warms, the ice caps melt, causing the water to be warmer, causing more ice to melt, causing the water to be warmer, and so on and so on.
- Coral bleaching—When the algae that lives in the coral animals dies or leaves the coral and causes the coral to die and turn white.
- Ocean warming—When Earth is getting warmer the oceans are also getting warmer. This is causing ice to melt, sea levels to rise, etc.
- Ocean acidification—As more carbon dioxide is added to the atmosphere it gets into the ocean causing the ocean to have a lower pH and harming things like coral animals.
- Invasive species—Nonnative species that are introduced to an environment and might outcompete the native species.
- Endangered species—Any species that is threatened to go extinct. Usually from one of the reasons in HIPPCO (see previous explanation).
- Habitat fragmentation—When a habitat is split up into smaller areas with roads, homes, and more in the middle, it leads to loss of biodiversity.

# Build Your Test-Taking Confidence

AP Environmental Science Practice Exam 1
AP Environmental Science Practice Exam 2

# AP Environmental Science Practice Exam 1
# Multiple-Choice Questions

**ANSWER SHEET**

| | | |
|---|---|---|
| 1 Ⓐ Ⓑ Ⓒ Ⓓ | 31 Ⓐ Ⓑ Ⓒ Ⓓ | 61 Ⓐ Ⓑ Ⓒ Ⓓ |
| 2 Ⓐ Ⓑ Ⓒ Ⓓ | 32 Ⓐ Ⓑ Ⓒ Ⓓ | 62 Ⓐ Ⓑ Ⓒ Ⓓ |
| 3 Ⓐ Ⓑ Ⓒ Ⓓ | 33 Ⓐ Ⓑ Ⓒ Ⓓ | 63 Ⓐ Ⓑ Ⓒ Ⓓ |
| 4 Ⓐ Ⓑ Ⓒ Ⓓ | 34 Ⓐ Ⓑ Ⓒ Ⓓ | 64 Ⓐ Ⓑ Ⓒ Ⓓ |
| 5 Ⓐ Ⓑ Ⓒ Ⓓ | 35 Ⓐ Ⓑ Ⓒ Ⓓ | 65 Ⓐ Ⓑ Ⓒ Ⓓ |
| 6 Ⓐ Ⓑ Ⓒ Ⓓ | 36 Ⓐ Ⓑ Ⓒ Ⓓ | 66 Ⓐ Ⓑ Ⓒ Ⓓ |
| 7 Ⓐ Ⓑ Ⓒ Ⓓ | 37 Ⓐ Ⓑ Ⓒ Ⓓ | 67 Ⓐ Ⓑ Ⓒ Ⓓ |
| 8 Ⓐ Ⓑ Ⓒ Ⓓ | 38 Ⓐ Ⓑ Ⓒ Ⓓ | 68 Ⓐ Ⓑ Ⓒ Ⓓ |
| 9 Ⓐ Ⓑ Ⓒ Ⓓ | 39 Ⓐ Ⓑ Ⓒ Ⓓ | 69 Ⓐ Ⓑ Ⓒ Ⓓ |
| 10 Ⓐ Ⓑ Ⓒ Ⓓ | 40 Ⓐ Ⓑ Ⓒ Ⓓ | 70 Ⓐ Ⓑ Ⓒ Ⓓ |
| 11 Ⓐ Ⓑ Ⓒ Ⓓ | 41 Ⓐ Ⓑ Ⓒ Ⓓ | 71 Ⓐ Ⓑ Ⓒ Ⓓ |
| 12 Ⓐ Ⓑ Ⓒ Ⓓ | 42 Ⓐ Ⓑ Ⓒ Ⓓ | 72 Ⓐ Ⓑ Ⓒ Ⓓ |
| 13 Ⓐ Ⓑ Ⓒ Ⓓ | 43 Ⓐ Ⓑ Ⓒ Ⓓ | 73 Ⓐ Ⓑ Ⓒ Ⓓ |
| 14 Ⓐ Ⓑ Ⓒ Ⓓ | 44 Ⓐ Ⓑ Ⓒ Ⓓ | 74 Ⓐ Ⓑ Ⓒ Ⓓ |
| 15 Ⓐ Ⓑ Ⓒ Ⓓ | 45 Ⓐ Ⓑ Ⓒ Ⓓ | 75 Ⓐ Ⓑ Ⓒ Ⓓ |
| 16 Ⓐ Ⓑ Ⓒ Ⓓ | 46 Ⓐ Ⓑ Ⓒ Ⓓ | 76 Ⓐ Ⓑ Ⓒ Ⓓ |
| 17 Ⓐ Ⓑ Ⓒ Ⓓ | 47 Ⓐ Ⓑ Ⓒ Ⓓ | 77 Ⓐ Ⓑ Ⓒ Ⓓ |
| 18 Ⓐ Ⓑ Ⓒ Ⓓ | 48 Ⓐ Ⓑ Ⓒ Ⓓ | 78 Ⓐ Ⓑ Ⓒ Ⓓ |
| 19 Ⓐ Ⓑ Ⓒ Ⓓ | 49 Ⓐ Ⓑ Ⓒ Ⓓ | 79 Ⓐ Ⓑ Ⓒ Ⓓ |
| 20 Ⓐ Ⓑ Ⓒ Ⓓ | 50 Ⓐ Ⓑ Ⓒ Ⓓ | 80 Ⓐ Ⓑ Ⓒ Ⓓ |
| 21 Ⓐ Ⓑ Ⓒ Ⓓ | 51 Ⓐ Ⓑ Ⓒ Ⓓ | |
| 22 Ⓐ Ⓑ Ⓒ Ⓓ | 52 Ⓐ Ⓑ Ⓒ Ⓓ | |
| 23 Ⓐ Ⓑ Ⓒ Ⓓ | 53 Ⓐ Ⓑ Ⓒ Ⓓ | |
| 24 Ⓐ Ⓑ Ⓒ Ⓓ | 54 Ⓐ Ⓑ Ⓒ Ⓓ | |
| 25 Ⓐ Ⓑ Ⓒ Ⓓ | 55 Ⓐ Ⓑ Ⓒ Ⓓ | |
| 26 Ⓐ Ⓑ Ⓒ Ⓓ | 56 Ⓐ Ⓑ Ⓒ Ⓓ | |
| 27 Ⓐ Ⓑ Ⓒ Ⓓ | 57 Ⓐ Ⓑ Ⓒ Ⓓ | |
| 28 Ⓐ Ⓑ Ⓒ Ⓓ | 58 Ⓐ Ⓑ Ⓒ Ⓓ | |
| 29 Ⓐ Ⓑ Ⓒ Ⓓ | 59 Ⓐ Ⓑ Ⓒ Ⓓ | |
| 30 Ⓐ Ⓑ Ⓒ Ⓓ | 60 Ⓐ Ⓑ Ⓒ Ⓓ | |

# AP Environmental Science Practice Exam 1
## Section I: Multiple-Choice Questions

Time: 90 minutes

**Directions:** For the multiple-choice questions that follow, select the best answer and fill in the appropriate letter on the answer sheet.

**Questions 1–3 refer to the information below.**

For many years, subsistence farmers in Brazil, Peru, Colombia, Bolivia, Venezuela, Suriname, Guyana, and French Guiana have cut down trees to grow crops for their families and to sell in local markets. This changed during the 1970s to mid-2000s as more than ¾ of the clear-cutting in the Amazon was for cattle ranching. Cattle ranching takes approximately 20 times more land to get the same calories from meat as it does from crops.

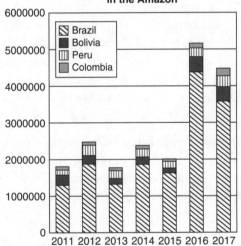

**Aggregate Annual Tree Cover Loss in the Amazon**

1. Based on the data in the graph, which country far exceeds the others in tree cover loss between 2011 and 2017?

   (A) Brazil
   (B) Bolivia
   (C) Colombia
   (D) Peru

2. Which is most likely the consequence of tree cover loss in the Amazon?

   (A) Lower levels of carbon dioxide
   (B) Decreased stream temperatures
   (C) Decreased need for pesticides
   (D) Soil erosion

3. Forest clearing began to decline in 2004 due to increased law enforcement, pressure from environmentalists, satellite monitoring, and protection of new areas. Changes in agricultural strategies and practices in order to increase food production including mechanization, genetically modifying organisms, fertilization, irrigation, and the use of pesticides can be attributed to what movement?

   (A) Agricultural Revolution
   (B) Green Revolution
   (C) Industrial Revolution
   (D) Cultural Revolution

4. Island biogeography is the theory and study of the species composition and species richness on islands. According to this theory, which island would have fewest number of species found on the island?

   (A) A large island far away from the mainland
   (B) A small island far away from the mainland
   (C) A small island close to the mainland
   (D) A large island close to the mainland

**Use the image below to answer questions 5–6.**

**Greenhouse Gas Forcings on Earth's Climate**

- ■ Water vapor
- ■ Clouds
- ▨ CO₂
- □ Other GHGs

5. As shown in the image above, water vapor and carbon dioxide are the two most abundant greenhouse gases on the planet. However, the greenhouse gas with the highest global warming potential (GWP) is which of the following?

(A) Methane
(B) Nitrous oxide
(C) Chlorofluorocarbons
(D) Water vapor

6. As more carbon dioxide is released into the atmosphere, a large part is also absorbed by the oceans. This increase in $CO_2$ causes a phenomenon known as ocean acidification. Which of the following is the greatest impact of ocean acidification?

(A) Corals are damaged due to the loss of calcium carbonate making it difficult for them to form shells.
(B) Ocean temperature drops causing salt to precipitate out and accumulate on the ocean floor.
(C) Marine mammals are forced to move farther north in search of food supplies.
(D) Beach erosion is accelerated due to stronger ocean currents.

7. The graph below shows many of the threats to wetlands worldwide. This loss has many impacts because of the ecosystem services that wetlands provide. Which of the following would be the best way to protect wetlands from further destruction?

**Wetland Converted to Other Uses**

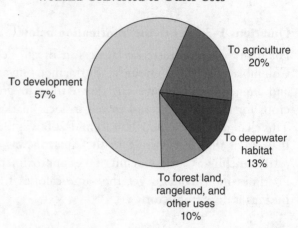

(A) Build dams to divert water from flowing downstream.
(B) Encourage commercial development to the area to bring in revenue and increase tourism.
(C) Strengthen legislation to regulate development and agriculture around wetlands areas.
(D) Regulate pesticide and fertilizer use on agriculture and rangeland areas.

8. The demographic transition describes population change over time. According to the four-stage demographic transition model, during what stage will the population be growing the fastest?

(A) Preindustrial
(B) Transitional
(C) Industrial
(D) Postindustrial

**9.** During what stage do births and deaths begin to fall but the population continues to increase due to population momentum?

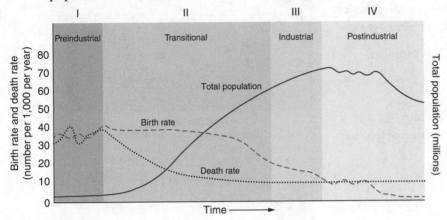

(A) Preindustrial
(B) Transitional
(C) Industrial
(D) Postindustrial

**10.** In which demographic stage seen in the graph above would the population growth be the highest?

(A) Preindustrial
(B) Transitional
(C) Industrial
(D) Postindustrial

**11.** A small lake in a deciduous forest has become covered in a thick bed of green algae. Large numbers of fish have died and the oxygen level in the water is extremely low. The diagram on the right shows an example of the lake over time.

What has most likely caused this problem?

(A) Ocean acidification
(B) An oil spill in the area
(C) Pesticide spraying on local crops
(D) Eutrophication caused by overuse of fertilizers on local crops

**Oligotrophic stage**
Deep and nutrient-poor system

Human pollution
($NO_3^-$, $PO_4^{3-}$, etc.)

**Mesotrophic stage**
Nutrient enrichment

Human pollution
($NO_3^-$, $PO_4^{3-}$, etc.)

**Eutrophic stage**
Nutrients saturated—shallow
algae and bacteria development

**Questions 12–14 refer to the information below.**

A local school district is looking to replace their current electricity source with a new, more reliable source that has less environmental consequences than the coal and oil they currently use. They hire an energy consultant to give them different options before going to the school board with their recommendation.

12. One option the energy consultant offers them is to use geothermal energy. The environmental consequences of this choice would be which of the following?

   (A) Hydrogen sulfide could possibly be released.

   (B) Excess carbon dioxide would be removed from the atmosphere.

   (C) Radioactive waste will be produced that must be stored for many years.

   (D) Fracking can cause groundwater contamination that will need to be remediated.

13. Another option the energy consultant brings to the school district is to use photovoltaic cells to generate active solar energy to produce power. Using the graph below, what does the data show would be the limitation of this source?

**Energy output of a photovoltaic solar system**

   (A) Active solar energy cannot be collected or stored for evening use without a battery.

   (B) Active solar energy may not generate enough energy during the winter months.

   (C) Methane is produced, which is a leading contributor to global climate change.

   (D) Excess solar energy production during summer months results in increased $CO_2$ emissions.

14. The final option given to the school district is to move to a cleaner renewable energy resource, hydroelectric power. Hydroelectric power is considered a cleaner energy source because it doesn't cause air pollution, but it does have some environmental problems. What would be an environmental solution to one of these problems?

   (A) Add a new dam with state-of-the-art technology to generate more kilowatts of electricity.

   (B) Make sure the dam is built on a river that leads to an estuary ecosystem.

   (C) Remove fish ladders that allow fish to migrate up and down the river.

   (D) Remove pollutants trapped behind the dam that can cause damage to wildlife.

**15.** Using the image below, explain what tectonic features you would find around the Pacific Plate and why these would be found here.

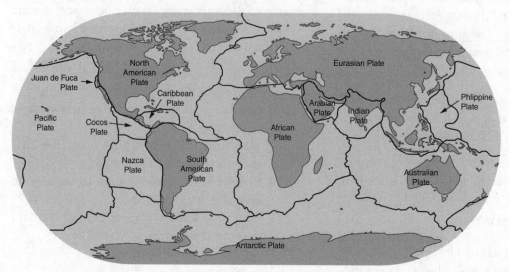

**Earth's tectonic plates**

(A) Divergent boundaries due to seafloor spreading
(B) Divergent boundaries due to excessive earthquakes and volcanoes
(C) Convergent boundaries, creating mountains, earthquakes, volcanoes, and island arcs
(D) Convergent boundaries, producing soil and sand due to erosion and sedimentation

**16.** In the Tropical Grasslands of Africa there is a relationship between a cheetah and a gazelle. Gazelles are herbivores that live in herds because there is really nowhere for the gazelle to hide. The cheetah can attack and try to outrun the gazelle. What type of relationship does this represent?

(A) Commensalism
(B) Mutualism
(C) Parasitism
(D) Predator-prey

**17.** Another example of this relationship is a lynx and hare. In 1865, the hare population in Canada was at an all-time high of 160,000. There was also a high of 80,000 lynx during that same year. Why would both organisms increase at the same time to reach such large populations?

(A) When the lynx was scarce, the hare numbers rose, which allowed for plenty of food for the lynx, who then increased in number due to so much food availability.
(B) When the lynx numbers were high, the hare numbers became even higher due to so much food availability.
(C) When the lynx numbers were at their lowest, the hare numbers were at their lowest due to increased environmental pressures.
(D) Lynx and hare numbers do not respond to one another because they are geographically isolated from each other.

**18.** The picture below is of a thermal inversion, when warm air traps the cooler air below. Why does this situation cause an atmospheric pollution problem?

(A) Sinking air pressure causes pollutants from high in the atmosphere to settle onto a city.

(B) Thermal inversions cause pollution to be trapped close to the ground, especially smog and particulates.

(C) The warm air trapped above the cooler air can lead to an increase in global climate change.

(D) When there is not a thermal inversion, the warm air is released into space causing global cooling and an increase in energy demand to cool populated areas.

**Questions 19–20 refer to the information below.**

In the 1960s and 1970s Texas horned toads and lizards were found all over Central and North Texas. However, in 1977 the Texas horned lizard was put on the threatened species list because of many reasons, one being the invasion of the invasive species, the fire ant. The fire ant pushed out the harvester ants (big red ant), which was the majority of the horned toad's/lizard's diet. In addition, farmers began to use pesticides to get rid of the fire ants, an action that also killed the red ants.

**19.** What is one solution that has helped bring the Texas horned toads and lizards back from endangerment?

(A) Texas Parks and Wildlife asked people to capture and breed these in their homes.

(B) A new invasive species was brought in to kill the fire ant.

(C) The Endangered Species Act was passed for protecting endangered and threatened animals and their habitat.

(D) Since the fire ant is a specialist species, Texas Parks and Wildlife just waited for the fire ant to die from lack of resources found in Texas.

**20.** In toxicology, many pesticides, like those used to control the fire ant, are tested according to their $LD_{50}$ levels. $LD_{50}$ levels are best described by which of the following?

(A) The level that kills 50 pests in 50 minutes

(B) The level that kills 50 pests out of 500

(C) The level that kills the pests but leaves 50 percent of the predators alive

(D) The level that kills 50 percent of the pest population of a particular species

**Use the figure below to answer questions 21–22.**

**21.** A scientist is trying to determine the best location for agriculture. After taking a sample of the soil and doing a texture analysis, the scientist plots the texture on the pyramid at point A. What are the proportions of sand, silt, and clay the scientist found for the soil at point A?

(A) 10 percent sand, 90 percent silt, 80 percent clay

(B) 10 percent sand, 10 percent silt, 80 percent clay

(C) 50 percent sand, 40 percent silt, 10 percent clay

(D) 0 percent sand, 90 percent silt, 10 percent clay

22. At which point would the scientist find the soil that is most porous and least permeable?

    (A) Point A
    (B) Point B
    (C) Point C
    (D) Point D

23. Which scenario best represents tragedy of the commons?

    (A) Farmers are allowing their cattle to graze on public land in the western United States, which results in overgrazing.
    (B) A tree farmer uses clear-cutting to bring in the highest profits on their own land.
    (C) A public municipality puts a tax on homes that use more than 10,000 liters of water per day.
    (D) Farmers in the Alps agree to keep cattle in barns in high altitude over the winter before allowing them to graze on the Alpine pastures in the summer.

24. Aquaculture has many benefits, both environmental and economical. What is one example of an economic benefit of aquaculture?

    (A) Aquaculture allows for competition and therefore lowers the number of fishing companies in the area.
    (B) Aquaculture uses large amounts of water and therefore brings revenue to the local economy.
    (C) Aquaculture promotes investment in large fishing boats.
    (D) Aquaculture requires small areas of water and little fuel.

**Use the image of Earth below to answer the following question.**

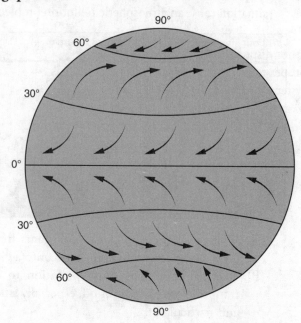

25. What is the cause of the global wind patterns seen in the image above?

    (A) The location of the land masses in relationship to the oceans
    (B) The amount of ice found on the planet, causing global climate change
    (C) The most intense solar radiation arrives at the equator and results in density differences and the Coriolis effect
    (D) Human-induced heat from energy production, causing global climate change

Use the following information to answer questions 26–27.

According to the Australian Department of Health, "Disease-causing germs can be spread from sewage if it is not disposed of properly or if people do not practice proper toilet hygiene (cleanliness). If a sewage disposal system is not properly maintained it will not be able to get rid of the sewage safely. For a sewage system to be properly maintained, all faulty (blocked, damaged, broken or worn-out) parts must be mended as soon as possible after they stop working correctly."

**26.** Which of the following properly names the order and processes of sewage treatment as seen in the image below?

**Sewage Treatment Plant**

| | PRIMARY | SECONDARY | TERTIARY |
|---|---|---|---|
| (A) | Physical removal of large objects with screens and grates | Bacteria break down organic matter | Ecological or chemical processes are used and the water is exposed to disinfectants |
| (B) | Bacteria break down organic matter | Physical removal of large objects with screens and grates | Ecological or chemical processes are used and the water is exposed to disinfectants |
| (C) | Bacteria break down organic matter | Ecological or chemical processes are used and the water is exposed to disinfectants | Physical removal of large objects with screens and grates |
| (D) | Ecological or chemical processes are used and the water is exposed to disinfectants | Physical removal of large objects with screens and grates | Bacteria break down organic matter |

**27.** A scientist is looking for ways to bring down the disease problems in a developing country. Which of the following human health issues would be linked to installing and properly maintaining sewage treatment plants?

(A) Zika
(B) Malaria
(C) Tuberculosis
(D) Dysentery

**Use the graph below to answer questions 28–30.**

**Agerage Global Temperature by Year**

**28.** According to the graph above, the temperature has been going up from 1900 to 2000. What could we attribute this increase in temperature to?

(A) Increase in ocean levels
(B) Increased levels of carbon dioxide
(C) Increased numbers of specialists living in fragile ecosystems
(D) Difference in seasonal amounts of plants that photosynthesize

**29.** What is the change in temperature from 1900 to 2000?

(A) 1.5 degrees
(B) 3 degrees
(C) 57 degrees
(D) 100 degrees

**30.** This increase in average global temperatures is warming both the land and the oceans. Which of the following would be an environmental impact of the warming of the oceans?

(A) Generalist species would risk becoming endangered.
(B) R-strategists would risk becoming endangered.
(C) Sea levels would fall, leading to specialists becoming endangered.
(D) Coral bleaching would occur because of loss of algae in the corals.

**31.** The image below is of the nitrogen cycle. Which of the following steps takes the most amount of nitrogen and adds it to the atmosphere?

(A) Plants
(B) Lightning
(C) Denitrifying bacteria
(D) Decomposers

**32.** What might be a result of a population over-shooting its carrying capacity?

(A) Famine and disease
(B) Decreased competition
(C) Increase in available resources
(D) Nitrogen levels reaching record high levels

**33.** As energy transfers from one trophic level to the next, energy is lost. If 1,000 kilocalories of energy are available at the producer level, how much would be available at the herbivore level?

(A) 1 kilocalorie
(B) 100 kilocalories
(C) 10,000 kilocalories
(D) 1,000 kilocalories

**34.** A population is growing at a rate of 3 percent per year. The population will double in approximately how many years?

(A) 3 years
(B) 210 years
(C) 23 years
(D) 300 years

**35.** A fire has burned its way through an oak-hickory deciduous forest. Which of the following claims can be supported in the graph?

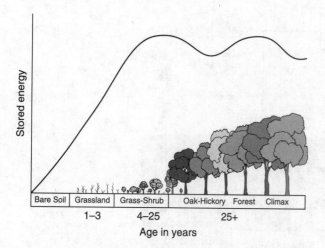

(A) The area will not begin to grow back for at least 25 years.
(B) The first plants move in in the first few years.
(C) The climax community takes a minimum of 100 years to establish.
(D) Soil must first be established from bare rock.

**36.** Which of the following would help reduce the problem of overfishing?

(A) Encourage the use of purse seines and long-line fishing to fish industry workers.
(B) Encourage bottom trawling near coral reefs.
(C) Pass legislation for catch limits per boat.
(D) Pass legislation to allow fishing in areas that are currently prohibited.

**37.** The fish industry workers off the coast of Chile have noticed that they are not catching near as many fish as in previous fishing seasons. The reason for this would most likely be which of the following?

(A) The melting of the sea ice has killed the fish due to warmer ocean temperatures.
(B) The fish have moved into the local rivers and streams to spawn.
(C) The fish industry workers have used new methods of fishing that are not sustainable.
(D) It is an El Niño event and the fish have moved to colder waters.

**38.** What causes the rain to fall on one side of the mountain and not on the other?

(A) As the air rises and cools it loses its moisture before it reaches the other side of the mountains.
(B) Dry air on the sea side rises and sinks on the other side of the mountain.
(C) The vegetation on the sea side of the mountain attracts all the moisture preventing it from reaching the other side.
(D) Cool air rises and sinks on the leeward side.

**Use the figure below to answer questions 39–40.**

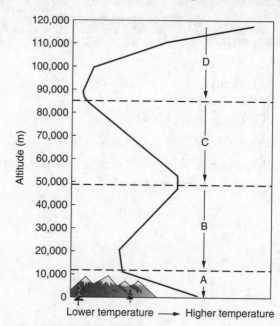

**39.** Which letter indicates where the protective ozone layer is found?

(A) A
(B) B
(C) C
(D) D

**40.** What gas would make up the majority of layer A?

(A) Oxygen
(B) Carbon dioxide
(C) Nitrogen
(D) Phosphorus

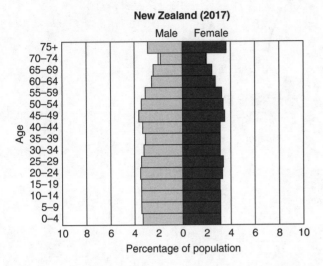

**New Zealand (2017)**

**41.** New Zealand's age-structure diagram is pictured above. What type of growth does the diagram demonstrate?

(A) Rapid growth
(B) Slow growth
(C) Stable growth
(D) Declining growth

**42.** Why would phytoplankton usually be found only in the first few meters of water?

(A) Red and blue light can only penetrate this deep.
(B) Zooplankton are their food source and this is where they are found.
(C) It becomes too salty below this level for phytoplankton to survive.
(D) Phytoplankton are unable to swim below 30 meters.

**43.** Which of the following would be considered a cultural ecosystem service of a river?

(A) Hiking, birdwatching, and photography
(B) Food sources
(C) Timber harvesting of hardwoods
(D) Water purification

**44.** The Montreal Protocol is a global agreement to phase out which of the following chemicals with the goal of reducing stratospheric ozone depletion?

(A) Carbon dioxide
(B) Organophosphates
(C) Volatile organic compounds
(D) Chlorofluorocarbons

**45.** A decrease in stratospheric ozone has led to which of the following?

(A) Melting of the polar ice caps
(B) Increased cases of lung cancer and COPD
(C) Skin cancer and cataracts
(D) An increase in atmospheric circulation

**Use the figure below to answer questions 46–47.**

**Food Webs**

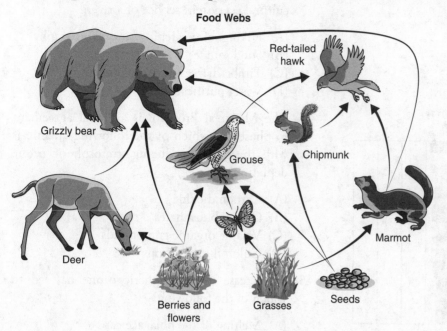

46. What organisms are missing in the above food web?

(A) Herbivores
(B) Decomposers
(C) Carnivores
(D) Producers

47. What would happen if you removed the marmot from the food web above?

(A) Red-tailed hawks would increase in number.
(B) The habitat for butterflies would be lost.
(C) The deer population would decline.
(D) The grasses would increase in number.

**Use the graph below to answer questions 48–49.**

48. Based on the graph above, global climate change has caused a rise in carbon dioxide levels to the highest in history. Which of the following would be an impact on biodiversity because of this anthropogenic event?

(A) Increased temperature will cause sea levels to rise.
(B) Decreased temperature will harm fragile generalist species.
(C) Ocean organisms would thrive because they now will live past the dangerous photic zone.
(D) The dangerous UV-B rays will be blocked by the higher levels of $CO_2$.

49. Which of the following human activities has caused the increase in $CO_2$ that is seen in the graph?

   (A) Overuse of hairsprays and aerosols
   (B) Production of Styrofoam
   (C) Use of Freon and other coolants
   (D) Burning of fossil fuels

50. The Clean Air Act regulations in the United States require coal-burning power plants to remove sulfur from their emissions. This legislation has greatly reduced what problem in the United States?

   (A) Global climate change
   (B) Acid rain
   (C) Ozone depletion
   (D) Radon poisoning in homes

**Use the diagram below to answer questions 51–52.**

**Nuclear Power Plant**

51. The presence of control rods, as seen in the diagram above, is required to regulate the fission reaction of which of the following?

   (A) Carbon-14
   (B) Uranium-235
   (C) Deuterium
   (D) Boron

52. What is an environmental problem with the generation of the energy above?

   (A) Air pollution
   (B) Noise pollution
   (C) Indoor air pollution
   (D) Thermal pollution

53. Photochemical smog is a problem in cities. The graph below shows the chemicals and when they peak during different times of the day. Nitrogen oxides peak early in the morning followed by an increase of ozone in the afternoon. This ozone peak is due to a reaction between oxygen and what other external input?

   (A) Sunlight
   (B) Carbon dioxide
   (C) Methane
   (D) Organophosphates

54. Indoor air pollutants are a problem in both developed and developing countries. According to the graph below, what is the biggest cause of death from indoor air pollutants?

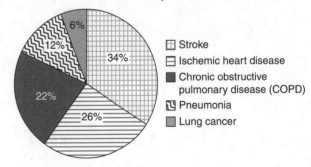

   (A) Ischemic heart disease
   (B) Lung cancer
   (C) Stroke
   (D) Pneumonia

**55.** A scientist is studying an area that has had an increase of acidification to its local soil and water. The scientist sets up an experiment to see what is causing the acidification of the soil. What would the scientist's experiment most likely point to as the cause of this acidification?

(A) A farmer spraying pesticides on corn crops
(B) Increased air traffic from a change in flight patterns
(C) A recently built hydroelectric dam above the area of concern
(D) A coal-burning power plant that is upwind from the area

**56.** Cockroaches can live in many different environments, can eat many different things, and can reproduce quickly. Which of the following best identifies a cockroach?

(A) An herbivore
(B) A carnivore
(C) A generalist
(D) A specialist

**57.** On the data table below, which species would most likely be considered an r-strategist?

| SPECIES | (A) MUSSEL | (B) RABBIT | (C) OPOSSUM | (D) BEAR |
|---|---|---|---|---|
| Number of off-spring produced per year | 1,000,000 | 14 | 2 | 2 |

**58.** A farmer uses a method of irrigation where there are furrows cut between crops, and these trenches are filled with water. Which of the following would be a disadvantage of this method?

(A) Wildlife would be attracted to the crops.
(B) One-third of the water is lost to evaporation and runoff.
(C) It is extremely expensive.
(D) Eutrophication of local groundwater would be a result.

**59.** Which of the following would result as a country becomes more developed?

**Annual Electric Power Consumption per Capita (kWh)**

Legend:
- Developed countries
- Southern Asia
- Sub-Saharan Africa

(A) Annual electrical power is inversely proportional to the GDP of the country.

(B) Annual electrical power consumption remains the same.

(C) Annual electrical power consumption decreases.

(D) Annual electrical power consumption increases.

**60.** Which of the following fossil fuels burns the cleanest?

(A) Coal
(B) Oil
(C) Nuclear
(D) Natural gas

**61.** Which of the following best describes an environmental cost of hydrologic fracturing?

(A) Release of volatile organic compounds
(B) Long-term storage of radioactive waste
(C) Energy produced is expensive
(D) Disrupts migratory birds

**62.** According to the USGS website: "Zebra Mussels are a fingernail-sized mollusk that is native to fresh waters in Eurasia. Their name comes from the dark, zig-zagged stripes on each shell. Zebra Mussels probably arrived in the Great Lakes in the 1980s via ballast water that was discharged by large ships from Europe. They have spread rapidly throughout the Great Lakes region and into the large rivers of the eastern Mississippi drainage. They have also been found in Texas, Colorado, Utah, Nevada, and California being spread by boats traveling from lake to lake with Zebra Mussels attached to the sides and bottom. Zebra Mussels negatively impact ecosystems in many ways. They filter out algae that native species need for food and they attach to—and incapacitate—native mussels. Power plants must also spend millions of dollars removing zebra mussels from clogged water intakes."

Which of the following would best stop the spread of this environmental problem?

(A) Add pesticides that kill all mussel species to lakes with zebra mussels.

(B) Find an invasive species that preys on Zebra Mussels and introduce that species to the lakes that contain zebra mussels.

(C) Inspect boats for Zebra Mussels and remove before moving the boat to a new lake.

(D) Drain rivers and physically remove the Zebra Mussels from the river beds.

**63.** How does ocean acidification damage coral reefs?

(A) Heat melts the tiny coral animals.

(B) Loss of calcium carbonate doesn't allow shell formation.

(C) Sea levels rise disrupting photosynthesis of the zooxanthellae.

(D) Minerals precipitate out and cover the coral shells.

**64.** Climate change is increasing the greatest in the polar regions due to a positive feedback loop. The graph below shows the sea ice extent over the past 35 years.

Which of the following best describes the phenomenon you see in the graph above?

(A) We have lost about 1 million square miles of sea ice in March and September in 35 years.

(B) We have gained about 1 million square miles of sea ice in March and September in 35 years.

(C) Sea ice extent has remained fairly constant over the past 35 years.

(D) Sea ice extent has dropped by over 4 million square miles in 35 years.

**65.** Which of the following would be the primary reason for ocean warming?

(A) Ocean acidification

(B) Thermal pollution from nuclear power plants

(C) Global temperature increase due to climate change

(D) Shifts in global wind patterns from El Niño

**66.** Which of the following is true of how an ecosystem can recover after a large fire breaks out in the area?

(A) The area will remain plant and animal free for many years.

(B) K-selected species will recover before r-selected species.

(C) Salinization of the soil will happen disrupting plant recovery.

(D) If the area had more species diversity it will generally recover more quickly than if it had lower species diversity.

**Use the graph below to answer questions 67–68.**

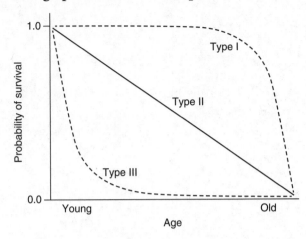

67. Kangaroos usually have one offspring per year. The joey will remain in the mother's pouch for nine months and will nurse until 17 months of age. Using this information and the graph above, which statement best characterizes a kangaroo?

    (A) Kangaroos are r-strategists and demonstrate a Type I survivorship curve.
    (B) Kangaroos are k-strategists and demonstrate a Type I survivorship curve.
    (C) Kangaroos are r-strategists and demonstrate a Type III survivorship curve.
    (D) Kangaroos are k-strategists and demonstrate a Type III survivorship curve.

68. Using the graph above, what can we expect from a species that demonstrates a Type III survivorship curve?

    (A) The species is a k-strategist that has many offspring that live a long time.
    (B) The species is a k-strategist that has many offspring that die young.
    (C) The species is a r-strategist that has many offspring that survive a short time.
    (D) The species is a r-strategist that has many offspring that survive a long time.

69. When rivers are dammed for recreation and hydroelectric power, there can be environmental problems that result. Which of the following would be a problem of this type of power?

    (A) The area downstream can flood and be disastrous to cities below the dam.
    (B) The area downstream can have huge amounts of soil and sediment buildup below the dam.
    (C) Less water may flow to the area downstream causing a decrease in nutrients and sediment below the dam.
    (D) The lake created above the dam may become a habitat for water fowl.

70. A farmer sprays an organophosphate pesticide on their crops. The first year the farmer notices a 90 percent reduction in the crops being eaten by the pest. In year two the farmer sprays again but this time notices a 50 percent reduction in the crops being eaten by the pest. In year three when the farmer sprays the crops with the same pesticide the farmer notices only a 10 percent reduction in the crops being eaten by the pest. What would be a solution the farmer could implement to stop this pesticide resistance?

    (A) Use genetically engineered crops that are resistant to the pest.
    (B) Continue adding the organophosphate because the resistance will stop in future years.
    (C) Move the crops to a neighboring field and use the organophosphate on the crop there.
    (D) Plant more of the same crops to get larger crop yields.

**71.** The graph below is from the United States Department of Agriculture website.

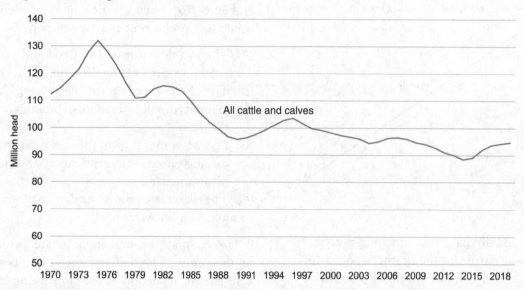

What could be a reason for the trend in the graph from 1996 to 2015?

(A) As demand for beef increased, ranchers bred more cattle.

(B) As drought conditions increased, ranchers slaughtered their cattle.

(C) The supply of domestic pork decreased.

(D) Ranchers began to use concentrated animal feeding operations (CAFOs) rather than free-range cattle farming.

**72.** Many resources are extracted from the ground by both surface and subsurface mining. These methods can have a large environmental impact such as groundwater contamination, habitat destruction, and methane production. Which of the following would be the best environmental solution to this problem?

(A) Rely more on subsurface mining than on surface mining.

(B) Switch to other methods such as hydraulic fracturing.

(C) Use the slag and tailings produced from the mining in manufacturing and building projects.

(D) Switch to a greater reliance on renewable energy resources.

**73.** Which of the following would be an environmental solution to the problem of urbanization?

(A) Provide private automobiles to allow easier commuting for citizens.

(B) Switch to fossil fuels to meet the greater energy demands from urbanization.

(C) Build homes that take up more land space rather than high-rise buildings.

(D) Use paving stones with grass in between for parking spaces rather than asphalt and concrete to allow water infiltration into aquifers.

**74.** Which of the following statements about renewable/nonrenewable energy resources is true?

(A) A nonrenewable example would be solar and a renewable would be coal.

(B) Nonrenewable energy can be replaced in a relatively short period of time.

(C) Nonrenewable energy has a fixed amount that can't be easily replenished.

(D) Nuclear energy is a renewable energy source.

**75.** Which of the following statements about geothermal energy is correct?

(A) Steam is generated from water that is heated from Earth's interior and is used to drive an electric generator.

(B) Geothermal energy is inexpensive.

(C) Geothermal energy is extremely inefficient.

(D) Geothermal energy is a nonrenewable resource.

**Use the graph below to answer questions 76–77.**

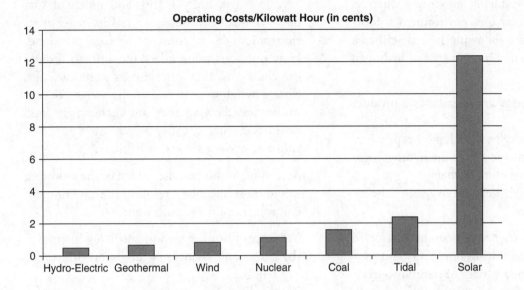

**Operating Costs/Kilowatt Hour (in cents)**

76. According to the graph above, solar energy has a much higher operating cost than any of the others. What is the percent increase in price of operating solar versus coal?

   (A) 5 times
   (B) 12 times
   (C) 100 percent
   (D) 550 percent

77. The costs above are associated with an active solar energy system. Which of the following would be an example of a passive solar energy system?

   (A) Photovoltaic cells that heat a liquid through mechanical and electric equipment
   (B) Solar energy farms that can be set up in desert ecosystems
   (C) Large windows to let heat from the sun into a building or home
   (D) Battery systems to collect solar power and store for evening use

78. Hydrogen fuel cells have many environmental benefits such as producing no carbon dioxide. However, they still have an environmental footprint. Which of the following best describes a negative environmental consequence of hydrogen fuel cells?

    (A) Water and energy are released as a product of these.
    (B) Hydrogen fuel cell technology is expensive.
    (C) Energy is needed to create the hydrogen gas which can cause climate change.
    (D) Combining hydrogen and oxygen in the air can form water.

79. A student enters a science fair competition with a project on demonstrating how $CO_2$ and particulates come from a variety of natural sources. Which of the following would the student's experiment most likely conclude?

    (A) $CO_2$ comes from decomposition and respiration and particulates from pollen and dust.
    (B) Volcanic eruptions do not produce $CO_2$ or particulates.
    (C) $CO_2$ is produced from nuclear energy power plants.
    (D) Particulate matter is completely anthropogenic.

80. According to the Australian Academy of Science: "We live in a noisy world, and much of that noise is made by humans. Traffic, machinery, electronics—it's a constant barrage of sound. How does our noise affect the animals around us? Unlike us, they can't put in some earplugs, close a window or turn off the stereo. Recent studies are showing that our increasingly loud world is having negative effects on a range of animals, across a variety of habitats."

According to this passage, which of the following would most likely be a result of the environmental problem of noise pollution?

    (A) Loss of hearing to humans living in cities
    (B) Stress and changes to migratory routes for wildlife
    (C) Acidification on soil from the machinery that causes noise pollution
    (D) Groundwater pollution from machinery and electronic production

**STOP. End of Section I.**

# AP Environmental Science Practice Exam 1
## Section II: Free-Response Questions

Time: 70 minutes

**Directions:** Answer all three questions below. Where an explanation or discussion is needed, support your answers with relevant information and/or specific examples. If a calculation is required, clearly show all your work and how you arrived at your answer.

1. **Design an investigation.**

    Park rangers throughout the state of Texas are investigating the impact of visitors on the water quality in state parks. Rangers from a local state park near San Antonio monitored water conditions in a slow moving river at the same site daily throughout the month of August. They collected samples every two hours beginning at 8 a.m. and ending at 6 p.m. The state park opens for visitors at 10 a.m. and closes at 6 p.m. The rangers take water samples in the park near a bathroom that has a septic tank. Park rangers are not sure of the condition of the tank and are investigating a possible leak. In addition, there is a large golf course located adjacent to the park, and the landscaping crew fertilizes and waters the golf course at 9 a.m. The park rangers collected the following data:

    | TIME OF DAY | DISSOLVED OXYGEN | CARBON DIOXIDE | TEMPERATURE OF WATER | pH | NITRATES | PHOSPHATES |
    |---|---|---|---|---|---|---|
    | 8 a.m. | 7.8% | 13 ppm | 23°C | 7 | 2.0 ppm | 0.1 ppm |
    | 10 a.m. | 7.8% | 13 ppm | 24°C | 7 | 2.0 ppm | 0.1 ppm |
    | 12 p.m. | 7.6% | 14 ppm | 25°C | 7 | 3.0 ppm | 0.2 ppm |
    | 2 p.m. | 7.4% | 15 ppm | 26°C | 7 | 3.2 ppm | 0.2 ppm |
    | 4 p.m. | 7.1% | 16 ppm | 27°C | 7 | 3.2 ppm | 0.3 ppm |
    | 6 p.m. | 7.1% | 17 ppm | 27°C | 7 | 3.2 ppm | 0.3 ppm |
    | 8 p.m. | 7.4% | 15 ppm | 25°C | 7 | 3.1 ppm | 0.2 ppm |

    (a) Based on the data in the table, **identify** the control group in this experiment.
    (b) **Identify** the scientific question for the investigation.
    (c) **Explain** how the results of this experiment would likely have been altered if the park rangers took water samples on a day when the park was closed for visitors.

    Park rangers determined that the level of nitrates and phosphates increases throughout the day.
    (d) **Identify** one possible reason for an increased level of nitrates and phosphates in the stream.
    (e) **Describe** one step that could be taken to reduce the levels of nitrates and phosphates in the river.
    (f) **Explain** one environmental consequence of high levels of nitrates and phosphates in a body of water.
    (g) Based on the data in the graph, **describe** the relationship between dissolved oxygen and temperature.

The park rangers are concerned about the number of visitors they see in the park because they know human activities might result in a loss of biodiversity in the park.

(h) **Identify** one specific activity, other than bathroom use, that might result in a loss of biodiversity in the park because of human interference.

(i) For the activity you identified in (h), **describe** how this activity could lower biodiversity.

(j) **Propose** a realistic solution to help reduce the loss of biodiversity you identified in (h).

2. **Analyze an environmental problem and propose a solution.**

According to the Everglades Cooperative Invasive Species Management Area, Tegu lizards are from South America and have escaped or been released into southern Florida. The three species that have been found in Florida are the Argentine black-and-white tegu, which can grow up to 4 feet long; the gold tegu, which can grow up to 3 feet long; and the red tegu, which can reach 4.5 feet long. The tegus are generalists, which eat many of the native wildlife, including small animals like lizards and rodents. They also dig in alligator and turtle nests and eat the eggs. They are becoming a threat to crocodiles, sea turtles, ground-nesting birds, and small mammals.

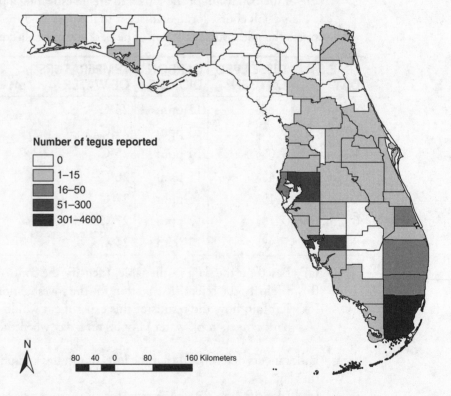

(a) Many invasive species are r-selected. **Identify** one characteristic of an r-selected species.

(b) **Explain** how invasive species are able to outcompete native species.

Florida scientists have recorded tegus eating eggs from an alligator nest—a behavior that could be a problem for the threatened American crocodile population that lives nearby.

(c) **Describe** one important characteristic of an endangered species that could cause it to be slow to recover.

Economic incentives have often helped solve environmental problems.

(d) **Identify** one example of an economic incentive that the government of Florida could offer to stop tegu lizards before they become a larger problem.

(e) **Explain** how the incentive identified in (d) could work to control the tegu population.

(f) **Describe** one impact the introduction of tegus could have on the ecosystem services provided by the Florida Everglades.

(g) **Propose** a realistic solution, other than the use of economic incentives, to help reduce the spread of the tegus from their current distribution seen on the map above.

(h) **Justify** the solution proposed in part (g) by providing an additional advantage.

(i) Based on the information given in the map above, **identify** where you expect the greatest number of tegus to be found in the next 10 years.

The following is an example of a simple food chain in the Florida Everglades:

$$\text{Plants} \rightarrow \text{Turtles} \rightarrow \text{Alligator}$$

(j) **Describe** what the arrows in the food chain above represent.

3. **Analyze an environmental problem and propose a solution using calculations.**

The graph below from the Our World in Data annual report shows the historical estimates of the world population and the UN projections until 2100.

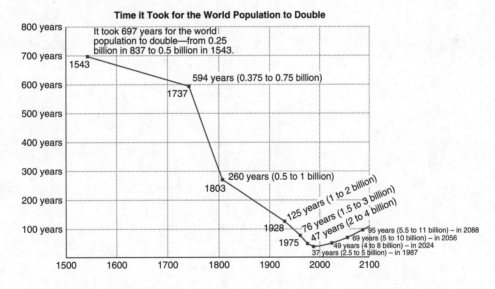

(a) **Calculate** the population growth rate between 1543 and 1803. **Show** your work.

(b) **Describe** the difference between a density-independent and a density-dependent factor.

(c) **Identify** one density-independent factor.

(d) **Identify** one action a government could do that would affect the growth or decline of a population.

(e) **Describe** an environmental problem associated with an increased human population.

An increased human population can have negative impacts on biodiversity.

(f) **Calculate** how much lithium was needed to produce the average electric cars that are currently registered in the United States. **Show** your work.

In an effort to lower the consumption of oil and gas, hybrid and electric cars have been produced. A plug-in hybrid uses about 12 kg of lithium, a standard electric car 22 kg, and a third popular model uses over 50 kg of lithium per car. There are currently 2,442,270 electric vehicles registered in the United States.

Assume the average electric car uses 25 kg of lithium per vehicle.
(g) **Calculate** how many gallons of water are needed to produce the average electric cars that are currently registered in the United States. **Show** your work.

Each ton (approximately 907 kg) of refined lithium uses up 500,000 gallons of water.

## STOP. End of Section II.

# Answers and Explanations for the Multiple-Choice Questions

1. **A**—Brazil makes up the majority of each of the bars in each year in the graph.

2. **D**—When deforestation occurs, the trees' roots no longer hold the soil in place and erosion becomes a huge problem.

3. **B**—The Green Revolution has allowed us to feed more people and has provided larger profits, tastier and more nutritious food, and less use of pesticides and water, but there are some consequences to these practices.

4. **B**—Island biogeography is the study of the species and distribution that would occur on islands. The theory states that islands closer to the mainland (where the animals/plants have moved from) and/or larger islands will have more species than islands farther away or smaller. The size of the island in theory matters because larger islands can support more and different species while smaller ones would be more limited.

5. **C**—

| GAS | GWP | ATMOSPHERIC LIFETIME |
|---|---|---|
| Carbon dioxide | 1 | 50–200 years |
| Methane | 21 | 12 years |
| Nitrous oxide | 310 | 120 years |
| Chlorofluorocarbons | 12,000–16,000 | 20–100 years |

6. **A**—As $CO_2$ enters the ocean it causes the ocean to become more acidic (lower pH). This acidity doesn't allow animals like clams and mussels to make protective shells, and can impact coral since they also make protective shells.

7. **C**—If laws regulating development and agriculture in wetland areas were strengthened, then wetlands would be protected and would recover.

8. **B**—Transitional countries are those where birth rates stay high but death rates begin to drop due to increases in health, food availability, and medicine. Infants begin to survive into childhood but because there are still so many births the country's population begins to explode. In addition, because education and birth control for women is limited, the TFR will remain high and the population will grow exponentially. The least developed countries today are in the transitional stage of the demographic transition.

9. **C**—Industrial, or stage 3, countries have birth rates that begin to drop due to access to reliable birth control, family planning, and women getting educations and jobs. This applies to most developing countries today. The population begins to slow, but not as quickly as you would think due to the concept of population momentum.

10. **B**—Transitional countries are those where birth rates stay high but death rates begin to drop due to increases in health, food availability, and medicine. Infants begin to survive into childhood but because there are still so many births the country's population begins to explode. In addition, because education and birth control for women is limited, the TFR will remain high and the population will grow exponentially. The least developed countries today are in the transitional stage of the demographic transition.

11. **D**—*Eutrophication* is the term used to describe a body of water that has many nutrients (fertilizers like nitrogen and phosphorus) that have run off from the land. These nutrients have "fertilized" the algae that live in the water. This can cause the water to become so thick and green with algae that no light can penetrate through the water.

12. **A**—Geothermal energy uses heat to create steam to turn a turbine that creates electrical energy with a generator. The cons are that it is expensive, can release hydrogen sulfide, requires a lot of water, and isn't readily available everywhere in the world.

13. **B**—The graph is showing that the solar energy output is much less in the winter months.

14. **D**—Hydroelectric power cons are when you build a dam you change the river ecosystem.

You flood an area above the dam, which was once a land habitat. If water is taken from the reservoir for irrigation or other purposes, you reduce the flow of water and the amount of nutrients available downstream. In some cases, the flow is so reduced that the water never reaches the sea. This can damage habitats and cause loss of biodiversity.

15. **C**—The Ring of Fire is an area around the Pacific Plate where a "ring" of volcanoes and earthquakes is found because of convergent plate boundaries.

16. **D**—In predator-prey relationships, a predator, such as a cheetah, eats its prey, such as a gazelle. The cheetah and gazelle are in a predator-prey relationship.

17. **A**—With many prey, there can be a lot of predators because of the ample prey availability.

18. **B**—A thermal inversion is a weather condition when warm, less dense air moves over dense, cold air over a city. Because of the thermal weather condition and the dense air, pollution, particularly smog and particulates, gets trapped near the ground and can't "escape" to space.

19. **C**—The Endangered Species Act is a law for the conservation of threatened and endangered plants and animals and the habitats where they are found.

20. **D**—Lethal Dose 50% is a term used in toxicology to indicate the amount of a toxin that kills 50 percent of the organism that is being tested. This can be any animal but usually refers to test rats and mice in a laboratory.

21. **B**—To do this, you start with the sand and find the percentage along the bottom of the triangle, in this case 10 percent, and follow the line that goes up and to the left for sand. Then, you move to the right side of the triangle and find the line for silt, in this case also 10 percent. Follow this line down and to the left until it hits the line you had drawn for sand. They should cross. Then, where they cross, if you draw a straight line to the left, where you find clay, you should be at the 80 percent line, which is your percentage of clay.

22. **A**—Porosity is having small spaces between the particles. The finer the particle size, the more porosity. This might seem backwards but clay has tiny holes and very fine particle sizes so clay has the highest porosity. Permeability is the ability of a material to allow liquid to flow through it. Clay has the lowest permeability, since water can't flow easily through it.

23. **A**—This is the concept where individuals tend to overexploit shared resources until the resource becomes unavailable to all. So, if farmers are overgrazing on public lands, it is a tragedy of the commons.

24. **D**—Aquaculture is a method of farm raising fish, shellfish, aquatic plants, and so on. A farmer can build large ponds and stock these ponds with large numbers of animals or plants, or use a natural river, lake, or ocean to do this with nets and holding pens. The benefits of these are: no depletion of our natural supplies of these organisms, feeding a large number of people, less use of water, increased profits, and the use of very little fuel.

25. **C**—The sun's radiation hits Earth with different intensities. It hits the equator most directly since it is nearly directly overhead most of the year.

26. **A**—The first step is known as primary treatment. In this step, the sewage is filtered with grates and screens for large items that are not liquid. In secondary treatment, we take the bacteria that is found in the sewage and give it lots of air so it can begin to consume the waste and break it down into carbon dioxide and inorganic sludge. In the last stage, known as tertiary treatment, chemicals like chlorine, ozone gas, or UV light kill any bacteria. Then the water is released to a river or lake.

27. **D**—Dysentery is an infection of the intestines resulting in severe diarrhea with blood and mucus in the feces. This comes from untreated sewage in streams and rivers that become drinking water or contaminates food.

28. **B**—Increases in carbon dioxide from burning fossil fuels have led to more heat being trapped and increased temperatures.

29. **A**—From 57 degrees to 58.5 degrees is a difference of 1.5 degrees.

30. **D**—Corals need zooxanthellae, an algae that lives in the tissues of coral and captures sunlight and converts it into energy for the coral animals. When the temperature of the ocean is too warm, the zooxanthellae come under stress and can die or leave their coral host, causing the coral to die and turn white, a process known as coral bleaching.

31. **C**—

| **D**—Denitrification | **N**— Nitrogen gas | Bacteria convert nitrogen in the soil back to an atmospheric form |
|---|---|---|
|  |  |  |

32. **A**—When there are more animals in an area than an area can support, the animals overconsume the plants and overcrowd one another. This can lead to disease and famine.

33. **B**—The 10 percent rule is the idea that as usable energy moves up the pyramid much of it is "lost" to the laws of thermodynamics. So if there were 1,000 kcal available at the producer level, there will be 100 available at the herbivore level.

34. **C**—70/3 = 23 years

35. **B**—In years 1–3 the grasses begin to move back in.

36. **C**—Laws that say how many fish or how big a fish can be when caught would help lessen overfishing problems.

37. **D**—During an El Niño–Southern Oscillation (ENSO), upwellings from the sea bed occur in normal years, bringing nutrients up for the plankton to feed on, and the plankton is food for the marine life up the food chain. In an El Niño year, that upwelling does not occur so the quantity of plankton is reduced, and in turn, so are the fish stocks.

38. **A**—The ocean provides a lot of moisture to the area. As the moist air rises, it cools and a lot of rain falls on the windward side of the mountain. However, because the air loses its moisture on the windward side of the mountains, it is dry on the other side.

39. **B**—The stratosphere is where the protective ozone layer is found.

40. **C**—Seventy-eight percent of the troposphere is made up of nitrogen.

41. **C**—The pyramid is stable.

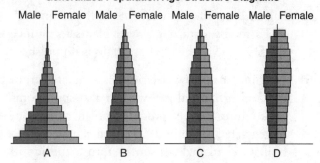

**Generalized Population Age-Structure Diagrams**

42. **A**—The primary productivity in water is dependent on how clear the water is and how deep the red and blue light can penetrate.

43. **A**—Cultural ecosystem services are not "things" we tangibly benefit from but rather interactions with nature, such as taking a walk and enjoying what you see or art that comes from looking at nature, etc.

44. **D**—The Montreal Protocol is an international treaty designed to protect the ozone layer by phasing out the substances, such as CFCs, that are responsible for ozone depletion.

45. **C**—Stratospheric ozone depletion allows more UV light to get through the stratosphere and to the surface of Earth. UV light is dangerous because it damages the DNA in skin cells, and leads to skin cancer, eye damage such as cataracts, premature aging, and can suppress the immune system.

46. **B**—Decomposers are not pictured in the food web but are a vital component of food webs.

47. **D**—Since marmots are shown to eat grasses, if you remove the marmot, the grasses would increase since you are removing the animal that eats them.

48. **A**—Carbon dioxide is a greenhouse gas that traps heat close to Earth, increasing temperatures on Earth. As Earth gets warmer, thermal expansion of the oceans occurs and land-based ice melts and runs off into the ocean. All of this contributes to sea levels rising.

49. **D**—When we burn fossil fuels, we emit carbon dioxide. As carbon dioxide levels in the atmosphere increase, so do temperatures on Earth.

50. **B**—Coal-burning power plants release nitrogen oxides ($NO_x$) and sulfur oxides ($SO_2$) into the atmosphere. When these chemicals go into the atmosphere and mix with the rain, snow, fog, hail or dust, they can become acid rain and fall to Earth. By requiring power plants to remove the $SO_2$, the problem of acid rain is diminished.

51. **B**—Similar to how electricity is generated from coal, oil or natural gas, we can also split atoms of uranium-235, a process known as fission, to generate a lot of heat. The heat can be used to boil water to make steam to turn a turbine to generate electrical energy.

52. **D**—Thermal pollution is often from a nuclear power plant where large amounts of heated water are dumped into a body of water.

53. **A**—Photochemical smog is formed when volatile organic hydrocarbons and nitrogen oxides, along with heat and sunlight, mix and pollution occurs.

54. **C**—According to the graph, 34 percent of deaths from indoor air pollutants are caused by stroke, the highest percentage of all categories.

55. **D**—Coal burning power plants, vehicles, manufacturing, and even volcanoes release nitrogen oxides ($NO_x$) and sulfur oxides ($SO_2$) into the atmosphere. When these chemicals go into the atmosphere and mix with the rain, snow, fog, hail or dust, they can form acid rain and fall to Earth.

56. **C**—Generalists can live in many different places and eat many different things. Generalists are less likely to be impacted by an environmental event.

57. **A**—Since the mussel has 1,000,000 offspring it is most likely an r-strategist.

58. **B**—Furrow irrigation is where trenches are dug between rows of crops and that area is flooded with water. This allows the farmer to flow water down these trenches and the water is absorbed by the roots of the plants. The advantages and disadvantages are similar to flood irrigation with about 35 percent being lost to evaporation.

59. **D**—The graph shows that as countries develop their annual consumption of electrical power increases.

60. **D**—Natural gas is the fossil fuel that burns the cleanest and can be used for energy. It is made up mostly of methane but contains other things like carbon dioxide, nitrogen, etc.

61. **A**—Fracking is an extraction method in which liquid is forced at very high pressures down into the rock to cause the oil or gas to be released. This can lead to groundwater contamination because the water that is used to release the oil or natural gas can contain contaminates that then run off into waterways. In addition, this process releases volatile organic compounds during the natural gas production process.

62. **C**—If people checked their boats for zebra mussels and removed any before moving on to a new lake or river, we would greatly reduce the numbers that are being introduced to new areas.

63. **B**—As oceans become more acidic, this acidity doesn't allow animals like clams and mussels to make protective shells. Coral are also affected similarly because of a loss of calcium carbonate from their shells.

64. **A**—In March the sea ice has gone from approximately 6.5 to 5.5 million square miles and in September from 3 to 2 million square miles. So, there is a loss of about 1 million square miles in both months.

65. **C**—The primary reasons that oceans (and land) are warming is from global climate change as a result of an increase in greenhouse gases from burning fossil fuels and agriculture.

66. **D**—Species diversity is the number of species and abundance of each species that live in a particular community. Species diversity helps to contribute to the health of an ecosystem because each species has an important role in this health. In addition, an area with a higher species diversity is an area that can recover faster from a disaster.

67. **B**—Humans and kangaroos are examples of Type I. According to the graph, almost 100 percent of kangaroos survive childhood and most survive a long time and into many years. These are often k-selected species.

68. **C**—A species with a Type III survivorship curve have very few who make it to adulthood. Think of frog eggs—most get eaten, dry out, and never mature, or they never hatch at all. Then, tadpoles are also a major food source for many species so lots of young frogs are also killed. However, a few make it to old age and become adult frogs. These are often r-selected species.

69. **C**—Hydroelectric power cons are that building dams is expensive, and when you build a dam you change the river ecosystem. You flood an area above the dam, which was once a land habitat, and you reduce the flow of water downstream, reducing the amount of nutrients available and changing the ecosystems.

70. **A**—If the farmer uses genetically modified/engineered crops that the bugs don't like and won't eat, then the farmer won't have to spray a large quantity of pesticides on the crop.

71. **D**—Ranchers began to use concentrated animal feeding operations (CAFOs) rather than free-range cattle farming. In CAFOs, the cattle reach market weight faster than in free-range cattle farming, resulting in fewer cattle than previously, as happened in the United States.

72. **D**—Switching to renewable resources would lower our dependence on mining and the environmental problems that are associated with mining.

73. **D**—One problem with urbanization is that large areas of soil have concrete or asphalt put down on them for parking lots, streets, etc. and water can't seep into aquifers. If we use paving stones for parking lots, then water can seep in between the stones rather than running off.

74. **C**—Nonrenewable resources are replaced slowly or not at all. These include things like coal, oil, natural gas, and nuclear energy resources.

75. **A**—Geothermal energy uses heat from deep in Earth to create steam to turn a turbine to create electrical energy.

76. **D**—To calculate the percentage increase you take the new (solar) and subtract the old (coal) and divide by the old (coal) and then multiply by 100 to make it a percent. Thirteen for solar minus 2 for coal equals 11 divided by 2 equals 5.5. 5.5 times 100 percent = 550 percent. Or $(13 - 2)/2 \times 100 = 550\%$.

77. **C**—Passive solar systems do not collect or store energy but can be used to heat or cool homes, etc. An example of this would be to build a home with large windows that face where the sun shines the most. Then, the sun will come in through the windows and heat the home. During the summer the homeowner could put thick curtains on the windows to prevent the heat from coming in.

78. **C**—The problem with hydrogen fuel cells is that to create the hydrogen gas through a process called electrolysis requires energy, possibly produced from nonrenewable sources such as coal. Partly because of this it is very expensive.

79. **A**—Every time you exhale, you add $CO_2$ to the atmosphere. $CO_2$ is also formed as things decompose and when volcanoes erupt. We measure $CO_2$ in parts per million (ppm). Natural sources of particulates are dust, sea salt, pollen, and particles from volcanic eruptions.

80. **B**—The author states "How does our noise affect the animals around us? Unlike us, they can't put in some earplugs, close a window or turn off the stereo. Recent studies are showing that our increasingly loud world is having negative effects on a range of animals, across a variety of habitats." So, the best answer would be that the noise is causing stress and possibly changes to the migration of animals.

# Explanations for the Free-Response Questions

**Question 1: Design an investigation**      **10 points**

(a) Based on the data in the table, **identify** the control group    **1 point**
in this experiment.

- 8 a.m.

(b) **Identify** the scientific question for the investigation.    **1 point**

Accept one of the following:

- Are visitors to the park having an impact on water quality in the park?
- Is the fertilizer from the golf course next to the park having an impact on water quality in the park?

(c) **Explain** how the results of this experiment would likely have been    **1 point**
altered if the park rangers took water samples on a day when the
park was closed for visitors.

Accept one of the following:

- The water quality in the park will increase/be better because no visitors will be using the bathroom when the park is closed.
- The water quality in the park will not change, because the golf course next to the park will still be using fertilizer and watering, which will run off into the water in the park.

Park rangers determined that the level of nitrates and phosphates increases    **1 point**
throughout the day.

(d) **Identify** one possible reason for an increased level of nitrates and
phosphates in the stream.

Accept one of the following:

- The bathroom septic system is leaking human waste into the river.
- The fertilizers used on the adjacent golf course are making their way into the river.

(e) **Describe** one step that could be taken to reduce the levels of nitrates    **1 point**
and phosphates in the river.

Accept one of the following:

- Repairing the septic system so it does not leak into the river
- Closing the bathrooms with the leaking septic system so visitors can't use it
- Planting plants to catch the fertilizer running off from the golf course
- Limiting/banning the amount of fertilizer used on the golf course
- Limiting the amount of watering the golf course does to slow the movement of fertilizer to the river

(f) **Explain** one environmental consequence of high levels of nitrates and    **1 point**
phosphates in a body of water.

Accept one of the following:

- Eutrophication, an excess of nutrients in a body of water due to runoff from the land

- Excess microorganism growth from runoff that can lower the oxygen content of the water
- Weed growth and algae blooms from the excessive nutrients in the water
- Dead zones that decrease aquatic life

---

(g) Based on the data in the graph, **describe** the relationship between dissolved oxygen and temperature.  **1 point**

Accept one of the following:

- As temperature goes up, dissolved oxygen goes down.
- As the water gets warmer, the amount of dissolved oxygen gets less.

---

The park rangers are concerned about the number of visitors they see in the park because they know human activities might result in a loss of biodiversity in the park.  **1 point**

(h) **Identify** one specific activity, other than bathroom use, that might result in a loss of biodiversity in the park because of human interference.

Accept one of the following:

- Car exhaust/air pollution
- Foot traffic
- Trash/littering
- Fishing
- Hunting
- Interfering with wildlife
- Food left behind that gets eaten by wild animals
- Invasive species/spores/plants/animals introduced to the environment
- Deforestation
- Fires

---

(i) For the activity you identified in (h), **describe** how this activity could lower biodiversity.  **1 point**

Accept one of the following:

- Habitat loss linked to one of the answers in (h), like deforestation
- Invasive species outcompeting native species if introduced into park
- Pollution from the car exhaust causing smog and harming plant/animal life
- People trampling the native vegetation so food is not available for animals or plants die
- Animals being overhunted/overfished reducing biodiversity numbers
- Animals coming into contact with humans where they move/migrate/die
- Animals eating trash/litter/human food and harming the species
- Fires that escape and cause a loss of plant/animal life

---

(j) **Propose** a realistic solution to help reduce the loss of biodiversity you identified in (h).  **1 point**

Accept one of the following:

- Limiting the number of visitors to the park each day
- Only allowing people to walk on designated trails
- Not allowing food/beverages into the park
- Making strict rules not allowing hunting, fishing, interacting with wildlife

- Not allowing campfires
- Not allowing visitors to cut down any trees/limbs/plants or collect limbs/brush
- Having guests park cars far from the park and bus/walk in to limit car exhaust

---

**Question 2: Analyze an environmental problem and propose a solution**     **10 points**

---

(a)  Many invasive species are r-selected. **Identify** one characteristic of an     **1 point**
r-selected species.

Accept one of the following:

- Produce a large number of offspring
- Contribute very little resources/energy to each individual offspring
- Little or no parental care
- High offspring mortality
- Small body size
- Short life spans
- Early maturity
- Can disperse offspring quickly
- Exponential growth
- May reproduce only once in their lifetime

---

(b)  **Explain** how invasive species are able to outcompete native species.     **1 point**

Accept one of the following:

- No natural predators
- Can outcompete for food, nesting sites, light, prey, and habitat
- Spread disease to native species
- May prey on native species or their young
- Are generalists

---

Florida scientists have recorded tegus eating eggs from an alligator nest—a     **1 point**
behavior that could be a problem for the threatened American crocodile
population that lives nearby.

(c)  **Describe** one important characteristic of an endangered species that
could cause it to be slow to recover.

Accept one of the following:

- Specific habitat requirements
- Limited diet
- Being hunted by humans for horns, tusks, meat
- Large size
- Small population size
- Limited geographic distribution

---

Economic incentives have often helped solve environmental problems.     **1 point**

(d)  **Identify** one example of an economic incentive that the government
of Florida could offer to stop tegu lizards before they become a
larger problem.

Accept one of the following:

- Buying tegu lizards (dead or alive) from people that capture them in the wild

- Making tegu lizards a food source for humans/animals
- Finding a use for tegu lizard hides such as leather-like products or other things humans will buy

---

(e) **Explain** how the incentive identified in (d) could work to control the tegu population.     **1 point**

Accept one of the following:

- If people have the incentive to collect the tegus in the wild because of a financial reward, then numbers of tegus will go down.
- If people or animals begin to consume tegus for food, then tegu numbers will go down.
- If tegu lizards are turned into a commercial item such as leather, people will collect tegus and their numbers will go down.

---

(f) **Describe** one impact the introduction of tegus could have on the ecosystem services provided by the Florida Everglades.     **1 point**

Accept one of the following:

- Provisioning—if the tegus harm any benefit to people such as food, water, wood, or biomedical
- Regulating—if the tegus harm anything from an ecosystem process such as flood prevention, erosion control, or control of pests
- Cultural—if the tegus harm a nonmaterial benefit from the ecosystem such as recreational, spiritual, or educational
- Supporting—if the tegus harm a service the ecosystem provides that helps other services such as biological diversity, nutrient recycling, or primary productivity

---

(g) **Propose** a realistic solution, other than the use of economic incentives, to help reduce the spread of the tegus from their current distribution seen on the map above.     **1 point**

Accept one of the following:

- Allow/encourage hunting of tegus.
- Make sure tegus are being moved from one place to another by things like cars accidentally transporting them.
- Introduce a predator to the tegus to help control them.
- Trap and remove tegus from the wild.

---

(h) **Justify** the solution proposed in part (g) by providing an additional advantage. **1 point**

Accept one of the following:

- By lowering the number of tegus in the wild, the native wildlife can rebound.
- Hunting tegus in the wild can provide food for humans/animals.
- Trapping/hunting tegus in the wild can provide commercial/material benefits to humans if their body parts can be used/sold.

---

(i) Based on the information given in the map above, **identify** where you expect the greatest number of tegus to be found in the next 10 years.     **1 point**

Accept one of the following:

- Southern Florida
- Western Florida

- Florida Keys
- Southeastern Florida

| | |
|---|---|
| The following is an example of a simple food chain in the Florida Everglades: | **1 point** |

$$\text{Plants} \rightarrow \text{Turtles} \rightarrow \text{Alligator}$$

(j) **Describe** what the arrows in the food chain above represent.

Accept one of the following:
- The flow of energy
- Where energy is being passed
- The direction of energy flow

---

| | |
|---|---|
| **Question 3: Analyze an environmental problem and propose a solution doing calculations** | **10 points** |

| | |
|---|---|
| (a) **Calculate** the population growth rate between 1543 and 1803. **Show** your work. | **1 point** |

One point for the correct setup to calculate the population growth rate.

The formula is: 70/growth rate = doubling time
- 70/growth rate = 260 years

| | |
|---|---|
| One point for the correct calculation of growth rate. | **1 point** |
- A 0.27 percent growth rate from 1543–1803.

**Total for part (a) 2 points**

| | |
|---|---|
| (b) **Describe** the difference between a density-independent and a density-dependent factor. | **1 point** |
- A density-independent factor exerts its influence regardless of the population's density, and a density-dependent factor intensifies as the population increases in size.

| | |
|---|---|
| (c) **Identify** one density-independent factor. | **1 point** |

Accept one of the following:
- Storm
- Fire
- Heat wave
- Drought

| | |
|---|---|
| (d) **Identify** one action a government could do that would affect the growth or decline of a population. | **1 point** |

Accept one of the following:
- Access to family planning
- Access to education
- Access to employment opportunities
- Encourage postponement of marriage
- Guarantee the availability of pensions

An increased human population can have negative impacts on biodiversity.    **1 point**

(e)  **Describe** an environmental problem associated with an increased human population.

Accept one of the following:
- Habitat destruction
- Invasive species
- Pollution
- Climate change
- Overexploitation

In an effort to lower the consumption of oil and gas, hybrid and electric    **1 point**
cars have been produced. A plug-in hybrid uses about 12 kg of lithium,
a standard electric car 22 kg, and a third popular model uses over 50 kg
of lithium per car. There are currently 2,442,270 electric vehicles registered
in the United States.

Assume the average electric car uses 25 kg of lithium per vehicle.

(f)  **Calculate** how much lithium was needed to produce the electric cars that are
currently registered in the United States. **Show** your work.

One point for the correct setup to calculate the amount of lithium needed.
- 25 kg of lithium × 2,442,270

One point for the correct calculation of the amount of lithium needed.    **1 point**
- 61,056,750 kg of lithium

**Total for part (f) 2 points**

Each ton (approximately 907 kg) of refined lithium uses up 500,000 gallons    **1 point**
of water.

(g)  **Calculate** how many gallons of water is needed to produce the average electric cars
that are currently registered in the United States. **Show** your work.

One point for the correct setup to calculate the amount of water needed.

Accept one of the following:
- $$\frac{907 \text{ kg}}{500,000 \text{ gallons of water}} = \frac{25 \text{ kg}}{X}$$
- $$\frac{500,000 \text{ gallons of water}}{907 \text{ kg}} = \frac{X}{25 \text{ kg}}$$

One point for the correct calculation of the amount of water needed.    **1 point**

Accept one of the following:
- 13,781.70 gallons of water
- 13,781.69 gallons of water
- 13,781 gallons of water

**Total for part (g) 2 points**

# AP Environmental Science Practice Exam 1
## Score Approximation

You can get a rough approximation of what your score on the AP Environmental Science Exam would be. Use this worksheet to compute an approximation of your score.

### Section I: Multiple Choice

Determine the number of multiple-choice questions you got right then enter that number below.

Number of questions answered correctly (80 possible)      _____

               × 1.125

This is your **Weighted Section I** Score      _____

### Section II: Free Response

Award yourself points as determined by the scoring guide given in the explanation for each question.

Question 1 (10 points possible)      _____
Question 2 (10 points possible)      _____
Question 3 (10 points possible)      _____

Add the three scores for the free-response section      _____

               × 2

This is your **Weighted Section II** Score      _____

Add your Weighted Section I Score and your Weighted Section II Score.      _____

This is your **Composite Score**.

### Score Conversion Chart

| COMPOSITE SCORE RANGE | APPROXIMATE AP SCORE |
|---|---|
| 110–150 | 5 |
| 89–109 | 4 |
| 77–88 | 3 |
| 63–76 | 2 |
| 0–62 | 1 |

# AP Environmental Science Practice Exam 2
## Multiple-Choice Questions

**ANSWER SHEET**

| | | |
|---|---|---|
| 1 (A) (B) (C) (D) | 31 (A) (B) (C) (D) | 61 (A) (B) (C) (D) |
| 2 (A) (B) (C) (D) | 32 (A) (B) (C) (D) | 62 (A) (B) (C) (D) |
| 3 (A) (B) (C) (D) | 33 (A) (B) (C) (D) | 63 (A) (B) (C) (D) |
| 4 (A) (B) (C) (D) | 34 (A) (B) (C) (D) | 64 (A) (B) (C) (D) |
| 5 (A) (B) (C) (D) | 35 (A) (B) (C) (D) | 65 (A) (B) (C) (D) |
| 6 (A) (B) (C) (D) | 36 (A) (B) (C) (D) | 66 (A) (B) (C) (D) |
| 7 (A) (B) (C) (D) | 37 (A) (B) (C) (D) | 67 (A) (B) (C) (D) |
| 8 (A) (B) (C) (D) | 38 (A) (B) (C) (D) | 68 (A) (B) (C) (D) |
| 9 (A) (B) (C) (D) | 39 (A) (B) (C) (D) | 69 (A) (B) (C) (D) |
| 10 (A) (B) (C) (D) | 40 (A) (B) (C) (D) | 70 (A) (B) (C) (D) |
| 11 (A) (B) (C) (D) | 41 (A) (B) (C) (D) | 71 (A) (B) (C) (D) |
| 12 (A) (B) (C) (D) | 42 (A) (B) (C) (D) | 72 (A) (B) (C) (D) |
| 13 (A) (B) (C) (D) | 43 (A) (B) (C) (D) | 73 (A) (B) (C) (D) |
| 14 (A) (B) (C) (D) | 44 (A) (B) (C) (D) | 74 (A) (B) (C) (D) |
| 15 (A) (B) (C) (D) | 45 (A) (B) (C) (D) | 75 (A) (B) (C) (D) |
| 16 (A) (B) (C) (D) | 46 (A) (B) (C) (D) | 76 (A) (B) (C) (D) |
| 17 (A) (B) (C) (D) | 47 (A) (B) (C) (D) | 77 (A) (B) (C) (D) |
| 18 (A) (B) (C) (D) | 48 (A) (B) (C) (D) | 78 (A) (B) (C) (D) |
| 19 (A) (B) (C) (D) | 49 (A) (B) (C) (D) | 79 (A) (B) (C) (D) |
| 20 (A) (B) (C) (D) | 50 (A) (B) (C) (D) | 80 (A) (B) (C) (D) |
| 21 (A) (B) (C) (D) | 51 (A) (B) (C) (D) | |
| 22 (A) (B) (C) (D) | 52 (A) (B) (C) (D) | |
| 23 (A) (B) (C) (D) | 53 (A) (B) (C) (D) | |
| 24 (A) (B) (C) (D) | 54 (A) (B) (C) (D) | |
| 25 (A) (B) (C) (D) | 55 (A) (B) (C) (D) | |
| 26 (A) (B) (C) (D) | 56 (A) (B) (C) (D) | |
| 27 (A) (B) (C) (D) | 57 (A) (B) (C) (D) | |
| 28 (A) (B) (C) (D) | 58 (A) (B) (C) (D) | |
| 29 (A) (B) (C) (D) | 59 (A) (B) (C) (D) | |
| 30 (A) (B) (C) (D) | 60 (A) (B) (C) (D) | |

# AP Environmental Science Practice Exam 2
## Section I: Multiple-Choice Questions

Time: 90 minutes

**Directions:** For the multiple-choice questions to follow, select the best answer and fill in the appropriate letter on the answer sheet.

1. A plant is found in an environment that receives very little rain and very high temperatures most of the year. The plant has special ways of storing and conserving water, has little to no leaves, and has extremely long roots. Which of the following biomes is this plant most likely found in?

   (A) Taiga
   (B) Desert
   (C) Boreal forest
   (D) Grassland

**Use the information below to answer questions 2–4.**

According to NOAA, most reef-building corals contain photosynthetic algae called zooxanthellae that live in their tissues. The coral provides the algae with a place to live and the algae produce oxygen for the coral and remove wastes. In addition, zooxanthellae are responsible for the beautiful colors of many corals. Sometimes when corals become stressed, as is the case when ocean temperatures become too warm, the polyps expel their algae cells and the colony looks white in appearance. This is known as "coral bleaching."

2. Which of the following best identifies the author's claim?

   (A) Zooxanthellae can become parasitic to coral in stressful environments.
   (B) Coral reefs are structures that can protect the estuaries from natural disasters such as hurricanes.
   (C) Zooxanthellae is an organism worthy of scientific study.
   (D) If a large area of coral reef is colored white, zooxanthellae have left the coral tissues because ocean temperatures are above the optimal growth range.

3. Zooxanthellae and coral are in which type of symbiotic relationship?

   (A) Mutualism
   (B) Commensalism
   (C) Parasitism
   (D) Predator-prey

4. Crown-of-thorns sea stars are a predator on coral reefs. Which of the following would be true of the crown-of-thorn sea stars?

   (A) Crown-of-thorn sea stars are herbivores.
   (B) Ten percent of the energy from the coral will go to the crown-of-thorn sea star when it eats the coral.
   (C) The crown-of-thorn sea star and the coral are in a commensalism relationship.
   (D) Crown-of-thorn sea stars return nitrogen in the form of atmospheric nitrogen back to the atmosphere.

**Use the information below to answer questions 5–6.**

Soil erosion costs the world billions of dollars every year. One reason for this economic cost is the number of pollutants washing into the streams and rivers and the loss of farmland due to erosion. A group of students decides to set up an experiment to see if they can reduce the amount of soil that is eroded after a rainfall.

5. Which of the following would the students discover as the best way to remediate the problem of soil erosion?

   (A) Allow animals to graze near the river/stream.
   (B) Clearcut the trees around the river/stream.
   (C) Plant plants near the river/stream.
   (D) Begin construction projects near the river/stream.

6. A large dam is built above the river, which changes the flow of the stream/river and prevents fish from migrating upstream. What would be a way to solve this environmental problem?

   (A) Build fish ladders to allow fish to bypass the dam and get upriver.
   (B) Construct new dams to replace older ones.
   (C) Dredge the river below the dam to move sediment back upstream.
   (D) Bring in nonnative species help repopulate the animals displaced by the dam.

**Use the graph below to answer questions 7–8.**

**Serengeti Wildebeests**

7. Based on the graph above, what would be the best estimate of the carrying capacity of the Serengeti wildebeests?

   (A) 50,000
   (B) 400,000
   (C) 800,000
   (D) 1,200,000

8. Which of the following factors might lower the carrying capacity of the herbivore wildebeests?

   (A) A significant amount of rainfall increases the grasses the wildebeests eat.
   (B) The predators of the wildebeests are culled to protect the local sheep population.
   (C) The Serengeti goes through a severe drought impacting local plant life.
   (D) A virus moves through the wildebeest predators killing 50 percent of the adult population.

**Use the data table below to answer questions 9–10.**

An ecological footprint compares resource demands and waste production for a person or for a society. The table below is a sample of an ecological footprint for five people in an office. Each number represents the amount of land, measured in hectares (10,000 square meters).

|          | FOOD (MEAT) | CARBON EMISSIONS | HOUSING | GOODS AND SERVICES | TOTAL |
|----------|-------------|------------------|---------|--------------------|-------|
| Person 1 | 1.8 | 2.9 | 2.4 | 1.6 | 8.7 |
| Person 2 | 3.2 | 3 | 1.6 | 1.2 | 9 |
| Person 3 | 1.4 | 2.7 | 2.2 | 2.0 | 8.3 |
| Person 4 | 2.7 | 3 | 1.5 | 2.9 | 10.1 |
| Person 5 | 2.8 | 3 | 3.4 | 1.9 | 11.1 |

9. If person 5 wanted to lower their ecological footprint to be more like person 3, what two activities would help the most?

(A) Take mass transit and buy fewer shoes and less clothing.
(B) Eat less meat and move to a smaller apartment.
(C) Eat less meat and buy fewer shoes and less clothing.
(D) Take mass transit and/or bike to work.

10. Person 1 and person 3 have the lowest ecological footprint when it comes to the food they eat. What is one reason why eating lower on the food chain can help lower your ecological footprint?

(A) Eating lower on the food chain takes approximately 20 times less land to produce the same number of calories as from meat.
(B) Eating lower on the food chain helps to lower your A1C and prevent diabetes.
(C) Eating lower on the food chain increases the amount of methane released into the atmosphere.
(D) Eating lower on the food chain uses more carbon helping to increase photosynthesis of land plants.

11. Which of the following would be a nonpoint source pollutant that would affect the health of a local forest?

(A) Smoke from a power plant in the area
(B) Wastewater from a drainage pipe
(C) Fire started from an irresponsible camper
(D) Acid rain

12. A doctor tells a patient that the patient is exhibiting the effects of an endocrine disrupter on the patient's body. What part of the body would the endocrine disruptor be impacting?

(A) Cardiovascular system
(B) Skin
(C) Hormones
(D) Nervous system

**Use the graph below to answer questions 13–14.**

13. Looking at the graph, what time of the day would photochemical smog be at its worst?

    (A) 4–6 h
    (B) 8–10 h
    (C) 12–14 h
    (D) 16–18 h

14. What is the human health impact of photochemical smog?

    (A) Respiratory problems and eye irritation
    (B) Cancer
    (C) Skin irritation and eczema
    (D) Nervous system problems

15. A family has an average utility use of 1,000 kWh per month. The family has a refrigerator that uses 40 kWh per month. Which of the following is the percentage of the family's total monthly electricity use to run the refrigerator?

    (A) 4%
    (B) 10%
    (C) 40%
    (D) 25%

16. Which of the following is the correct order from cleanest and most heat generated to least clean and least heat generated when burned?

    (A) Anthracite – lignite – bituminous
    (B) Bituminous – lignite – anthracite
    (C) Lignite – anthracite – bituminous
    (D) Anthracite – bituminous – lignite

17. Bird, butterfly, and bat migration have been a concern among many people when it comes to wind farms. What would be one way to minimize the impact of wind farms on these migrations?

    (A) Move wind farms offshore rather than on land.
    (B) Slow the speed or turn off the turbines during migration periods.
    (C) Lower the height of the wind turbine to 50 meters.
    (D) Paint the wind farms a bright color so birds and bats will see and avoid them.

**Use the graph below to answer questions 18–20.**

18. What would be the most likely cause of the trend in the graph above?

   (A) Global migration of mammal species
   (B) A severe El Niño year off the coast of South America
   (C) The effects of climate change
   (D) A normal fluctuation in hurricane activity

19. The trend in the graph will most likely lead to what environmental concern?

   (A) Increased air pollution
   (B) Overexploitation of marine species
   (C) Habitat loss along coastlines
   (D) Increased human population growth

20. What would be the best way to slow the cause of the trend in the graph?

   (A) Slow the expansion of nuclear energy
   (B) Limit the use of fossil fuels
   (C) Stop construction in coastal areas
   (D) Limit the use of pesticides and fertilizers on farmland

**Use the image below to answer questions 21–23.**

**Eutrophication**

21. What would be the environmental consequence of the additional nitrogen and phosphorus entering the lake?

(A) A decrease in dissolved oxygen and a large die-off of fish and other aquatic organisms
(B) Temperature increase due to the algae bloom
(C) Increased lake levels from the algae decay
(D) An increase in pathogens and infectious diseases from local industry

22. A student is trying to find the source of the nitrogen and phosphorus that is causing eutrophication. Where should the student first begin the investigation?

(A) The local coal-burning power plant
(B) The large multi-use construction project in the neighboring city
(C) The pesticide plant producing organophosphates
(D) The runoff from agricultural land

23. What is one suggestion the student could give the city to mitigate the problem of eutrophication?

(A) Take large nets and scoop out the algae that are blocking the sunlight.
(B) Introduce fish such as the Bristlenose Plecostomus that eat algae.
(C) Plant plants around the lake known as a riparian buffer.
(D) Encourage herbivores like cattle to graze near the river.

**Farmed Fish is the most Resource Efficient Protein on the Planet.**
**[The Perfect Protein]**

| | Feed | Fresh water |
|---|---|---|
| | 1.2 Pounds | 1 Gallons |
| | 2.3 Pounds | 2,000 Gallons |
| | 6 Pounds | 3,500 Gallons |
| | 13 Pounds | 2,500 Gallons |

24. The graphic above shows how aquaculture or farming fish is the most efficient form of animal protein saving millions of gallons of water and needing much less food to feed the fish. However, which of the following is an environmental consequence of aquaculture?

(A) The surrounding water can be contaminated with organic waste.
(B) Fish are inexpensive and therefore do not generate economic profits.
(C) Soil erosion can occur trapping light and preventing photosynthesis.
(D) Pesticides must be sprayed to stop fish disease which contaminates the water.

25. Which of the following environmental problems are associated with burning fossil fuels, vehicle emissions, and deforestation?

(A) Eutrophication
(B) Island biogeography
(C) Ocean acidification
(D) Thermal pollution

26. Which of the following best describes the greenhouse effect?

(A) Acid rain can cause a positive feedback loop further heating Earth.
(B) Gases in Earth's atmosphere trap heat from the sun.
(C) The principal greenhouse gases are hydrogen, nitrogen, and helium.
(D) The greenhouse effect is Earth's ability to mitigate the rising sea levels.

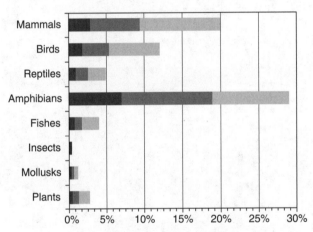

The percentage of species in several groups that are listed on the 2007 IUCN Red List:

■ Critically endangered
■ Endangered
■ Vulnerable

27. A student was researching endangered species. What should the student conclude from the data above?

(A) There are no insects on the vulnerable list.
(B) Fish and reptiles both have the same environmental stressors.
(C) Mollusks and insects should not be an environmental concern.
(D) Amphibians have the greatest impact from changes to their environment.

**Use the image below to answer questions 28–29.**

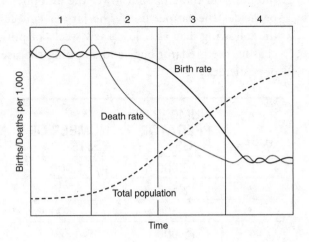

28. In the graph above, at which phase does the population stay relatively stable?

(A) 1 and 4
(B) 1 and 2
(C) 2 and 3
(D) 3 and 4

29. In which phase above would the country's population be growing exponentially?

(A) 1 and 4
(B) 2 and 4
(C) 2 and 3
(D) 1 and 2

**30.** A farmer purchases wasps and ladybugs to eat the pests on the crop and lower the amount of pesticides the farmer uses. The farmer collects the following data after just a few weeks of purchasing the predator bugs and stopping the use of pesticides.

| WEEK | NUMBER OF PREDATOR BUGS | NUMBER OF PESTS |
|------|-------------------------|-----------------|
| 1 | 2,000 | 1,000 |
| 2 | 2,500 | 700 |
| 3 | 3,500 | 300 |
| 4 | 5,000 | 20 |

What can we conclude from the data on the farm and what benefit does that pose to the environment?

(A) The farmer is adding a new pest to the farm that could potentially damage local wildlife.

(B) The farmer is using integrated pest management and reducing the risk of pesticides to the wildlife in the area.

(C) The farmer's method is not working and the farmer will need to switch to a new form of the pesticide.

(D) The predator bugs are overpopulating the farm which will lead to devastating financial problems in the future.

**31.** What type of biome would we expect to find at 30°N and 30°S?

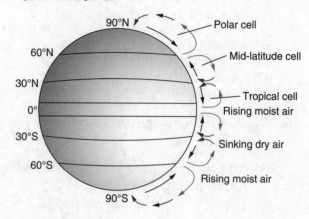

(A) Rainforest
(B) Savannah
(C) Tundra
(D) Desert

**32.** What relationship can we assume about phosphorus from the diagram below?

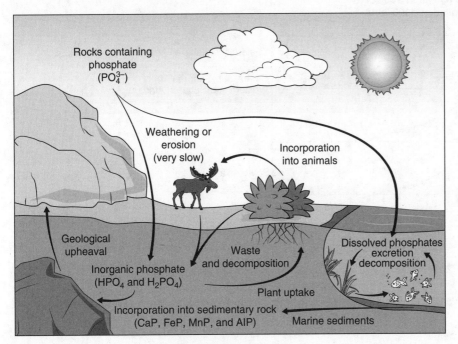

**Phosphorus Cycle**

(A) Rocks and soil contain phosphorus and, since there is no atmospheric form, the phosphorus cycle is slow.

(B) The atmosphere and soil contain phosphorus so we can assume phosphorus is also prevalent and abundant in aquatic ecosystems as well.

(C) The rocks and the atmosphere contain phosphorus that comes directly from animals as they undergo cellular respiration and decompose after death.

(D) Lakes and the atmosphere contain phosphorus so we can assume the phosphorus cycle is a fast cycle that replenishes very quickly.

**33.** If the population of a country grows at a rate of approximately 4 percent per year, how many years will it take for the population to double?

(A) 280 years

(B) 17.5 years

(C) 175 years

(D) 5.7 years

**34.** The pesticide dichlorvos, an insecticide used in household pesticide strips, is determined to have an $LD_{50}$ of 61 mg/kg. If a typical mouse weighs .30 kg, which of the following would be the appropriate dose to kill mice?

(A) 61 mg/kg × 50% × 0.30 kg

(B) 61 mg/kg × 0.30 kg

(C) 61 mg/kg × 0.30 kg/50%

(D) 61 mg/kg/50%

**Use the graph below to answer questions 35–36.**

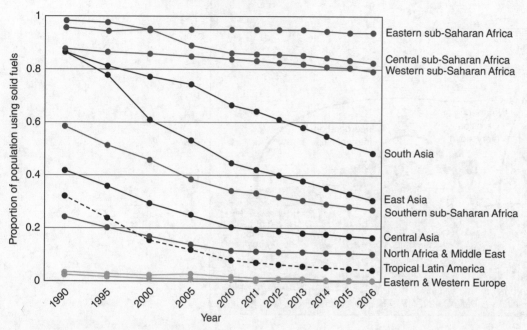

Proportion of Population Subject to Indoor Air Pollution, 1990–2016

**35.** According to the graph above, much of the world is subjected to indoor air pollution from burning solid fuels for cooking or heating. Which of the following would be correct according to the trend in the graph?

(A) East Asia is going through the demographic transition process.
(B) Western sub-Saharan Africa is seeing the greatest decrease in indoor air pollutants over the past 30 years.
(C) The number of people exposed to indoor air pollution is dropping.
(D) Western Europe has never had an indoor air pollution problem.

**36.** What can you conclude from the graph about Eastern sub-Saharan Africa?

(A) This is a developed country.
(B) Indoor air pollution is being addressed in this country.
(C) Industrial smog is a problem in this country.
(D) There is widespread use of solid fuels for cooking and heating.

**37.** The graph below shows the development of primary energy consumption worldwide and makes projections until 2030. Which of the following can you conclude from the graph?

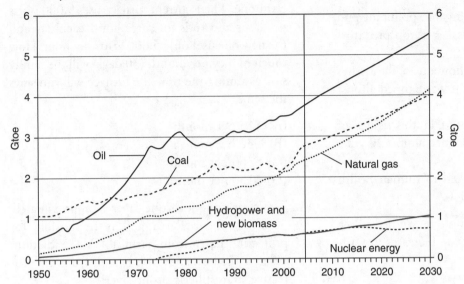

(A) Oil will increase by 5 Gtoe from 1950 to 2030.

(B) Hydropower will not increase at all from 1950 to 2030.

(C) Nuclear has the greatest slope and therefore the greatest potential for future use.

(D) Natural gas will increase exponentially from 1950 to 2030.

**38.** Based on the data in the graph below, how many million tons of paper was sent to MSW before recycling in 2008?

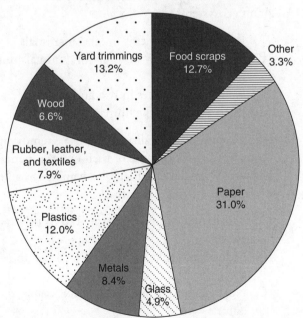

Total MSW Generation (by material), 2008
250 Million Tons (before recycling)

(A) 172.5 million tons

(B) 77.5 million tons

(C) 31 million tons

(D) 310 million tons

39. A scientist is studying the effects of DDT, a synthetic organic compound banned worldwide in 2001. Which of the following best identifies a testable hypothesis for the scientist's study?

(A) DDT is a persistent organic pollutant and will show up in the tissues of top predators for many decades.

(B) DDT is unlikely to show up in the tissues of top predators since it was banned almost 20 years ago.

(C) DDT will not be found in the tissues of plants because it was banned almost 20 years ago.

(D) DDT will not be linked to human health impacts in the year 2030.

40. Which of the following should be studied to see if a geologic feature is causing increases in $CO_2$ and particulate matter?

(A) Plant pollen

(B) Burning of fossil fuels

(C) Respiration from local wildlife

(D) Volcanoes

41. Which of following would be an effect of an endocrine disruptor chemical on the biodiversity of an ecosystem?

(A) Respiratory problems in land mammals

(B) Stress and anxiety in migratory animals due to the noise

(C) Gender imbalances in fish and other species

(D) Birth defects in the human population

42. Many environmentalists propose removing dams from rivers because of their environmental impact. What environmental advantage would occur by removing old dams?

(A) The habitat would be restored to its original condition.

(B) Sediment would be allowed back to above the dam.

(C) Nutrient flow would be reduced below the dam.

(D) Hydroelectric power could now be generated.

43. A family's electricity bill is $160 using 1,600 kWh at the cost of $0.10/kWh. The family is considering ways to lower this cost by replacing their old electric furnace with a newer, more energy efficient one. Their current furnace uses 9,000 watts per hour and runs for three hours each day and the new one uses only 5,000 watts per hour. How much money per month (30 days) will the family save assuming the time the furnace will run stays the same?

(A) $15 per month

(B) $36 per month

(C) $360 per month

(D) $150 per month

44. The stratospheric ozone layer is approximately 30 miles above Earth and is responsible for protecting Earth from harmful UV-C radiation. What is the human health benefit from the protective stratospheric ozone layer?

(A) Cases of asthma and emphysema are reduced.

(B) Cases of insect vector diseases are reduced.

(C) Cases of nervous system poisonings are reduced.

(D) Cases of skin cancer are reduced.

45. In 1996 leaders from around the world met in Montreal, Canada, and banned chlorofluorocarbons (CFCs). Why did these world leaders want to ban CFCs?

(A) CFCs are known carcinogens.

(B) CFCs destroy ozone in the stratosphere.

(C) CFCs are mined in fragile ecosystems and destroy habitats.

(D) CFCs are harmful organophosphates that bioaccumulate up the food web.

46. The greenhouse effect is a process that occurs when gases in Earth's atmosphere trap the sun's heat. This is important to life on Earth. Which of the following is one of the main greenhouse gases?

(A) Nitrogen

(B) Argon

(C) Water vapor

(D) Hydrogen

47. The map below shows where huge floods may be normal by 2050. Which of the following would be an expected effect of climate change?

(A) Coastal populations will be displaced.
(B) Greenland will have extensive habitat loss.
(C) Invasive species will become a larger concern in Africa.
(D) Island nations will need to switch to renewable energy.

48. A local forest has had a large wildfire go through it with many plant species burned. A scientist goes back three years later to discover grasses, bushes, and even small trees are thriving. What can the scientist determine about the forest?

(A) The forest was a former tree farm with one monocrop.
(B) The forest had a high species diversity before the fire.
(C) The forest had a low species diversity before the fire.
(D) The forest was part of a coniferous forest biome.

**49.** The graph below shows the population density, deforestation, and soil erosion associated with long-term Maya settlement in the Peten lowlands.

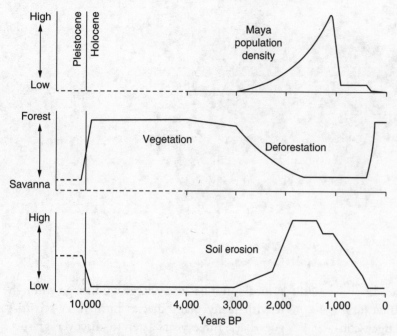

Which of the following can you determine from the data?

(A) The Mayans were hunter/gatherers.
(B) Soil erosion is directly proportional to deforestation.
(C) As the Mayan population increased, they planted large areas of forests.
(D) As the Mayan population increased, environmental damage occurred.

**50.** The graph below shows the effects of climate change on birds. Which of the following can you derive from the graph that demonstrates how birds have adapted to their environment from 1966 to 2013?

**Change in Latitude of Bird Center of Abundance, 1966–2013**

(A) Birds have begun breeding with different species.

(B) Birds have bred and increased in number.

(C) Birds have moved an average of 20 to 60 miles north.

(D) Birds have reacted to climate change by eating different food sources.

**51.** A scientist is studying the number of species on a particular island chain. Island A is 20 km from the mainland, island B is 50 km from the mainland, island C is 75 km from the mainland, and island D is 150 km from the mainland. The scientist notices that there are many fewer species on island D than on any of the other islands. What could the scientist conclude as the reason for this?

(A) Island D was hit by a large hurricane in the last century.

(B) Island D had less species able to travel the 150 km from the mainland.

(C) Island D is a larger island.

(D) Island D has no native plants on it.

**52.** A group of students notice that the playground near the local elementary school is experiencing a large amount of runoff, which is not allowing the rainfall to soak into the soil. They design an experiment to test the best ways to increase infiltration and limit runoff. Which of the following would be the likely results of this experiment?

(A) Covering the land with nonporous asphalt will increase infiltration.

(B) Covering the playground with an impermeable rubber mat will decrease injury and increase infiltration.

(C) Covering the playground with permeable pavement like gravel will increase infiltration.

(D) Removing all plants, trees, and shrubs that use water will increase infiltration.

53. Chinese farmers have been using rice terraces since ancient times. This method of growing rice on hilly and mountainous land has continued into modern day. What is one environmental benefit of this practice of rice terracing?

    (A) Terracing limits soil erosion.
    (B) Terracing allows for larger profits.
    (C) Terracing increases overgrazing.
    (D) Terracing decreases the need for pesticides.

54. The image below shows how floods will increase and impact coastal areas over the next 50–100 years. What is the environmental cause of this increase in coastal flooding?

    **Amplification of Moderate Floods**

    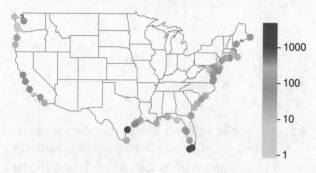

    (A) Deforestation
    (B) Habitat loss
    (C) Overharvesting
    (D) Climate change

55. According to the U.S. National Oceanic Atmospheric Administration (NOAA), the temperature in the upper few meters of the ocean has increased by approximately 0.13°C per decade over the past 100 years. Which of the following is the primary reason for this increased ocean temperature?

    (A) Increased El Niño–Southern Oscillation events in the past century
    (B) Increased greenhouse gas emission causing global temperatures to rise
    (C) Decreased albedo effects
    (D) Decreased solar activity in the form of solar flares

56. Kudzu is an invasive vine plant to North America that is native to eastern Asia, Southeast Asia, and some Pacific Islands. Kudzu smothers other plants and trees under a blanket of leaves, blocking all sunlight and eventually killing the native plants. Some environmentalists have suggested looking at economic means of controlling the kudzu. Which of the following would be an example of an economic means of solving this environmental problem?

    (A) Spray kudzu with a nonpersistent pesticide to avoid the pesticide treadmill.
    (B) Encourage chefs to find new ways to harvest and cook kudzu for profit.
    (C) Slash and burn large areas to destroy the kudzu and allow native plants to regrow.
    (D) Import a predator from Asia that eats kudzu and release it to areas where kudzu is found.

57. According to the U.N., about 61 percent, or 1,393,000 hectares, of Belize is forested but between 1990 and 2010, Belize lost an average of 9,650 hectares, or 0.61 percent, per year, adding up to 12.2 percent of its forest cover, or 193,000 hectares, being lost to deforestation. Which of the following methods would most benefit the Belizean environment and help to mitigate the human impact on forests?

    (A) Use and buy wood only from sustainable forestry techniques.
    (B) Build large networks of roads through the forest and encourage replanting.
    (C) Import fast-growing trees from other countries that can repopulate the forest.
    (D) Spray broad-spectrum pesticides to limit damage to trees from pests.

58. Clear-cutting forests can have many environmental effects. Which of the following would be the most immediate environmental effect of clear-cutting a forest?

    (A) Decreased stream temperatures around the forest
    (B) Decreased flooding around the forest
    (C) Increased profits for the lumber industry
    (D) Increased soil erosion around the forest

59. A farmer is noticing an increased loss of crops to a pest. The farmer wants to solve this problem without using even more pesticide, which causes environmental problems. Which of the following would be a good solution for the farmer to employ?

(A) Switch to a less toxic pesticide
(B) Plant monocrops
(C) Plant trees to provide shade to her crops
(D) Plant genetically engineered crops resistant to pests and disease

60. The diagram below shows a thermal inversion over the UK.

Which of the following would be the most likely result from this temperature inversion?

(A) Sunlight would be diminished for many days.
(B) Temperatures would decrease during the day.
(C) Smog and particulates would be trapped close to the ground.
(D) Tornadoes will form due to the difference in temperatures above the city.

61. Living fences are used in many places as a permanent hedge that is tight enough and tough enough to serve the same functions as a manufactured fence. What would be the environmental benefits of a living fence?

(A) Living fences are cheaper to build than using manufactured wood.
(B) Living fences provide edge habitat that support ecological diversity.
(C) Living fences are never eaten and destroyed by livestock.
(D) Living fences can be invasive.

**Use the image below to answer questions 62.**

### Carbon Cycle

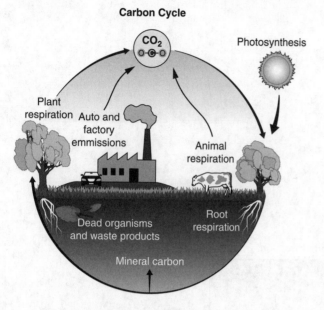

**Use the diagram below to answer questions 64–65.**

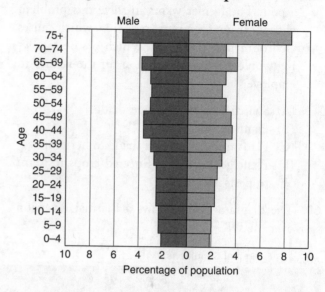

**62.** Which of the following is true and seen in the image above?

(A) Carbon cycles between cellular respiration and photosynthesis.

(B) Carbon does not have an atmospheric component.

(C) Carbon is found only nonanthropogenically.

(D) Carbon makes up the majority of our atmosphere.

**63.** Coyotes are native to North America and are highly versatile in their choice of food. Their diet consists of 90 percent meat including bison, rodents, birds, lizards, and snakes. Koalas on the other hand are herbivores with most of their diet consisting of eucalyptus leaves, which are found mainly in Australia. Which of the following best describes these two species?

(A) Koalas are herbivores and coyotes are detritovores.

(B) Koalas are specialists and coyotes are generalists.

(C) Koalas are prey to the predator coyotes.

(D) Koalas and coyotes live in a mutualistic relationship with one another.

**64.** Which of the following characteristics are most associated with the country that demonstrates the age structure above?

(A) More than 50 percent of people are in their postreproductive years and the population will shrink.

(B) A company looking to profit in this country would want to invest in baby diapers and baby formula.

(C) This country is in the first stage of the demographic transition.

(D) This country lacks universal health care, governmental food benefits, and other support systems for a struggling, poverty-stricken country.

**65.** Which of the following might be true of the country that demonstrates the age structure above?

(A) There are high infant mortality rates in this country.

(B) A baby boom has increased population size for generations.

(C) Access to education and health care is low in this country.

(D) Women are putting careers before thoughts of marriage and children.

66. Identify the type of plate boundary shown in the image below.

**Strike-Slip**

(A) Transform boundary
(B) Divergent boundary
(C) Convergent boundary
(D) Ring of fire

67. Using the diagram below, which area receives the most solar radiation during any time of the year and why?

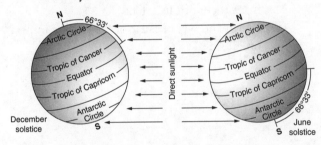

(A) The Arctic Circle because it is located at the North Pole.
(B) The Tropic of Cancer because it is tilted toward the sun during the June solstice.
(C) The equator because it receives the most direct sunlight during all seasons.
(D) The Tropic of Capricorn because it is tilted toward the sun during the December solstice.

68. Which of the following is true during an El Niño–Southern Oscillation event in the United States?

(A) It will be colder and drier in Canada.
(B) It will be rainier in California.
(C) The East Coast will experience extreme rainfall events.
(D) There is no relationship between weather and El Niño in the United States.

69. A housing developer has decided to cut down a large part of a forested area to build a neighborhood. A group of students discovers that the plan is to clearcut the entire area to make it cheaper and easier to build homes on. The students want to prove to the developer that clearcutting is going to cause extensive soil erosion. What would be the best way for the students to prove their point to the housing developer?

(A) Take soil samples and test for the amounts of nitrogen, phosphorus, and potassium.
(B) Set up an erosion experiment to show that plants and trees help prevent soil runoff.
(C) Take temperature data around the planned housing area and provide that data to the developer.
(D) Take soil samples to find the amount of sand, silt, and clay and provide that information to the developer.

**70.** The image below shows the different layers of the atmosphere.

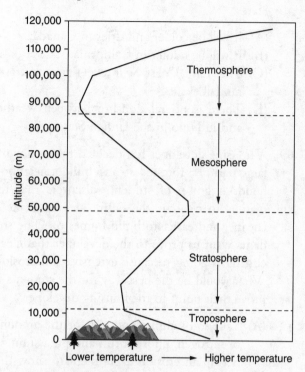

Which layer is where all weather on Earth occurs?

(A) Troposphere
(B) Stratosphere
(C) Mesosphere
(D) Thermosphere

**71.** What kind of weather pattern would you expect in the circled region below and why would you expect to see that pattern there?

(A) Warm and dry because it is in the southern United States
(B) Cool and wet because of the ocean's impact on all sides
(C) Cool and dry because of the wind patterns from the Coriolis effect
(D) Warm and wet because of the ocean's impact on all sides

**72.** Which of the following graphs would be indicative of a k-selected species?

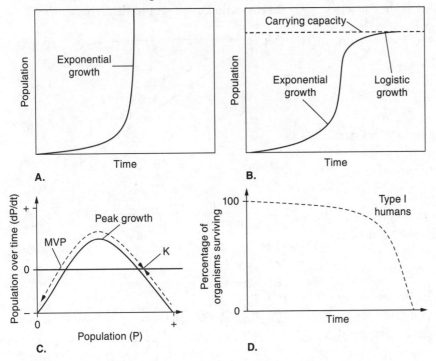

(A) A
(B) B
(C) C
(D) D

**73.** The image below shows a nuclear power plant. What is the environmental concern that occurs at the area labeled A?

(A) Release of carbon dioxide
(B) Nuclear radiation leaks
(C) Thermal pollution
(D) Production of soot

**74.** Humans have impacted biodiversity in many ways. For example, by building roads and inhabiting wild areas. Which of the following is the biggest impact of this human activity on biodiversity?

(A) Habitat fragmentation
(B) Overexploitation
(C) Water turbidity in local streams
(D) Climate change

**75.** Ocean acidification is a local and regional human activity that has global impacts. Which of the following is the cause of ocean acidification?

(A) Generation of nuclear energy
(B) Increased $CO_2$ levels in the atmosphere
(C) Invasive oceanic species in the Southern Hemisphere
(D) Expansion of the Green Revolution

**76.** If the graph below showed the numbers of lionfish found in the Western Atlantic Ocean, Caribbean Sea, and Gulf of Mexico, what could we conclude from the data?

(A) The resources needed for lionfish growth are abundant.
(B) Lionfish are k-strategists.
(C) Lionfish eat phytoplankton, a resource abundant in the Western Atlantic Ocean, Caribbean Sea, and Gulf of Mexico.
(D) Lionfish have reached their carrying capacity.

**77.** Many fish have many offspring at one time that they do not take care of. Which of the following survivorship curves would fish represent?

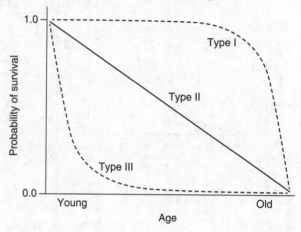

(A) Type I
(B) Type II
(C) Type III
(D) Types I and III

**78.** A student is on a walk and decides to test some of the soil they find. After testing the student discovers it is 40 percent sand, 30 percent silt, and 30 percent clay. Which of the following soil types would the student classify the soil as?

(A) Silty clay
(B) Clay loam
(C) Sandy clay loam
(D) Clay

**79.** Which of the following would be classified as a provisioning ecosystem service?

(A) Food
(B) Carbon sequestration
(C) Habitats for species
(D) Tourism

**80.** Which of the following explains why ecosystems have very few tertiary consumers compared to the numbers of primary and secondary consumers?

(A) The net primary productivity levels in areas with tertiary consumers is low.
(B) Ecological tolerance demonstrates less tertiary than primary consumers.
(C) Bioaccumulation of persistent pesticides up the food chain limit the numbers and distribution of tertiary consumers.
(D) Energy is lost as heat as you move upward to higher trophic levels and therefore cannot support as many tertiary consumers.

**STOP. End of Section I.**

# AP Environmental Science Practice Exam 2
## Section II: Free-Response Questions

Time: 70 minutes

**Directions:** Answer all three questions, which are weighted equally; the suggested time is 23 minutes for answering each question. Your answers should completely answer all parts of the question. Where explanation or discussion is needed, support your answers with relevant information and/or specific examples. If a calculation is required, clearly show all your work and how you arrived at your answer.

1. **Design an investigation.**

   A group of students have a concern about coral bleaching and want to know if it is linked to climate change. In their research they find that coral typically grows at 27°C. They set up an experiment to test their hypothesis. To do this, they prepare 6 salt water tanks to include the same number and types of species of coral. They set each tank at a different temperature as seen in the chart below:

   | TEMPERATURE | PERCENTAGE OF CORALS THAT ARE BLEACHED |
   |-------------|----------------------------------------|
   | 26°C | 0% |
   | 27°C | 0% |
   | 28°C | 10% |
   | 29°C | 22% |
   | 30°C | 45% |
   | 31°C | 80% |
   | 32°C | 82% |

   (a) **Identify** the scientific question for the investigation.
   (b) **Identify** the control in this experiment.
   (c) **Identify** the independent variable in this experiment.
   (d) The original experiment contained 35 grams of salt per kilogram of water (or 35 ppt). The students repeated the experiment by modifying the amount of salt in each tank from 35 ppt to 40 ppt. **Explain** how the results of the experiment could be altered with this modification.
   (e) An increase in atmospheric temperatures is one reason oceans are warming. **Identify** one process that leads to anthropogenic carbon dioxide emissions.
   (f) **Propose** a realistic solution to reduce the atmospheric warming impacts of the process you identified in part (e).

   Clear-cutting forests can cause environmental problems.
   (g) **Describe** a negative environmental effect of clear-cutting.
   (h) **Propose** a solution for mitigating the impacts of clear-cutting.

(i) After a forest has been clear-cut, secondary succession can occur. Describe how biodiversity changes during secondary succession.

(j) **Describe** how the amount of sediment and fertilizer runoff into nearby waterways would be expected to differ when comparing an area with an undisturbed forest to an area where the forest has been clear-cut.

2. **Analyze an environmental problem and propose a solution.**

*Science Daily* published an article titled "U.S. and Canada Have Lost More Than 1 in 4 Birds in the Past 50 Years." The article states "A study published today in the journal *Science* reveals that since 1970, bird populations in the United States and Canada have declined by 29 percent, or almost 3 billion birds, signaling a widespread ecological crisis. The results show tremendous losses across diverse groups of birds and habitats— from iconic songsters such as meadowlarks to long-distance migrants such as swallows and backyard birds including sparrows."

(a) **Identify** one factor that could have led to an almost 30 percent decline of bird populations in the United States and Canada.

(b) **Explain** how the factor you named in (a) might impact other species, such as amphibians.

(c) While bird populations are declining, there have been some success stories of bird species that have recovered. **Identify** one example of a bird species whose population has recovered due to human involvement.

(d) For the species you named in (c), **describe** what was done to help the species recover.

(e) **Identify** one characteristic of an organism that could make them particularly vulnerable to becoming threatened or endangered.

(f) **Explain** one economic argument for protecting endangered/threatened species.

(g) **Describe** one ecological service that animals provide.

Air pollution can be harmful to many birds, which are known to be indicator species. One specific air pollutant that seems specifically dangerous to birds is ozone.

(h) **Explain** what it means to be an indicator species.

(i) **Describe** how ozone is formed in the troposphere.

(j) **Describe** the health impact of tropospheric ozone on the human body.

3. **Analyze an environmental problem and propose a solution using calculations.**

The average American produces 4.3 pounds of waste per day, adding up to a total amount of waste by Americans of 220 million tons per year. Much of the waste produced in the United States ends up in landfills, which can generate large amounts of methane. In fact, landfills are the third-largest source of anthropogenic methane in the United States, accounting for approximately 14.1 percent of methane emissions. One ton of methane causes 72 times more warming than does one ton of carbon dioxide.

One way to lower the environmental impact of landfill methane is to capture the methane to produce electricity. One million tons of landfill waste per day can generate 0.78 MW of electricity.

(a) **Calculate** how many pounds of waste an average family of four would produce per year. **Show** your work.

(b) If all the trash produced in a year in the United States were put in landfills and converted into electricity, **calculate** how much electricity could be generated. **Show** your work.

(c) Methane has a high warming potential. **Identify** one environmental problem associated with a warmer environment.

(d) For the environmental problem you identified in (c), **explain** how that could reduce biodiversity.

(e) **Identify** one gas other than methane and carbon dioxide that contributes to climate change.

(f) For the gas you identified in (e), **describe** a human activity that leads to its release.

(g) Country X produces 33 percent less waste per year than Americans. **Calculate** how much electricity per year could be produced in Country X if all methane emissions from waste were converted to electricity. **Show** your work.

## STOP. End of Section II.

# Answers and Explanations for the Multiple-Choice Questions

1. **B**—Desert. This biome covers about 20 percent of the land on our planet and is characterized by less than 50 cm of rain a year. Trees are usually absent and there is little vegetation.

2. **D**—According to the author, "Sometimes when corals become stressed, as is the case when ocean temperatures become too warm, the polyps expel their algae cells and the colony looks white in appearance."

3. **A**—Mutualism is when both species benefit from the relationship. The coral provides the algae with a place to live and the algae produce oxygen for the coral and remove wastes.

4. **B**—The 10 percent rule is the idea that as usable energy moves up the pyramid much of it is "lost" to the laws of thermodynamics.

5. **C**—Plant roots hold in soil and prevent erosion, so by planting plants you would help remediate the problem of soil erosion.

6. **A**—Fish ladders would allow fish to bypass the dam that would otherwise be blocking their migration path.

7. **D**—Carrying capacity is the number of organisms an ecosystem can support over time. This is often shown in a graph like the one below. The population of wildebeests, once established, fluctuates around the 1,200,000 mark. The carrying capacity of wildebeests is about 1,200,000.

**Population Changes and Carrying Capacity**

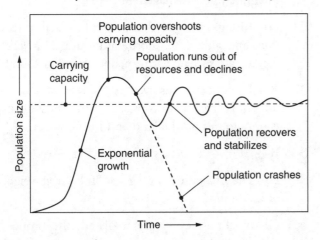

8. **C**—Herbivores eat grass. If there were a severe drought that killed off all the grass, we would have a loss of the herbivore, among them the wildebeests.

9. **B**—Person 5's greatest ecological footprint is in food and housing, so by lowering both of these this person would lower their ecological footprint the most.

10. **A**—Eating less meat has some big environmental advantages. It takes almost 20 times less land to get the same number of calories from growing plants rather than animals.

11. **D**—Nonpoint source pollution is pollution that can't point to just one particular source. Acid rain on a forest is caused by numerous things.

12. **C**—Endocrine disruptors are chemicals that can mimic hormones in organisms and can come from a variety of things, such as pesticides, food, and pharmaceuticals.

13. **B**—This type of smog occurs in warm places that have a lot of people, cars, factories, power plants, etc. It is formed when volatile organic hydrocarbons and nitrogen oxides, along with heat and sunlight, mix, causing pollution. The hydrocarbons and nitrogen oxides peak on the chart between hours 8 and 10.

14. **A**—Photochemical smog can cause eye irritation and respiratory illness. It also produces ground-level ozone.

15. **A**—40 kW/1000 × 100% = 4%

**16. D**—See picture below.

← Increasing heat and carbon content →

← Increasing moisture content →

Peat (not a coal) — Heat/Pressure → Lignite (brown coal) — Heat/Pressure → Bituminous (soft coal) — Heat/Pressure → Anthracite (hard coal)

**17. B**—If you slow the speed or turn off the turbines during migration periods, you would harm fewer birds, butterflies, and bats because they could fly through the blades without being harmed.

**18. C**—The graph is showing the increase in temperatures on Earth due to climate change.

**19. C**—As temperatures increase, sea levels are rising, a fact that would harm the organisms living in the estuaries and coastlines.

**20. B**—Burning fossil fuels emits carbon dioxide, and carbon dioxide increases global temperatures. To stop the increase of global temperatures, we could limit the burning of fossil fuels.

**21. A**—*Eutrophication* is the term used to describe a body of water that has so many nutrients (fertilizers like nitrogen and phosphorus) that the nutrients have "fertilized" the algae that live in the water. Then, when the algae die, microbes like bacteria and fungi that live in the water eat the algae and in doing so use nearly all of the dissolved oxygen in the water. This creates what is called a dead zone.

**22. D**—Agriculture uses a great deal of nitrates and phosphates to fertilize crops so that they grow faster, larger, etc. If the student is trying figure out who is causing the eutrophication, then starting by looking at farming would make the most sense.

**23. C**—Since plants use nitrates and phosphates, if the student wants to limit the amount of nitrates and phosphates going into the lake, the student could plant plants around the lake. The plants could take up the nutrients before they enter the lake.

**24. A**—The environmental problem of aquaculture is that the large numbers of fish or shellfish can produce huge quantities of waste (fish poop, excess fish food, etc.), which can pollute the river, lake, or ocean.

**25. C**—The oceans absorb almost a quarter of global $CO_2$ emissions we create from burning fossil fuels and deforestation. As the $CO_2$ enters the ocean, it causes the ocean to become more acidic (lower pH), causing ocean acidification.

**26. B**—In the greenhouse effect, solar radiation (infrared) from the sun is absorbed by Earth's surface. It warms the surface, and some is reflected back to space. The main gases that are in our atmosphere that absorb the solar radiation are carbon dioxide, methane, water vapor, nitrous oxide, and chlorofluorocarbons.

**27. D**—The chart shows that nearly 30 percent of amphibians are listed as endangered, critically endangered, or vulnerable. So, they must have the greatest threats to their environment.

**28. A**—During both stages 1 and 4, births and deaths are the same, so the population is not growing.

**29. C**—In stages 2 and 3, births are greater than deaths, so the population is growing.

**30. B**—Biological methods like predator bugs that a farmer buys to eat the pests (biocontrol) or rotating crops to reduce pests are examples of integrated pest management.

**31. D**—Rising, moist air that goes off in both directions and sinks at 30° north and south. This sinking, dry air is where Earth's major deserts are found.

**32. A**—The phosphorus cycle is a slow cycle and it does not have an atmospheric form. Phosphorus is only found on the land and in the water.

**33. B**—70/4 = 17.5 years to double

**34. B**—The $LD_{50}$ is 61 mg/kg × 0.30 kg (the weight of the mouse).

**35. C**—In almost every region listed, the proportion of the population using solid fuels is going down. So, indoor air pollution is dropping.

36. **D**—In eastern sub-Saharan Africa the line has stayed relatively flat over the years shown in the graph and is still above 90 percent. This tells us that the use of solid fuels is still widespread.

37. **A**—Oil rises from .5 Gtoe to 5.5 Gtoe, for a difference of 5 Gtoe.

38. **B**—250 million tons × .31 = 77.5 million tons

39. **A**—DDT (dichlorodiphenyltrichloroethane) is a synthetic organic chemical used as an insecticide and PCBs (polychlorinated biphenyls) are used as dielectric and coolant fluids in electrical equipment. POPs do not break down in the environment very quickly and can build up in the tissues and fat of animals. This bioaccumulation of POPs in an organism's tissues can be toxic. Because POPs don't break down, and because animals migrate long distances, and because these chemicals can travel very far in wind and water, there are POPs in almost all parts of our planet.

40. **D**—Volcanoes are geologic features that emit $CO_2$ and particulates.

41. **C**—Endocrine disruptors have been linked to developmental, reproductive, neural, immune, and other problems in animals. A gender imbalance would be a reproductive example.

42. **A**—Since dams can cause habitat damage by flooding an area that used to be land and lowering the water flow downstream, by removing the dam you could begin to restore the natural habitat.

43. **B**—

| 9000 Watts | 1 kW | $.10 | 3 hours | 30 days |
|---|---|---|---|---|
| | 1000 Watts | 1 kWh | 1 day | 1 month |

= $81 month

| 5000 Watts | 1 kW | $.10 | 3 hours | 30 days |
|---|---|---|---|---|
| | 1000 Watts | 1 kWh | 1 day | 1 month |

= $45 month

$81 − $45 = $36 per month savings

44. **D**—More UV light is able to get through the stratosphere and to the surface of Earth. UV light is dangerous because it can damage the DNA in skin cells, lead to skin cancer, cause cataracts, cause premature aging, and suppress the immune system.

45. **B**—The sun's UV energy breaks up CFC molecules, releasing chlorine atoms. The chlorine atoms then react with the $O_3$ molecules breaking up the $O_3$ and taking one oxygen atom to form chlorine monoxide and $O_2$. Ozone absorbs UV light, so CFCs lower the stratosphere's ability to absorb UV light.

46. **C**—The main gases in our atmosphere that absorb the solar radiation are carbon dioxide, methane, water vapor, nitrous oxide, and chlorofluorocarbons.

47. **A**—Sea levels are rising, which can flood coastal communities, displace coastal populations, and impact ocean organisms that are subsequently too deep to photosynthesize.

48. **B**—Species diversity is the number of species and abundance of each species that live in a particular community. Species diversity helps to contribute to the health of an ecosystem because each species has an important role in this health. Since the area rebounded quickly, it can be concluded that it has a high species diversity.

49. **D**—As the Mayan population increased, so did soil erosion and deforestation.

50. **C**—The bottom line shows that birds have moved 20 miles and the top line shows they have moved 60, so they have moved somewhere between 20 and 60 miles north.

51. **B**—Island biogeography is the study of the species and the distribution that would occur on each of these islands. The theory states that islands closer to the mainland (where the animals/plants have moved from) and/or larger islands will have more species than islands farther away or smaller.

52. **C**—Covering the playground with permeable pavement like gravel will increase infiltration and allow more water to seep into the soil.

53. **A**—Terracing is similar to contour plowing, but when an area is very hilly or mountainous, the farmer will make step-like rows and plant the crops on these rows. This helps to reduce soil erosion.

54. **D**—As climate change is melting the ice caps and causing thermal expansion of ocean waters, coastal cities could have increased flooding.

55. **B**—Our oceans get warmer because of climate change from greenhouse gases.

56. **B**—If invasive species could become profitable, such as becoming a form of food, then people would make sure to collect them, helping lower their numbers.

57. **A**—If we stopped clear-cutting forests and instead used sustainable forestry methods, we would decrease the problem of deforestation.

58. **D**—Trees have roots that hold in the soil. When we clear-cut areas of land, we expose this soil, leaving it vulnerable to erosion and/or flooding. Furthermore, this soil may end up in a river, lake, or stream, leading to problems there.

59. **D**—Genetically engineered crops are grown so the pests don't or can't harm them. This has pros and cons. The pros are increased profits for farmers, helping to keep the cost of food affordable, and reduced need for pesticides. Reduced use of pesticides is good for the environment since pesticides can often harm other organisms that they weren't designed to harm. However, the con is loss of diversity in the crop.

60. **C**—This is a weather condition when warm, less dense air moves over dense, cold air. Because of the thermal inversion, the dense air traps pollution, particularly smog and particulates, near the ground and it can't "escape" to upper atmosphere.

61. **B**—Living fences are used instead of regular fences. These trees or hedges can become a biological corridor for animals to use as a habitat or a means of travel.

62. **A**—Photosynthesis and cellular respiration are how carbon cycles in living things and is known as short-term cycling.

63. **B**—Specialists are organisms that require particular habitats, food, etc. An example of a specialist species would be a koala that can only eat eucalyptus. If the habitat where koalas live is damaged and their specific food source is gone, this could be particularly devastating to the population of koalas. Generalists are the opposite.

They can live in many different places and eat many different things. Generalists are less likely to be impacted by an environmental event.

64. **A**—The population will shrink. Countries like Germany, Bulgaria, and Russia are considered negative- or declining-growth countries because more than 50 percent of the population is past the age of reproduction.

65. **D**—In these countries, parents may only be having one child, so when mom and dad die the family (and the country) get smaller. Often, this is because women are working and putting off having children until they are older. This limits the number of children women can have because their reproductive age is limited.

66. **A**—Transform boundaries are where the plates slide side-by-side one another. The most common example you will be familiar with is California's San Andreas fault. Earthquakes are common along these faults as the plates move past each other and stored energy is released as energy of motion.

67. **C**—The equator is always nearly directly facing toward the sun.

68. **B**—The impact of El Niño includes changes to rainfall, wind, and ocean circulation patterns. It is particularly rainy during an El Niño year on the West Coast of the United States and South America.

69. **B**—Since trees have roots that hold in the soil, when we clear cut large areas of land we expose this soil, leaving it vulnerable to erosion and/or flooding. This soil may end up in a river, lake, or stream leading to problems there.

70. **A**—All weather on our planet is found in the troposphere. No weather phenomenon happens in any other layer of the atmosphere.

71. **D**—The area circled is Florida, which is surrounded on all sides by the ocean. This regulates the temperature and keeps it relatively warm and wet all year.

72. **D**—Humans are an example of a k-selected species. The graph shows a Type I survivorship curve, which is indicative of a k-selected species. Almost 100 percent of humans survive childhood and most humans survive for many years.

73. **C**—Nuclear energy generation produces so much heat that it must be "dumped" into a water source. Thermal pollution is often the result of a nuclear power plant where large amounts of heated water are being dumped into a body of water. The heated water doesn't have to have any pollutants in it, but just being warm can cause problems. This is because warm water can't hold as much oxygen as cold water. The oxygen diffuses out of the water and into the air.

74. **A**—The greatest reason for loss of biodiversity is habitat loss. We harm habitats by cutting down forests, by building roads, and by inhabiting areas where there used to be large areas of uninhabited land (habitat fragmentation).

75. **B**—The ocean absorbs carbon dioxide from the atmosphere. This is caused by the wind producing waves and turbulence, resulting in the water absorbing the carbon dioxide. The oceans absorb almost a quarter of global $CO_2$ emissions we create from burning fossil fuels and deforestation. As the $CO_2$ enters the ocean it causes the ocean to become more acidic (lower pH).

76. **A**—The lionfish are growing exponentially, which means that there must be plenty of food and habitat for them so they can keep reproducing until they reach their carrying capacity.

77. **C**—Type III. If they have many babies and don't take care of them, they are indicative of Type III.

78. **B**—To do this, start with sand and find the percentage along the bottom of the triangle, in this case 40 percent, and follow the line that goes up and to the left for sand. Then, move to the right side of the triangle and find the line for silt, in this case 30 percent. Follow this line down and to the left until it intersects the line you found for sand. Then, where they cross, draw a straight line to the left, where you find clay. You should be at the 30 percent line, which is your percentage of clay. Where these three lines intersected is the type of soil you have. In this case, clay loam.

79. **A**—Provisioning ecosystem services are things like food and clean water.

80. **D**—The 10 percent rule is the idea that as usable energy moves up the pyramid much of it is "lost" to the laws of thermodynamics. The first law of thermodynamics states that energy cannot be created or destroyed but the second law states that it can be transferred or transformed. So, there can't be as many top predators as there are primary and secondary consumers.

# Explanations for the Free-Response Questions

**Question 1: Design an investigation**                                          **10 points**

(a) **Identify** the scientific question for the investigation.                    **1 point**

Accept one of the following:

- Is coral bleaching linked to climate change?
- Does climate change affect coral?
- Does climate change make coral bleach?

(b) **Identify** the control in this experiment.                                   **1 point**

- 27°C

(c) **Identify** the independent variable in this experiment.                       **1 point**

Accept one of the following:

- Temperature
- Temperature of the water
- Temperature of the salt water

(d) The original experiment contained 35 grams of salt per kilogram of water       **1 point**
(or 35 ppt). The students repeated the experiment by modifying the
amount of salt in each tank from 35 ppt to 40 ppt. **Explain** how the
results of the experiment could be altered with this modification.

Accept one of the following:

- The percentage of corals that are bleached will increase/go up.
- The percentage of corals that are bleached will decrease/go down.
- The percentage of corals that are bleached will not change.

(e) An increase in atmospheric temperatures is one reason oceans are              **1 point**
warming. **Identify** one activity that leads to anthropogenic carbon
dioxide emissions.

Accept one of the following:

- Burning fossil fuels
- Power generation
- Transportation
- Agriculture
- Deforestation
- Manufacturing

(f) **Propose** a realistic solution to reduce the atmospheric warming             **1 point**
impacts of the process you identified in part (e).

Accept one of the following:

- Use renewable resources (wind, solar, geothermal) rather than coal, oil, natural gas.
- Carpool.
- Take mass transit (bus, train, subway).
- Replant areas that are deforested.
- Expand the use of plug-in vehicles.

Clear-cutting forests can cause environmental problems. **1 point**

(g) **Describe** a negative environmental effect of clear-cutting.

Accept one of the following:

- Soil erosion
- Increased soil and stream temperatures
- Flooding
- Release of carbon dioxide
- Climate change

(h) **Propose** a solution for mitigating the impacts of clear-cutting. **1 point**

Accept one of the following:

- Reforestation
- Using and buying wood harvested by ecologically sustainable forestry techniques
- Reusing wood

(i) After a forest has been clear-cut, secondary succession can occur. **1 point**
**Describe** how biodiversity changes during secondary succession.

Accept one of the following:

- After a forest is cut down, secondary succession can occur. Soil is present so pioneer species will move in followed by other species replacing them. Finally, a climax community (forest) will be present.
- Succession is a process in which species present at one stage are gradually replaced by new species. As succession continues, there is an increase in complexity and biodiversity.

(j) **Describe** how the amount of sediment and fertilizer runoff into nearby **1 point**
waterways would be expected to differ when comparing an area with
an undisturbed forest to an area where the forest has been clear-cut.

Accept one of the following:

- There would be an increased amount of sediment and fertilizer runoff in a clear-cut forest.
- There would be a decreased amount of sediment and fertilizer runoff in a natural forest.

## Question 2: Analyze an environmental problem and propose a solution 10 points

(a) **Identify** one factor that could have led to an almost 30 percent **1 point**
decline of bird populations in the United States and Canada.

Accept one of the following:

- Habitat loss
- Cats and other predators
- Pesticide use
- Climate change

(b) **Explain** how the factor you named in (a) might impact other species, such as amphibians.                    **1 point**

Accept one of the following:

- Habitat loss will impact other species by removing areas for the species to live.
- Cats can be predators on other species, which could lower species numbers.
- Pesticides can kill/harm other species, which could lower species numbers.
- Climate change can impact other species by making it too warm and outside their natural range.

(c) While bird populations are declining, there have been some success stories of bird species that have recovered. **Identify** one example of a bird species whose population has recovered due to human involvement.                    **1 point**

Accept one of the following (other examples could be correct as well):

- Bald eagle
- California condor
- Piping plovers
- Purple martin
- Golden-winged warblers
- Whooping crane
- Brown pelicans
- Florida scrub-jay

(d) For the species you named in (c), **describe** what was done to help the species recover.                    **1 point**

Accept one of the following:

- Banning DDT and other persistent pesticides
- Habitat restoration
- Creating protected areas
- Habitat corridors
- Promoting sustainable land use practices

(e) **Identify** one characteristic of an organism that could make them particularly vulnerable to becoming threatened or endangered.                    **1 point**

Accept one of the following:

- Specialized feeding behaviors
- Specialized food sources
- Require a large territory
- Limited geographic range or habitat
- Compete with humans for space or food (might be hunted)
- Exploited for economic value
- Introduced/exotic species prey on them
- Limited range of tolerance
- Lack of genetic diversity
- Feeds at high trophic levels
- Biomagnification of chemicals that have harmed the species

(f) **Explain** one economic argument for protecting    **1 point**
endangered/threatened species.

Accept one of the following (other answers not listed could be correct):
- Food supplies
- Pollination
- Pest control
- Tourism
- Genetic diversity
- Disease prevention
- Hunting/fishing
- Cycling water and nutrients
- Medicinal plants/pharmaceuticals
- Oxygen production
- Wastewater treatment

(g) **Describe** one ecological service that animals provide.    **1 point**

Accept one of the following (other answers not listed could be correct):
- Food for other species
- Pollinators for plant species
- Detritivores that recycle nutrients
- Cycling water and nutrients

(h) **Explain** what it means to be an indicator species.    **1 point**

Accept one of the following:
An indicator species is
- a plant or animal that by its presence, abundance, scarcity, or chemical composition demonstrates that some distinctive aspect of the character or quality of an ecosystem is present
- an organism that serves as a measure of the environmental conditions that exist in a given area
- living organisms that tell us that something has changed or is going to change inter environment

(i) **Describe** how ozone is formed in the troposphere.    **1 point**

Accept one of the following:
- Volatile organic compounds and nitrogen oxides in the presence of heat and sunlight form ozone.
- Chemical reactions between oxides of nitrogen and volatile organic compounds form ozone.

(j) **Describe** the health impact of tropospheric ozone on the human body.    **1 point**

Accept one of the following:
- Respiratory problems
- Lung function lowered
- Asthma

- Emphysema
- COPD
- Chest pain
- Coughing
- Throat irritation
- Congestion
- Bronchitis
- Inflammation of the lining of the lungs
- Scar lung tissue

---

**Question 3: Analyze an environmental problem and propose a solution doing calculations**  **10 points**

(a)  **Calculate** how many pounds of waste an average family of four would produce per year. **Show** your work.  **1 point**

One point for the correct setup to calculate the amount of waste a family of four would produce per year.

- 4 people × 4.3 pounds of waste per day × 365 days in a year

---

One point for the correct calculation of the amount of waste a family of four would produce per year.  **1 point**

- 6,278 pounds of waste per year

---

**Total for part (a) 2 points**

---

(b)  If all trash produced in a year in the United States were put in landfills and converted into electricity, **calculate** how much electricity could be generated. **Show** your work.  **1 point**

One point for the correct setup to calculate how much electricity could be generated.

- $\dfrac{220 \text{ million} \times 0.78 \text{ MW}}{1 \text{ million}}$

---

One point for the correct calculation how much electricity could be generated.  **1 point**

- 171.6 MW of electricity

---

**Total for part (b) 2 points**

---

(c)  Methane has a high warming potential. **Identify** one environmental problem associated with a warmer environment.  **1 point**

Accept one of the following:

- Sea level rising
- Loss of habitat for species living in coastal regions
- Melting permafrost
- Erosion

- Invasive species
- Stronger storms
- Melting sea ice

---

(d) For the environmental problem you identified in (c), **explain** how that could reduce biodiversity.  **1 point**

Accept one of the following:

- Habitat loss from sea level rising can mean less available land/resources for a species to survive.
- Invasive species can outcompete native species.
- Stronger storms can displace species from where they naturally occur.

---

(e) **Identify** one gas other than methane and carbon dioxide that contributes to climate change.  **1 point**

Accept one of the following:

- Ozone
- Nitrous oxide
- CFCs
- HFCs
- HCFCs

---

(f) For the gas you identified in (e), **describe** a human activity that leads to its release.  **1 point**

Accept one of the following:

- Ozone—released in vehicle exhaust from internal combustion engines
- Nitrous oxide—released by burning of petroleum products, biomass, and nitrogen-rich fuels (particularly coal); also released by feedlots (concentrated animal feeding operations, CAFOs) and dairy farms
- CFCs—released through their usage in refrigerators and air conditioners, in foam production, for cleaning electronics, and formerly as a propellant
- HFCs—released through their usage in refrigerators and air conditioners, in foam production, for cleaning electronics, and formerly as a propellant
- HCFCs—released through their usage in refrigerators and air conditioners, in foam production, for cleaning electronics, and formerly as a propellant

---

(g) Country X produces 33 percent less waste per year than Americans. **Calculate** how much electricity per year could be produced in Country X if all methane emissions from waste were converted to electricity. **Show** your work.  **1 point**

One point for the correct setup to calculate the amount of methane produced.

| 0.67 | 220,000,000 tons of waste per year | 0.78 MW of electricity |
|------|-----------------------------------|------------------------|
|      |                                   | 1 million tons         |

One point for the correct calculation the amount of methane produced.    **1 point**

Accept one of the following:

- 114.972 MW of electricity
- 114.97 MW of electricity

**Total for part (g) 2 points**

# AP Environmental Science Practice Exam 2
## Score Approximation

You can get a rough approximation of what your score on the AP Environmental Science Exam would be. Use this worksheet to compute an approximation of your score.

### Section I: Multiple Choice

Determine the number of multiple-choice questions you got right then enter that number below.

Number of questions answered correctly (80 possible)     _____

$\times 1.125$

This is your **Weighted Section I** Score     _____

### Section II: Free Response

Award yourself points as determined by the scoring guide given in the explanation for each question.

Question 1 (10 points possible)     _____
Question 2 (10 points possible)     _____
Question 3 (10 points possible)     _____

Add the three scores for the free-response section     _____

$\times 2$

This is your **Weighted Section II Score**     _____

Add your Weighted Section I Score and your Weighted Section II Score.     _____

This is your **Composite Score**.

### Score Conversion Chart

| COMPOSITE SCORE RANGE | APPROXIMATE AP SCORE |
| --- | --- |
| 110–150 | 5 |
| 89–109 | 4 |
| 77–88 | 3 |
| 63–76 | 2 |
| 0–62 | 1 |